The State of America's Children

A REPORT FROM THE

CHILDREN'S DEFENSE FUND

INTRODUCTION BY **MARIAN WRIGHT EDELMAN**

BEACON PRESS

BOSTON

Beacon Press
25 Beacon Street
Boston, Massachusetts 02108-2892
www.beacon.org

Beacon Press books are published under the auspices of
the Unitarian Universalist Association of Congregations.

03 02 01 00 99 98   8 7 6 5 4 3 2 1

Library of Congress Cataloging-in-Publication Data

The state of America's children: a report from the
Children's Defense Fund / introduction by Marian Wright
Edelman.
    p. cm.
  ISBN 0-8070-4147-5 (pbk.)
    1. Child welfare —Finance—United States. 2.
Children's rights—United States. 3. Child welfare—
United States. I. Children's Defense Fund (U.S.)
HV741.S735 1998
362.7'0973—dc21   97-39587

Years
LEAVE NO CHILD BEHIND.

This book is dedicated to the memories of:

Mother Teresa,
God's voice, hands, and feet for the poor

≈

Dr. Samuel DeWitt Proctor,
preacher, teacher, and mentor,
exemplar of the gospel of Jesus Christ,
protector of children, and
pastor emeritus of Abyssinian Baptist Church, New York City

≈

Dr. Thomas Kilgore,
pastor emeritus of the Second Baptist Church in Los Angeles,
former chair of Morehouse College Board of Trustees, and
former president of the Progressive Baptist and
American Baptist Conventions

≈

Dr. Aaron Henry,
a fighter for civil rights in Mississippi

≈

Esther Peterson,
who fought tirelessly
for all American consumers, workers, and citizens

Acknowledgments

Susanne Martinez, director of programs and policy at the Children's Defense Fund (CDF), oversaw development of this book and provided overall editorial direction. Kathryn Kline Dahl was the principal editor, with assistance from Diane Minor, director of publications. Many individuals at CDF and elsewhere contributed to the content and may be contacted for further information about their subjects. CDF contributors include MaryLee Allen and Jamila Larson (children and families in crisis); Helen Blank, Gina Adams, and Karen Schulman (child care); Stan Dorn, Martha Teitelbaum, and Jill Jones (child health); Kim Wade and Holly M. Jackson (children and violence); and Deborah Weinstein, Arloc Sherman, and Nancy Ebb (family income). Data were produced and analyzed by Paul Smith and Janet Simons. Elizabeth Reynolds assisted with copyediting and proofreading, and Jennifer Leonard managed production. Joanne Pittman provided administrative support.

Special thanks go to outside contributors: Robert Greenstein of the Center on Budget and Policy Priorities (child nutrition); Melissa Ludtke (adolescent pregnancy); Wayne Sherwood (housing); and Alan Zuckerman of the National Youth Employment Coalition (youth employment). Feroza Fitch of Lexicon Graphics provided typesetting and design services.

The creation, publication, and distribution of this book were underwritten by an endowment gift from the DeWitt-Wallace Reader's Digest Fund.

Media inquiries should be directed to Sarah Howe.

Contents

Figures

Preface

In 1998 the Children's Defense Fund celebrates 25 years of research, public education, policy development, and advocacy for children. We also celebrate the 30th anniversary of the Washington Research Project, CDF's parent organization and a pioneer in the public interest law movement.

The Poor People's Campaign, Dr. Martin Luther King Jr.'s last crusade, attempted to move America beyond civil rights to address social and economic needs to assure families', children's, and America's future. That is what CDF has been trying to do and will continue to do until we succeed. I never dreamed it would be so hard for America to do what is right and sensible for children. But I am very proud and grateful for the significant progress that we and others have achieved for children. Billions of dollars in new child investments and major new education, child care, child health, and child welfare laws, regulations, and protections now reach millions of children.

For example, the Education for All Handicapped Children Act of 1975 (94-142), the forerunner of today's Individuals with Disabilities Education Act, established a federal right to education for children with disabilities. It has yielded $40.4 billion in special education funding since Fiscal Year 1976. CDF's first report, *Children Out of School in America,* documented the exclusion of children with disabilities. Before 94-142, Office of Education data showed 37.5 percent of school-age children with disabilities were unserved by schools. Today fewer than 1 percent are neither evaluated nor served.

The Child Care and Development Block Grant has provided $7.1 billion since 1991 to help parents work and children receive better-quality child care. We seek to expand its funding in our 1998 campaign to ensure quality and affordable options for all parents of preschool and school-age children.

The $48 billion State Children's Health Insurance Program (CHIP), created in 1997, will reach 5 million children over 10 years when fully implemented. Past Medicaid child health expansions have given millions more children a Healthy Start, and child immunization rates are rising again, thanks to the Vaccines for Children Program. An unpaid Family and Medical Leave Act was finally enacted in 1993. More than 17 million children have received a Head Start and are succeeding in school and in life. Millions more children have new protections against child abuse and neglect, live in permanent adoptive homes, and are able to get enough food, thanks to the expansion of family and child nutrition programs.

But no victories are ever final, as we have seen in repeated attacks to dismantle the safety net for poor, disabled, and immigrant children and families. That is why we are continuing to build a movement by developing a critical mass of leaders and strengthening community capacity in order to make it un-American to hurt children and to finish the task of giving all children a decent, safe, and happy future. The nearly 300,000 people who stood for children on June 1, 1996, at the Lincoln Memorial and who continue to stand in their communities provide the foundation for the next stage of movement-building for children and families.

My deepest gratitude goes to the over 2,000 past and present CDF staff and Board members, numerous supporters, and funders all over America who have brought children's needs to the center of national awareness. Now we must translate this awareness into effective personal and national *action*. With God's help and yours, we will succeed.

In faith and gratitude,

Marian Wright Edelman

A Child Shall Lead Us

America is great because America is good, and if America ever ceases to be good, America will cease to be great.

Alexis de Tocqueville

Capitalism forgets that life is social, and the kingdom of brotherhood is found neither in the thesis of communism nor the antithesis of capitalism but in a higher synthesis. It is found in a higher synthesis that combines the truth of both. . . . It means ultimately coming to see that the problem of racism, the problem of economic exploitation, and the problem of war are all tied together! These are the triple evils that are interrelated."

Dr. Martin Luther King Jr.
Where Do We Go from Here:
Chaos or Community?

You shall not pervert the justice due to your poor.

Exodus 23:6

America appears to be riding high on the cusp of the 21st century and third millennium. Wall Street is booming. Excess, Russell Baker says, has become a way of life for the very rich. In what may be the ultimate in corporate hubris, Miller Brewing Company has applied for a trademark or been recently registered as the "official sponsor of the Millennium" according to *Harper's Magazine*. Corporate CEOs, who earned 41 times what their workers made in 1960, made 185 times as much as their workers in 1995. The average CEO in 1995 earned more every two days than the average worker earned in a whole year. Fortune 500 CEOs averaged $7.8 million each in total compensation. This exceeds the average salaries of 226 school teachers a year.

The rosy view of American prosperity at the top hides deep and dangerous moral, economic, age, and racial fault lines lurking beneath the surface. Unless we heed and correct them, they will destroy America's fundamental ideals of justice and equal opportunity, family and community stability, economic productivity, and moral legitimacy as the democratic standard bearer in the next era.

In the 25 years since the Children's Defense Fund began, great progress has been made in improving children's lives in many areas. Millions of children with disabilities have a right to education; millions of poor children have received a Head Start, health care, immunizations, better child care, and permanent adoptive homes. But shamefully high child poverty rates persist, and children are the poorest group of Americans. The gap between America's poor and rich has grown into a chasm, the wages of young families with children have eroded, and many middle class families are treading economic water.

Since 1989 the poorest fifth of families have lost $587 each and the richest 5 percent have gained $29,533 each. We have five times more billionaires but 4 million more poor children. While millions of stock options helped quintuple the earnings of corporate CEOs between 1980 and 1995, those same employers threw millions of children out of health insurance plans at their parents' workplaces, and parental wages stagnated.

More than 11 million children are uninsured, 90 percent of whom have working parents. More parents worked longer hours and more families sent a second or only parent into the labor force to meet family necessities. But for millions of families, work did not pay a family-supporting wage, and a minimum wage no longer prevents poverty. Sixty-nine percent of poor children live in working families. Ending welfare as we know it will not help them. Ending poverty as we know it will. Sustained economic investment in rebuilding our communities and in stable jobs with decent wages, quality affordable child care, and health insurance must become top American priorities.

Six years of economic expansion with low inflation and a soaring stock market have not filtered down to 36.5 million poor people, including 14.5 million children. In 1996 the number of *very* poor people who live below half the poverty line (a mere $8,018 for a family of four) increased, while the current income of households in the top 5 percent increased by $12,500. Today more than one in five children is growing up poor and one in 11 is growing up extremely poor. This is shameful and unnecessary.

If we are truly concerned about preventing welfare, teen pregnancy, youth violence, school dropouts, and crime, then we need to start first by preventing child poverty and ensuring every child a fair start in life. The moral, human, and economic costs of permitting 14.5 million children to be poor are too high.

- A baby born poor is less likely to survive to its first birthday than a baby born to an unwed mother, a high school dropout, or a mother who smoked during pregnancy.
- Poverty is a greater risk to children's overall health status than is living in a single-parent family.
- Poor children face greater risk of stunted growth, anemia, repeated years of schooling, lower test scores, and less education, as well as lower wages and lower earnings in their adult years.
- Poverty puts children at a greater risk of falling behind in school than does living in a single-parent home or being born to teenage parents.

Dr. Laura D'Andrea Tyson, former chair of the President's Council of Economic Advisors, says, "Policies to reduce the poverty rate among children—which typically remains higher in the United States than in any other advanced industrial countries—must be a fundamental part of our efforts to build a healthy economy for the 21st century." Nobel laureate in economics Robert M. Solow of the Massachusetts Institute of Technology states, "In optimistic moments, I like to believe that most Americans would want to lift children out of poverty even if it cost something. It is hard to blame little children for the problems that surround them now and will damage their future health, ability, and learning capacity. Doing nothing about it seems both immoral and unintelligent."

All segments of society pay the costs of child poverty and would share the gains if child poverty were eliminated. America's labor force is projected to lose as much as $130 billion in future productive capacity for every year 14.5 million American children continue to live in poverty. These costs will spill over to employers and consumers, making it harder for businesses to expand technology, train workers, or produce a full range of high-quality products. Additional costs will be borne by schools, hospitals, and taxpayers and by our criminal justice system. Poor children held back in school require special education and tutoring, experience a lifetime of heightened medical problems and reliance on social service, and fail to earn and contribute as much in taxes.*

When legitimate avenues of employment are closed, poor youths and adults turn to illegitimate ones, especially the lethal underground economy of drugs and crime fueled by out-of-control gun trafficking. Since 1970 America's prison population has increased more than fivefold at an annual taxpayer tab exceeding $20 billion. Almost one in

---

*These and other findings are detailed in a CDF report by Arloc Sherman, *Poverty Matters: The Cost of Child Poverty in America.*

three young Black and one in 15 young White males between ages 20 to 29 are under some type of correctional control (incarceration, probation, or parole). Two-thirds of state prison inmates in 1991 had not completed high school and one-third had annual incomes under $5,000. Joseph Califano, head of Columbia University's National Center on Addiction and Substance Abuse, reports that if present trends persist, one of every 20 Americans born in 1997 will spend some time in jail, including one of every 11 men and one of every four Black men.

Is this America's dream for its children and itself? Can an $8.7 trillion American economy not afford decent jobs, quality child care, education, and health care for all its children?

What Kind of Ancestors Will We Be? What Is America's Legacy?

It is time for every American to see and excise the moral tumors of child neglect, violence, poverty, and racism eating away the core of our national soul. What kind of billboard are we for democracy or capitalism—in a world where more than 3 billion people live on less than $2 per day and 200 million children suffer malnutrition every year—when millions of American children are hungry, homeless, neglected, abused, and dying from diseases we have the money and power but not the decency to prevent?

How will we lead a world where 5 of 6 billion citizens are not White, when young Black and Latino males see no jobs, hope, or future choices beyond prison and death? How do we fill our privileged children—who, like many poor children, are longing for a sense of purpose things cannot meet—with spiritual anchors and worthwhile goals? Will our children have something besides drugs and booze and cigarettes and rollicking good times to turn to when life's rough seas batter their souls?

How will they remember us as parents and leaders? Will they remember the jets, second mansions, and multiple nannies, or will they remember how often we watched their games and plays and concerts and were home to soothe over a bad nightmare? Will their memory books be chock-full of expensive toys and designer clothes, or of regular mealtimes, shared conversation, family games, prayer, and worship? Are they able to get our attention in the small daily ways that matter and say I

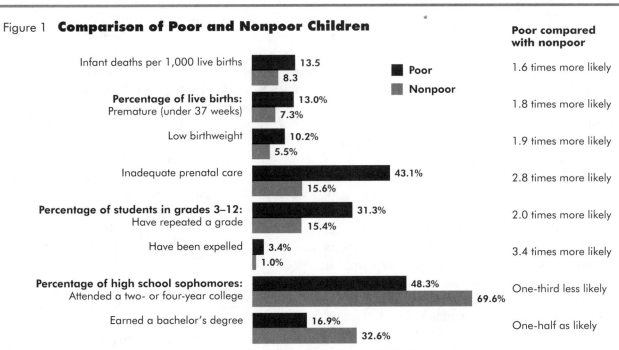

Figure 1 **Comparison of Poor and Nonpoor Children**

	Poor	Nonpoor	Poor compared with nonpoor
Infant deaths per 1,000 live births	13.5	8.3	1.6 times more likely
Percentage of live births: Premature (under 37 weeks)	13.0%	7.3%	1.8 times more likely
Low birthweight	10.2%	5.5%	1.9 times more likely
Inadequate prenatal care	43.1%	15.6%	2.8 times more likely
Percentage of students in grades 3–12: Have repeated a grade	31.3%	15.4%	2.0 times more likely
Have been expelled	3.4%	1.0%	3.4 times more likely
Percentage of high school sophomores: Attended a two- or four-year college	48.3%	69.6%	One-third less likely
Earned a bachelor's degree	16.9%	32.6%	One-half as likely

Source: Arloc Sherman, *Poverty Matters: The Cost of Child Poverty in America* (CDF, 1997), p. 3.

Table 1   **Poor Outcomes for Poor Children**

Outcome	Poor children's higher risk relative to nonpoor children
Health	
Death in childhood	1.5 to 3 times more likely
Stunted growth	2.7 times more likely
Iron deficiency in preschool years	3 to 4 times more likely
Partial or complete deafness	1.5 to 2 times more likely
Partial or complete blindness	1.2 to 1.8 times more likely
Serious physical or mental disabilities	About 2 times more likely
Fatal accidental injuries	2 to 3 times more likely
Pneumonia	1.6 times more likely
Education	
Average IQ score at age 5	9 points lower
Average achievement scores at age 3 and above	11 to 25 percentiles lower
Learning disabilities	1.3 times more likely
Placement in special education	2 or 3 percentage points more likely
Below-usual grade for child's age	2 percentage points more likely for each year of childhood spent in poverty
Dropping out between ages 16 and 24	2 times more likely than middle-income youths; 11 times more likely than wealthy youths

Source: Arloc Sherman, *Poverty Matters: The Cost of Child Poverty in America* (CDF, 1997), p. 4.

love you, or only through desperate screams of violence, gangs, guns, sexual promiscuity, and substance abuse?

Does what we do every day really matter for anyone besides ourselves and our immediate family? Is our example one we would like our children to emulate and pass on to our grandchildren and the children of the world? Will we leave them a country and Earth more just, virtuous, and safe than we inherited? What messages do our lives convey about the brotherhood and sisterhood of humanity?

How will each of us add to or subtract from America's moral bank account when the God of the universe asks for an accounting? Will God care how many times our excessive nuclear stockpiles can blow up humankind? Will God be proud that we sell more weapons to other nations than any other country, which fuel wars all over the globe that kill mostly women and children? Will God ask how many billionaires and millionaires we created with the land and water and talents God blessed us with and praise us for developing the cleverest ads

to sell tobacco's deadly poisons to our children? Will God agree that a child's life in Bangladesh is less precious than one in Bangor, Maine, as America's tobacco industry markets its deadly wares to developing nations? Or will God ask did we feed the hungry, heal the sick, visit the prisoner, protect the widow, orphan, and stranger? How will America answer? How will you and I answer? How will we teach our children to answer as citizens of the richest nation on earth blessed with the opportunity to abolish want and disease?

America's children will make or break America's greatness and future. One in four current Americans is a child. Children are the future tense of our humanity. Its quality will depend largely upon our present-tense care of them. The Rev. Dr. Gardner Taylor, the dean of American preachers, says:

If we do not bequeath to them something worth calling life, then we cannot expect of them any lives that are worthwhile. . . . Might it be that this land with all of its richness, with all of its opportunity for true

Key Facts About American Children

1 in 2	preschoolers has a mother in the labor force.
1 in 2	will live in a single-parent family at some point in childhood.
1 in 2	never completes a single year of college.
1 in 3	is born to unmarried parents.
1 in 3	will be poor at some point in childhood.
1 in 3	is a year or more behind in school.
1 in 4	is born poor.
1 in 4	is born to a mother who did not graduate from high school.
1 in 4	lives with only one parent.
1 in 5	is poor now.
1 in 5	lives in a family receiving food stamps.
1 in 5	is born to a mother who received no prenatal care in the first three months of pregnancy.
1 in 6	has a foreign-born mother.
1 in 7	has no health insurance.
1 in 7	lives with a working relative but is poor nonetheless.
1 in 8	never graduates from high school.
1 in 8	is born to a teenage mother.
1 in 11	lives at less than half the poverty level.
1 in 12	has a disability.
1 in 13	is born at low birthweight.
1 in 24	is born to a mother who received late or no prenatal care.
1 in 25	lives with neither parent.
1 in 132	dies before age 1.
1 in 680	is killed by gunfire before age 20.

greatness, its opportunity to present itself before the world as what a nation ought to be, might now be sowing the seeds of its very destruction in abandonment of its children?

I believe so. That is why the Children's Defense Fund has been struggling for 25 years to plant seeds for a massive moral movement to Leave No Child Behind and to ensure every child of every race born in every place in America a healthy, fair, safe, and moral start in life and a successful passage to adulthood, with the help of caring families and communities.

Children are life, power, hope, and the chance for renewal and immortality. Children will carry on our families, communities, institutions, and values. How then do we honestly examine and transform the values and priorities of the wealthiest nation in history, which lets its children be the poorest group of Americans and lets a child be killed by guns every hour and a half? How do we reverse the prevailing political calculus that would rather pay three times more to lock children up *after* they get into trouble than to give them incentives to stay in school and out of trouble, through good after-school and summer programs, jobs, and service opportunities? How do we make it easier rather than harder for parents to balance work and family responsibilities and to get the community and financial support they need to carry out the most important role in America?

Five Questions All American Citizens Should Ask Ourselves and Our Political Leaders About National Priorities

As a Democrat, as a Christian, as a southern Baptist, as someone who fundamentally believes in the words of the Bible . . . I [do not] believe that God's response to the poor is to treat them as though they are the least priority, almost as though they are a nuisance to be dealt with. . . . With all due respect to the Christian Coalition, where does it say in the Scriptures that the character of God is to give more to those who have and less to those who have not? . . . If there is one thing evident in the Scriptures, it is that God gives priority to the poor.

> U.S. Representative Glenn Poshard
> Democrat, Illinois 19th district
> Speech to the House of Representatives

No one may claim the name Christian and be comfortable in the face of hunger, hopelessness, insecurity, and the injustice found in this country and around the world. . . . Every economic decision and institution must be judged in light of whether it protects or undermines the dignity of the human person.

> National Conference of Catholic Bishops
> Pastoral Letter on the Economy

The time has come for an all-out world war against poverty. The rich nations must use their vast resources of wealth to develop the underdeveloped, school the unschooled and feed the unfed. The well-off and the secure have too often become indifferent and oblivious to the poverty and deprivation in their midst. The poor in our countries have been shut out of our minds, and driven from the mainstream of our societies, because we have allowed them to become invisible. Ultimately a great nation is a compassionate nation. No individual or nation can be great if it does not have a concern for "the least of these."

> Dr. Martin Luther King Jr.
> Where Do We Go from Here:
> Chaos or Community?

1. Why is our nation continuing to spend $265 billion a year, $5.1 billion a week, $727 million a day, and $30 million an hour on "National Defense" in a post–Cold War era with no towering external enemies? Our military budget exceeds the total military expenditures of the 12 next-largest spenders—including Russia, France, Great Britain, Germany, and China—combined. Congress gave the Pentagon $9 billion more than it requested in 1996, while cutting $54 billion from child nutrition programs for poor and legal immigrant children and families. The military plans to purchase three new tactical fighter systems that will cost $355 billion—systems the U.S. General Accounting Office says we don't need and can't afford—at a time when millions of struggling parents left behind in the global economy need better-paying jobs and millions of children need health care, quality child care, education, and housing.

As President Dwight Eisenhower reminded us in 1953, "Every gun that is made, every warship launched, every rocket fired signifies . . . a theft from those who hunger and are not fed, those who are cold and not clothed. This world in arms is not spending money alone. It is spending the sweat of its laborers, the genius of its scientists, and the hopes of its children."

■ Every 14 hours we spend more on the military than we do annually on programs to prevent and treat child abuse.

■ Every 29 hours we spend more on the military than we do annually on summer jobs for unemployed youths.

■ Every six days we spend more on the military than we do annually on the Child Care and Development Block Grant for child care for low-income working parents.

■ Every six days we spend more on the military than we do annually on Head Start, which still serves only one in three eligible children.

■ Every 11 days we spend more on the military than we do annually on Title I compensatory education for disadvantaged children.

It takes only a few nuclear weapons to blow up humankind. America spends tens of billions of dollars to maintain a nuclear overkill "advantage" at a time when irresponsible leaders and gangsters seek access to inadequately secured nuclear weapon stockpiles and a cheap computer chip can accidentally launch a nuclear war. "Can't we do better than condone a world in which nuclear weapons are accepted as commonplace?" asks retired General George Lee Butler, former head of the Strategic Air Command. "The elimination of nuclear weapons," Butler states, "is called utopia by people who forget that for so many decades the end of the Cold War was considered utopia."

As we near the close of a 20th century marked by dazzling scientific and technological progress, but also the bloodiest century in history, we all need to reassess the meaning of power and of life. More than 109 million human beings lost their lives in wars during this century, and far more civilians than soldiers died due to military con-

---

Key Facts About Poor Children

3 in 5   are White.

1 in 3   lives in suburban America.

1 in 3   lives in a family with married parents.

2 in 3   live in a working family.

---

flicts. We must heed General Omar Bradley's warning on Armistice Day in 1948:

> We have grasped the mystery of the atom and rejected the Sermon on the Mount. . . . Ours is a world of nuclear giants and ethical infants. We know more about war than we know about peace, more about killing than we know about living. The way to win an atomic war is to make certain it never starts. And the way to make sure it never starts is to abolish the dangerous costly nuclear stockpiles which imprison humankind.

2. Why, with over 200 million guns in circulation already killing a child every hour and a half, does our country manufacture or import a new gun every eight seconds? American children under age 15 are 12 times more likely to die from gunfire than children in 25 other industrialized nations combined. Virtually all violent youth crime is gun-driven. Yet many politicians seek to return to the barbaric practice of locking up children (the majority of whom are neither violent nor repeat offenders) in adult jails instead of locking up the adults who sold or gave them the guns. Why seek to protect guns rather than protect children from guns?

When the polio virus killed 2,700 children and adults in its peak year—seven a day—we declared a national emergency. Why don't we declare a national emergency to stop the deadly gun virus that kills almost twice as many children—5,285 a year, 14 a day—in their homes, neighborhoods, schools, and parks? It is ironic that the world's leading military power stands by as White militia gangs and Black, Latino, Asian, and White street gangs stockpile arsenals that endanger all citizens.

Moments in America for Children

Every 9 seconds	a child drops out of school.
Every 10 seconds	a child is reported abused or neglected.
Every 15 seconds	a child is arrested.
Every 25 seconds	a child is born to an unmarried mother.
Every 32 seconds	a child sees his or her parents divorce.
Every 36 seconds	a child is born into poverty.
Every 36 seconds	a child is born to a mother who did not graduate from high school.
Every minute	a child is born to a teen mother.
Every 2 minutes	a child is born at low birthweight.
Every 3 minutes	a child is born to a mother who received late or no prenatal care.
Every 3 minutes	a child is arrested for drug abuse.
Every 4 minutes	a child is arrested for an alcohol-related offense.
Every 5 minutes	a child is arrested for a violent crime.
Every 18 minutes	an infant dies.
Every 23 minutes	a child is wounded by gunfire.
Every 100 minutes	a child is killed by gunfire.
Every 4 hours	a child commits suicide.

3. How much do we truly value children and families when we don't put our money and our respect behind our words? Is a child care worker who earns $6.12 an hour, $12,058 a year, and receives no benefits 182 times less valuable to America's future than the average professional basketball player who earns $2.2 million a year, or 162 times less valuable than the average HMO head who made $1.95 million in 1996? Is she only one-fourth as important to America's well-being as an advertising manager for a tobacco brand who makes $23.32 an hour? Most states require 1,500 hours of training to become a manicurist or hair stylist, but more than 30 states do not require a single hour of training for child care workers.

What family values dictate a public policy in many states that pays more to nonrelatives than to relatives to care for children whose parents cannot nurture and protect them? Why are we willing to spend $10,000 a year to place a child in a foster home and much more to place a child in an institution *after* the family fails but refuse to invest $4,500 in job creation, child care, and income supplements for poor parents? Why does an average welfare payment of $365 a month to a poor family undermine personal responsibility when billions in "subsidies and incentives"—euphemisms for government welfare for the nonpoor and powerful—do not?

4. Why should every 66-year-old in the United States be guaranteed health coverage and not every 6-year-old or 16-year-old? Is one life more valuable than the other? Why should a child in one state have a chance to live and grow up healthy and not a child in another state? Why should our leaders decide it is acceptable to provide health insurance to *every other child?* And why are some of our political leaders and powerful lawyers so eager to protect a tobacco industry that saps 420,000 lives a year, $50 billion in direct health costs, and entices nearly 2 million children to smoke and shorten their lives? Former Surgeon General C. Everett Koop and former Food and Drug Administration head David Kessler propose a $2 a pack tobacco tax to deter teen smoking. That money not only could save millions of young lives by preventing them from smoking but also fund millions of children's hopes and dreams. A $2 tobacco tax would yield more than $100 billion dollars. That is enough to end childhood poverty, fund child care for working families, and ensure every child the healthy start that the tobacco industry has done so much to destroy.

5. Why is the United States, save Somalia (which lacks a legally constituted government to act), alone among nations in failing to ratify the Convention on the Rights of the Child? All the other nations of the world are willing to commit to the convention's goals of ending illegal child labor, sexual exploitation, violent abuse of, and capital punishment for children. Why do we refuse to pledge to make reasonable efforts to give all of our nation's children the adequate health care, food, shelter, and education that should be every child's birthright?

How We Can Stand for Children and Help Transform America

1. We can affirm rather than undermine our children's strengths and differences. A wonderful animal parable illustrates how so many institutions and professionals hurt rather than help children.

Once upon a time the animals decided they must do something heroic to meet the problems of the new world. So they organized a school. They adopted an activity curriculum consisting of running, climbing, swimming, and flying. And to make it easy to administer, all of the animals had to take all of the subjects.

The duck was excellent in swimming—better, in fact, than his instructor—and made passing grades in flying. Since he was slow in running, he had to stay after school and drop swimming to practice running. The duck kept this up until his feet were badly worn and he was only average, at last, in swimming. But average was acceptable in that school, so nobody worried about that except the duck.

The rabbit started at the top of the class in running but had a nervous breakdown because of so much makeup work in swimming. The squirrel was excellent in climbing until he became frustrated in the flying class, where his teacher made him start from the ground up instead of from the treetop down. He also developed charley horses from overexertion and got a C in climbing and a D in running. The eagle was a problem child and was disciplined severely in the climbing class, for even though he beat all the others to the top of the tree, he insisted on using his own way to get up there.

At the end of the year an abnormal eel who could swim exceedingly well and also run, climb, and fly a little had the highest average and was valedictorian. Prairie dogs kept their child out of school and fought the tax levy because the administration would not add digging and burrowing to the curriculum. They apprenticed their child to a badger and later joined the groundhogs and gophers to start a successful private school.

2. We can work collaboratively. No single person, institution, or government agency can meet all of our children's and families needs. But each of us, taking one or more of those needs, can together weave the seamless web of family and community and private sector support children need. We must work together and resist the political either/or-ism and organizational turf-ism that plague so much policy development, advocacy, service, and organizing today. Good parenting and good community, employer, and governmental supports for parents are inextricably intertwined.

Good moral principles that are professed *and* practiced at home, on the job, in our communities and public life together create a positive culture for raising good children. Good volunteers *and* good voters who take both service and advocacy seriously are required. Good policy arises out of good politics, which arises out of informed and active parents and citizens who stand up for and organize effectively for children. Good mentoring programs require committed, sensitive people who will stick with children over a sustained period and full-time staff and management infrastructures to train, deploy, and monitor them.

Great visions remain simply that unless they are broken down into manageable and achievable pieces for action that then are well implemented.

Where America Stands

Among industrialized countries, the United States ranks:

1st	in gross domestic product
1st	in the number of millionaires and billionaires
1st	in health technology
1st	in military technology
1st	in military exports
1st	in defense spending
10th	in eighth-grade science scores
16th	in living standards among the poorest one-fifth of children
17th	in rates of low-birthweight births
18th	in the income gap between rich and poor children
18th	in infant mortality
21st	in eighth-grade math scores
Last	in protecting our children against gun violence

According to the Centers for Disease Control and Prevention, U.S. children under age 15 are:

12	times more likely to die from gunfire,
16	times more likely to be murdered by a gun,
11	times more likely to commit suicide with a gun, and
9	times more likely to die in a firearm accident

than children in 25 other industrialized countries *combined*.

Good implementation requires massive public awareness and citizen involvement so that children and parents know about and can actually benefit from policies and programs intended to serve them. Bureaucratic leaders and front-line administrators need good training, high expectations, and an ethic of serving children and families rather than bureaucratic convenience.

3. We can counter the idols of our culture and pervasive adult hypocrisy that are confusing and leading so many children astray. Parents, child advocates, and spiritual leaders must become profoundly and doggedly countercultural. We must reject our culture's glorification of violence, excessive materialism, and easy feel good–ism. We must know and teach our children the difference between heroism and celebrity, not to confuse money with meaning, educational degrees with wisdom and common sense, or power with worthwhile purpose. Someone

has said, "The hero is known for achievements, the celebrity for being well known. Celebrities make the news, heroes make history. Time makes heroes, time dissolves celebrities."

Children need heroes and role models with integrity who struggle to live what they preach and admit it when they make mistakes. I would have been devastated as a child to find that my parents, teachers, and preachers were not who I believed them to be and that they told me one thing and did another. Adult hypocrisy is the number one cause of family, community, national, and moral disintegration today. Our children are confused because we adults are confused about right and wrong.

4. We can have the courage to try to see and speak the truth like the little boy who cried out that the emperor had no clothes amidst the crowd pretending not to see the naked, preening king. Let's not let the spinmeisters in Washington, state capi-

CDF's 1998 Priorities

■ Ensuring every—not every other—American child a Healthy Start in life. We seek to ensure effective state implementation of the recently enacted $48 billion State Children's Health Insurance Program (CHIP), to educate families about CHIP and Medicaid, and to enroll all eligible children.

■ Ensuring every child a Head Start in life by providing parents quality, affordable child care options for all preschool and school-age children, with the assistance of employers, community institutions, and federal, state, and local governments.

■ Ensuring every child a Fair Start in life by educating the public and policy makers about the unacceptable moral, human, and economic costs of permitting 14.5 million children to grow up poor and by mobilizing the nation to end child poverty as we know it. Jobs with decent wages, community economic development, and a quality education for every child must become overarching national priorities.

■ Ensuring every child a Safe Start in life by preventing violence against and by children. Every community must be safe from violent adult and youth offenders. But we oppose the growing criminalization of youths, especially minority youths, and the detention of nonviolent youth offenders and children who are truants and runaways in adult jails, a practice forbidden by current law. We support more effective community-based prevention and interventions like after-school and summer programs, mentoring, and parent training.

■ Ensuring every child a Moral Start in life through creative leadership development and community capacity building to ensure an intergenerational cadre of effective servant-leaders committed to building and sustaining a movement to Leave No Child Behind.

tals, or Hollywood blind us to the unjust budgets and laws that enrich the rich and impoverish the poor, increase the gaps between the have-too-muchs and the have-not-enoughs, and maintain the status quo in our society and world.

Do not be deterred by critics. Sojourner Truth, an illiterate but brilliant slave woman, when told that the building where she was about to speak would be burned if she attempted to address her waiting audience, replied, "Then I will speak to the ashes." A famous evangelist, confronted by a critic saying "I don't like your way of doing things," replied, "I am not very satisfied with them myself. How do you do it?" "Oh, I don't do that sort of thing," the critic responded. "In that case," the preacher said, "I prefer my way of doing it to your way of not doing it." Just keep saying what children need, and keep working and mobilizing until those needs are put first in our nation regardless of opinion poll politics.

5. We must never lose hope and make it contagious. Pass it around. South African President Nel-

son Mandela in his inaugural speech reminded us, "As we let our light shine, we unconsciously give other people permission to do the same." Czech Republic President Vaclav Havel defines hope as an orientation of the spirit that transcends immediate experiences: "It is not the conviction that something will turn out well, but the certainty that something makes sense regardless of how it turns out. The more unpropitious the situation in which we demonstrate hope, the deeper the hope is. It is this hope, above all, which gives us the hope to live and continually try new things, even in conditions that seem hopeless as ours do here and now."

Who would have predicted oppressive apartheid's peaceful overthrow in South Africa and Nelson Mandela walking out of prison after 27 years ramrod straight, preaching reconciliation and forgiveness? Who would have believed that the walls of the Soviet and East European communism would crumble in a heap, as much from decay within as from enemies without? Who thought that child advocates could get the legislative dream team of conservative Utah Republican Orrin Hatch and liberal Massachusetts Democrat Edward Kennedy to introduce bipartisan child health legislation in 1997, successfully take on the powerful tobacco industry, and get a $48 billion state child health insurance program included in a balanced budget agreement partially funded by a tobacco tax? And who would have predicted in 1998 how many politicians in both parties and interest groups who pooh-poohed the request by Senators Hatch and Kennedy for a 43 cent tobacco tax are now lined up seeking a windfall from proposed tobacco tax legislation only a few months later?

6. We can make a commitment to reach out to and save at least one child not our own. Each of us, by making a difference in the life of at least one child, can make a difference in the lives of our communities and nation. Over 3,000 years ago five women saved a people by saving one child. Jochebed, Moses' mother; Miriam, Moses' sister; and the Egyptian pharaoh's daughter who rescued the Jewish slave baby boy Moses from the bulrushes transcended class, caste, religion, and ethnic boundaries to save one boy child who later saved a whole people. Two Hebrew slave midwives, Shiphrah and Puah, also were crucial in the salvation of the Hebrew people. They disobeyed Pharaoh's order to kill all male Hebrew babies because they feared and respected God's law more than the king's. These five unlikely social revolutionaries—a mother, a sister, a royal daughter, and two slave midwives—were God's instruments for the liberation of an entire people and changed the course of human history. Remember their examples when you fear challenging powerful opponents and barriers to child protection and investment. Just do what is right for the child—every child—every time.

7. We can stand together and keep building a powerful moral movement to Leave No Child Behind. Through prayer, service, organized advocacy, action, and through our votes we can and will move America to protect and invest in all our children and in its future. On June 1, 1996, nearly 300,000 citizens of every age, race, faith, and political persuasion stood at the Lincoln Memorial in the largest demonstration of commitment to children in American history.

On June 1, 1997, we stood again for healthy children in more than 700 local events in all 50 states and on the Internet. This Stand for Healthy Children, together with a broad-based national Child Health Now coalition CDF co-convened with the American Cancer Society, helped enact the landmark $48 billion bipartisan State Children's Health Insurance Program (CHIP). Over the next 10 years CHIP will provide health insurance to 5 million of the more than 11 million uninsured children—if states are held accountable.

On June 1, 1998, we will Stand for Quality Child Care in all 50 states and in a Cyber Stand. Our goal is to ensure quality affordable child care options for millions of preschool and school-age children. We reject any efforts by anyone to provoke a "mommy war." We believe that all parents should have a chance to stay at home and care for their children without fear of poverty or should be able to work without worrying about the safety and quality of the care their children receive.

And we will stand every year, for as long as it takes to eliminate physical and spiritual child poverty and the teen pregnancy, violence, school dropout, hopelessness, and moral drift it spawns in children of every race and income group. Jobs, not jails; families, not phantom jets; conscience, not consumerism; morality, not money must become our personal and collective values if America is to be truly great.

It is a long, hard road from Egypt to Canaan and from slavery to freedom. The journey takes perseverance, sacrifice, and faith. It takes good leaders and good followers. Let us continue to move forward together until no child is left behind and our Creator can say well done!

Marian Wright Edelman

FAMILY INCOME

More than 14 million American children—one in five—live in poverty, according to U.S. Census Bureau data. The situation is even more acute for the very young: close to one in four children under age 6 is poor. Moreover, the rate of child poverty has grown over the past several decades, despite rising prosperity in the nation. In 1973, 14.4 percent of all children in America were poor; by 1996 the rate had increased to more than 20 percent. This is a shameful record for one of the world's wealthiest countries.

The cost of child poverty is enormous, both for the children themselves and for society. Poor children suffer more health problems, are more likely to fall behind in school, and are less likely to get a well-paying job after they grow up. The burden thus gets passed along to schools, hospitals, the criminal justice system, and other segments of society. It is both irrational and unconscionable that a nation as rich as America has not done a better job of protecting its most vulnerable members—its children—from the pain and costs of poverty.

The best antidote to child poverty is employment that provides parents with adequate wages to support their families. However, as figure 1.1 shows, many parents of poor children are already in the work force; their earnings are simply too meager to give their children a decent standard of living. We need to help these families become more economically secure and self-sufficient, so that every child has the chance to grow up free from the constraints of poverty.

Family Income: 1973 to 1998

For most of the period since the Children's Defense Fund was founded, the earning and buying power of the typical family with children has remained stagnant. According to Census Bureau data, the median inflation-adjusted income of families with children remained unchanged at about $41,000 from 1976 to 1996, while income rose 18 percent for childless families. At the same time, certain families with children—including young families, those headed by poorly educated parents, lower-income families, and minority families—suffered deep income losses.

A greater struggle for many. Young families (headed by parents under 30) were among the hardest hit. Their median income plunged 33 percent between 1973 and 1994, from nearly $30,000 to less than $20,000 (in 1994 dollars). Median income for families headed by a high school dropout likewise shriveled by close to one-third between 1973 and 1996, while that for families headed by a college graduate rose slightly. During the same period, income gaps between upper- and lower- income families widened (see figure 1.2). The poorest one-fifth of families (with or without children) in 1996 had incomes 9 percent lower than in 1973, while family income for the wealthiest fifth increased 35 percent. Families in the top 5 percent gained most; their incomes were 55 percent higher in 1996 than similar families two decades before.

Minorities in particular have lost ground. While White families with children gained 4 percent from 1976 to 1996, Black families lost 4 percent and Hispanic families, 9 percent. Among young families the racial disparities in the income decline are especially wide, although minority households in every age group sustained losses. From 1973 to 1994, income dropped 46 percent among young Black families with children, compared with 28 percent among young Hispanics and 22 percent among young Whites.

Two-parent families would have lost far more if mothers had not increased their participation in the paid labor force. Between 1975 and 1994, married mothers ages 25 to 29 increased their average annual work time by more than 60 percent, according to CDF's calculations. Even so, young married couples with children typically had incomes 12 percent lower in 1994 than in 1973 because the mother's additional work could not offset the 30 percent decline in the father's earnings in the same period.

The need for both parents to work in order to staunch the loss of wages has had far-reaching consequences for children. More money must be spent on child care and other job-related expenses. The availability of private health insurance through work has plummeted (see chapter 2), so working families with children must spend more out of pocket to meet their health care needs. These burdens are difficult enough for two-parent families but even more challenging for single parents. Their incomes are low; Census Bureau data reveal that in 1996 nearly half (49 percent) of all children in

Figure 1.1 **The Working Poor**

Work does not guarantee that families will escape poverty. A large and growing proportion of poor families with children are headed by someone who works.

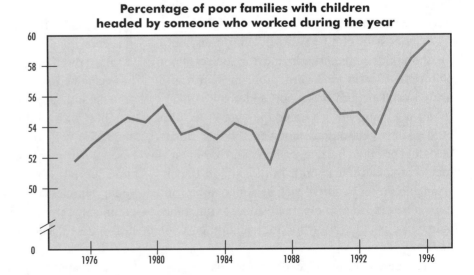

Percentage of poor families with children headed by someone who worked during the year

Source: U.S. Department of Commerce, Bureau of the Census. Calculations by Children's Defense Fund.

families headed by single mothers were below the poverty threshold ($12,516 for a three-person family in that year), compared with 10 percent for children in married-couple families. And the number of single-parent families has increased. Just under a quarter of all American children (23 percent) lived in female-headed families in March 1997—more than double the 1970 rate.

More poverty among children. As already noted, Census Bureau data show that in 1973, 14.4 percent of all children in America were poor; by 1996 the rate had climbed to 20.5 percent. For young families, whose incomes have dropped the most, the child poverty rate doubled, from 20 percent in 1973 to 41 percent in 1994.

Children are more likely to be poor than adults, and their disproportionate poverty is getting worse. CDF calculations of Census Bureau data show that children in the 1960s were, on average, 34 percent more likely to be poor than persons 18 or older. In 1996 children were 81 percent more likely than adults to be poor (20.5 percent of children lived in poverty versus 11.3 percent of adults).

Government cash transfer programs like Social Security lifted 78 percent of otherwise poor elderly Americans (over age 65) out of poverty in 1996. Cash assistance programs for children, including the now-abolished Aid to Families with Dependent Children (AFDC), did a far worse job, raising only 13 percent of children above the poverty line in 1996. Between 1970 and 1996, AFDC benefits lost about half their value, according to CDF calculations based on Congressional Research Service data. In contrast, Social Security, the main source of income security for senior citizens, has maintained its value through automatic cost-of-living adjustments that keep pace with inflation.

Major expansions in the Earned Income Tax Credit (EITC) since 1993 have been of some help to poor families. Census Bureau estimates indicate that the EITC provided enough aid in 1996 to lift nearly one in six poor children out of poverty—more than twice the proportion in 1993. The EITC increases have partially offset increases in child poverty that resulted from the welfare benefit cuts of the early 1980s, at least for families able to obtain work.

Figure 1.2 **Income Inequality**

Since 1985 the richest 5 percent of American families have received a larger share of the nation's income than the poorest 40 percent.

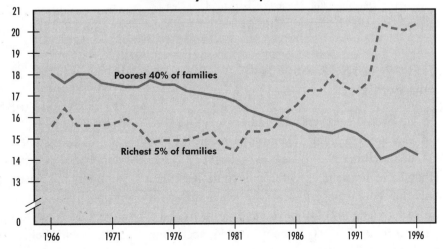

Percentage of total U.S. family income received by rich and poor families

Poorest 40% of families

Richest 5% of families

Source: U.S. Department of Commerce, Bureau of the Census.

Table 1.1 **Children in Poverty, 1996**

Characteristic	Number (thousands)	Percent
Total	14,463	20.5%
Race or ethnicity		
Hispanic[a]	4,237	40.3
Black	4,519	39.9
Asian or Pacific Islander	571	19.5
White	9,044	16.3
Place of residence		
Central city	6,509	30.8
Rural (nonmetropolitan) area	3,167	22.4
Suburb	4,787	13.5
Region		
South	5,543	22.9
West	3,842	22.9
Northeast	2,489	19.2
Midwest	2,590	15.5
Family type[b]		
Female-headed	7,990	49.3
Male-headed	779	22.8
Married couple	5,035	10.1
Family employment status		
Family member works	9,471	14.7
Part-time and/or part-year	5,793	51.9
Full-time and year-round	3,678	6.9

a. Persons of Hispanic origin may be of any race.
b. Data are for children related to the head of household by birth, marriage, or adoption.
Source: U.S. Department of Commerce, Bureau of the Census. Calculations by Children's Defense Fund.

Child Poverty: Pervasive and Persistent

The overall numbers of children living in poverty are deplorable. Even more disturbing, the proportion of children in extreme poverty (that is, in households with an income less than half the federal poverty level, or less than about $6,250 for a family of three) actually grew from 8.5 percent in 1995 to 9.0 percent in 1996, according to Census Bureau data. No racial group is immune: 40.3 percent of Hispanic children, 39.9 percent of

Black children, and 16.3 percent of White children were poor in 1996 (the first year that child poverty among Hispanics outpaced that among Blacks). And poverty afflicts children in every region of the country, in suburbs and rural areas as well as in the cities, and in households headed by couples and by single parents alike (see table 1.1).

The workings of the economy alone will not eradicate child poverty. Although the nation was in its fifth year of economic recovery in 1996, child poverty crept down only to 20.5 percent, from 20.8 percent in 1995. The proportion of poor children living in families where an adult worked at least some of the time soared to 69 percent in 1996, up from 61 percent just three years earlier. The average poor family with children in 1996 got more than twice as much income from work as from welfare (see figure 1.3).

Why Poverty Matters

A new CDF report, *Poverty Matters*, compiles findings from recent research confirming that child poverty is associated with a host of ills. Notably, Jeanne Brooks-Gunn and Greg Duncan, who reviewed several new child poverty studies in their recent volume, *Consequences of Growing Up Poor*, concluded that children living in extreme or prolonged poverty tend to suffer disproportionately from conditions such as stunted growth and lower test scores, and that poverty among preschool children is likely to have damaging effects on school completion many years later. Brooks-Gunn, Duncan, and others report that poor children's worse odds in these areas appear to be linked to poverty itself and not merely to other family characteristics such as parental age, IQ, or marital status.

As U.S. social welfare policy moves toward a work-based system, it is striking that a very strong economy has failed to prevent either an increasing proportion of extremely poor children or more poverty among children younger than 6. Replacing welfare with below-poverty wages will not lessen a poor child's likelihood of suffering from a serious disability, iron deficiency, or falling behind in school. Yet these ills are preventable. To the extent that family income can be increased, outcomes for children improve.

When families were provided with a guaranteed minimum income for at least 18 months in federally funded experiments in the 1970s and early 1980s (the Seattle and Denver Income Maintenance Experiments, or SIME/DIME), school enrollment among the 2,000 16- to 21-year-olds studied increased from 42 percent to 51 percent. More recently, Duncan and others found that a $10,000 annual increase in family income during the first five years of life was linked to nearly a full year's increase in completed schooling.

When poor children drop out of school (and they are twice as likely to do so as middle-income youths), their future earnings are limited. For example, Census Bureau data show that in 1996, 40 percent of families with children headed by a high school dropout were poor, compared with 3 percent of families headed by a college graduate. CDF estimates that for every year that 14.5 million children remain poor, the diminished productivity that results will cost a total of $130 billion in lost future economic output.

Wall Street economist John Mueller, a self-described "conservative Reagan Republican," notes that human capital investments, including such investments in children as school funding and family expenditures on children's development, bring a real rate of return of 12.5 percent in the business economy. This compares favorably to other capital investments such as business equipment, which have a 10.4 percent rate of return, Mueller observes. Investing in children pays off.

Legislative Progress in 1997

Several notable developments last year will help children. The minimum wage increased, changes in the tax laws included a credit for children in low- and moderate-income families, and a new welfare-to-work grant program was funded to help families moving into the work force.

Minimum wage hike. The second installment of the minimum wage increase enacted in 1996 took effect in September 1997, raising the minimum wage to $5.15 per hour. The increase still leaves full-time, year-round minimum wage employment at only 82 percent of the 1998 poverty level

Figure 1.3 **Income Sources for Poor Families**

Earnings provide poor families with more than twice as much income as welfare does.

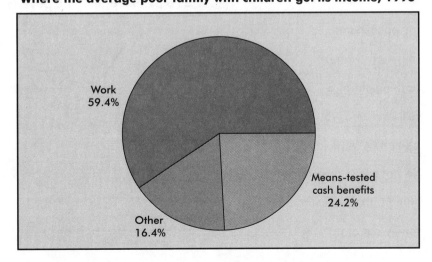

Where the average poor family with children got its income, 1996

Work 59.4%

Means-tested cash benefits 24.2%

Other 16.4%

Source: U.S. Department of Commerce, Bureau of the Census. Calculations by Children's Defense Fund.

for a family of three (see figure 1.4). Although the minimum wage needs to be boosted further to reach the above-poverty levels that existed during most of the 1960s and 1970s, the 1996–97 increase was well-targeted. According to the Economic Policy Institute, 10 million workers (almost 9 percent of the U.S. labor force) will benefit from the 90-cent increase phased in over two years. These are largely adult breadwinners in the lowest brackets of the income scale. (Contrary to the assertion by opponents of the increase that most minimum wage workers are teens, more than 70 percent are over 18.)

Tax relief. In 1997 Congress passed a child tax credit that is worth $400 per child in 1998 and rises to $500 per child in subsequent years. Some 45 million children in 27 million families are expected to benefit from this credit. However, another 20 million children in families with too little income to have a tax liability will *not* be helped.

Efforts by the Clinton Administration and Democratic leaders in Congress succeeded in making the new credit available to some moderate-income working families who would not have benefited from earlier House and Senate versions. As

enacted, the child tax credit is computed before the Earned Income Tax Credit. Thus a two-parent family with two children and an income of $23,000 in 1997 will get $675 from the credit to wipe out its income tax liability and will still qualify for a $1,668 refund through the EITC. Families with three or more children can receive a higher child tax credit, available as a refund, to the extent that their Social Security payroll taxes exceed their EITC. If the credit had also been made refundable for low-income families with fewer children, it would have reached more poor children in working families. As it stands, two-parent families with incomes as high as $110,000 and single-parent families with incomes up to $75,000 will benefit from the credit.

As noted earlier, the EITC continues to be one of the most significant forms of assistance to low-income working families. In 1996 the EITC was worth $25 billion to 18.7 million low-income families—considerably more than the $16 billion disbursed each year through the Temporary Assistance for Needy Families (TANF) block grant, the successor to AFDC. In 1997 families with two or more children received a maximum EITC of $3,656 if their earnings were between $9,140 and

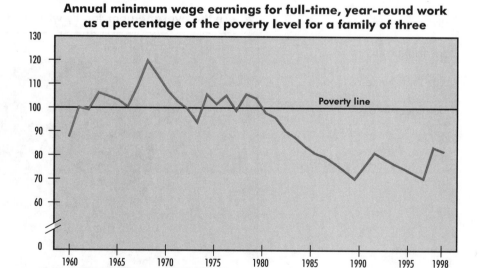

Figure 1.4 **Inadequacy of the Minimum Wage**

Even after the 1997 increase in the minimum wage, earnings from a full-time, year-round, minimum wage job do not come close to lifting a three-person family out of poverty.

Annual minimum wage earnings for full-time, year-round work as a percentage of the poverty level for a family of three

Poverty line

Source: U.S. Department of Commerce, Bureau of the Census. Calculations by Children's Defense Fund.

$11,930. Above that threshold, the credit gradually diminishes, phasing out when the family's income reaches $29,290. The value of the EITC will be adjusted upward for inflation annually.

Welfare-to-work funding. The new federal welfare-to-work grant program provides $3 billion in 1998 and 1999 for employment-related services targeted to those welfare recipients likely to have the most trouble finding stable jobs on their own. States can use the funds to create or subsidize jobs and to support work through child care, transportation, and counseling or training services.

Implementing the 1996 Welfare Law

The welfare law enacted in August 1996 radically changed cash assistance programs for millions of families when it replaced AFDC with TANF. It also eliminated food stamp benefits for immigrant families and restricted eligibility for Supplemental Security Income (SSI)—cash assistance for low-income seniors and persons with disabilities.

A great deal of attention in 1997 was focused on the precipitous drop in welfare caseloads across the nation. Between January 1993 and August 1997, caseloads plunged 27 percent, a drop of 1.35 million families. Many argue that the caseload decline means the new TANF program is working. However, if the goal of the welfare changes is to help families with children move into work and out of poverty, we must take a closer look at what states have actually done under the new law and what happens to families when they leave the public assistance rolls.

Little movement from welfare to work. Few states track families when they leave welfare. We do know that in the quarter ending June 30, 1997, states reported that only 15 percent of closed cases were due to the increased earnings of recipients. This figure understates earnings because some parents may not inform welfare agencies of their employment after they leave welfare. Even so, it is clear—and alarming to anyone concerned about children's well-being—that most of those losing welfare benefits are not gaining paychecks that can support a family.

Stringent sanctions. Many families are losing benefits because of stiff penalties for failure to

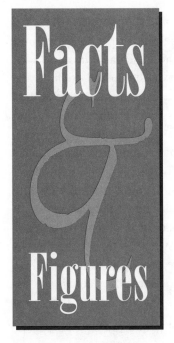

Facts & Figures

- One in five American children lives in poverty. Poor children numbered almost 14.5 million in 1996.

- In 1996, 69 percent of poor children lived in families where someone worked—up from 61 percent just three years earlier.

- Among young families (headed by a parent under 30), median income plunged 33 percent between 1973 and 1994, and the child poverty rate doubled from 20 to 41 percent.

- More than 1.3 million families have lost welfare benefits since 1993—a drop of 27 percent. Former welfare recipients who find jobs typically earn less than $10,000 a year.

- Families with children accounted for more than a third of the homeless Americans in urban areas who sought shelter in 1997.

- Work alone is not always a ladder out of poverty. For young mothers who began the 1980s on welfare and later worked, average hourly wages rose only 6 cents per year—reaching just $6.85 in 1990.

meet work requirements or follow various other program rules, such as signing a personal responsibility contract. About two-thirds of states will terminate cash benefits for the whole family if a parent does not participate in work activities, even though federal law mandates only a cut in assistance. In the second quarter of 1997, failure to comply with program rules accounted for about 40 percent of all cases closed, and one in five states cited noncompliance as the reason for closing more than half of the cases.

A May 1997 study from the General Accounting Office (GAO) reported on benefit terminations in states operating welfare demonstration programs before the new law was implemented. These terminations involved losses of assistance not because of time limits, which had not yet taken effect, but because of penalties for noncompliance. Of 18,000 terminations in 33 states, 13,000 occurred in just three—Iowa, Massachusetts, and Wisconsin. Of the Massachusetts families who lost aid, only 48 percent received income afterward from the three most common sources of cash income: earnings, pensions, or child support. Only 23 percent specifically had earnings, which could have been generated by anyone in the household, not necessarily the parent. It is worth noting that about half of these 23 percent had income from earnings *before* leaving welfare, combining cash aid with low wages. That is, only a little more than one in 10 actually moved from welfare to new earnings, whether their own or someone else's. These findings do not encourage optimism that children and families will rise out of poverty when they leave welfare.

In the rush to reduce caseloads, states have in some cases been too quick to terminate benefits when families are really complying with the rules. When Wisconsin began implementing its welfare changes in late 1996 and early 1997, about half the appeals for restoration of benefits were successful. In other states, such as South Dakota and Tennessee, anecdotal evidence suggests that some parents who have sought outside help after losing assistance have had their benefits restored.

When families do not follow the rules, early evidence indicates there are factors making compli-

ance difficult. Minnesota asked its welfare case managers to assess whether their clients who had been receiving aid for at least two years had any of a long list of "barriers to employment": illiteracy, physical or mental disability, substance abuse, experience of family violence, and so forth. They found that 34 percent of the caseload had at least one of those barriers, and 16 percent had more than one. Among families penalized for noncompliance, however, barriers to employment were far more prevalent—between two-thirds and three-quarters of the families had at least one. And not surprisingly, mothers suffering from depression, caring for a child with a disability, or trying to escape from an abusive partner were more likely to miss appointments or work or to refuse to cooperate in establishing paternity.

Time limits. About three-quarters of the states have set a lifetime limit of 60 months on benefits—the maximum allowable using federal TANF funds. Eleven of these states have chosen shorter time limits followed by periods of ineligibility, but families are allowed to accumulate 60 months of benefits in a lifetime. (For example, benefits may be collected two years out of every five, up to a cumulative maximum of five years.) Another nine states have opted for lifetime limits shorter than five years. (See box 1.1 for more details.)

Although federal dollars cannot be used for aid to families beyond the 60-month lifetime limit (with 20 percent of the caseload allowed to be exempt), some states have established exempt categories of families and have committed state dollars to pay for their benefits. For instance, Illinois and parts of Maine are using state funds to provide cash aid in every month that families work at wages low enough to qualify for partial assistance. These months therefore do not count toward the time limit. New Jersey gives state-funded benefits to families with an incapacitated parent or primary caregiver. Maine and Wyoming assist families in which the parent or caregiver is pursuing education or training, including postsecondary study.

In marked contrast to the states that have sought to preserve aid to certain families, Indiana

Box 1.1 **Welfare Time Limits: State Choices**

The 1996 welfare law allows recipients of Temporary Assistance for Needy Families (TANF) to collect federally funded benefits for a maximum of 60 months. States can, however, use state funds or waivers to extend benefits; they can also set shorter lifetime limits and/or restrict the number of consecutive months during which recipients may collect assistance. About three-quarters of all states have chosen lifetime limits of 60 months, although some impose earlier restrictions, as detailed below.

Time triggers for states are as follows:

- **12 months:** *Texas* (with no statutory lifetime limit) restricts aid to 12, 24, or 36 months for adults, depending on work experience and education, followed by 60 months of ineligibility for the adult; makes exceptions in cases of hardship.

- **18 months:** *Tennessee* (with a 60-month lifetime limit) restricts aid to 18 consecutive months followed by three months of ineligibility, with countywide extensions when unemployment is twice the state average.

- **21 months:** *Connecticut* sets a 21-month lifetime limit, with extensions possible.

- **24 months:** *Arkansas* and *Idaho* set 24-month lifetime limits. *Arizona* (with a 60-month lifetime limit) restricts aid to 24 of 60 months for adults, with extensions possible; families receive reduced aid after 24 months. *Florida* (with a 48-month lifetime limit) restricts aid to 24 of 60 months, or 36 of 72 for long-term recipients and parents under age 24 with poor job skills. *Illinois* (with a 60-month lifetime limit) restricts aid to 24 cumulative months for families whose youngest child is 13 or older, followed by 24 months of ineligibility. *Indiana* sets a 24-month lifetime limit for adults in state work programs, with extensions possible; after adults lose aid, families receive reduced benefits until the 60-month lifetime limit is reached. *Louisiana* (with a 60-month lifetime limit) restricts aid to 24 of 60 months. *Massachusetts* (with no lifetime limit) restricts aid to 24 of 60 months. *Nebraska* (with no lifetime limit) restricts aid to 24 of 48 months, with extensions possible. *Nevada* (with a 60-month lifetime limit) restricts aid to 24 months followed by 12 of ineligibility. *North Carolina* (with a 60-month lifetime limit) restricts aid to 24 cumulative months, followed by 36 of ineligibility; allows variation in pilot counties. *Oregon* (with no lifetime limit) restricts aid to 24 of 84 months. *South Carolina* (with a 60-month lifetime limit) restricts aid to 24 of 120 months. *Virginia* (with a 60-month lifetime limit) restricts aid to 24 months, followed by 12 of Medicaid, child care, and transportation aid, followed by 24 of ineligibility.

- **36 months:** *Missouri* sets a 36-month lifetime limit for adults who have completed self-sufficiency agreements, after which the family may receive reduced benefits until the 60-month lifetime limit is reached. *New Mexico* sets a 36-month lifetime limit. *Ohio* (with a 60-month lifetime limit) restricts aid to 36 cumulative months followed by 24 months of ineligibility, with extensions possible. *Utah* sets a 36-month lifetime limit, with extensions possible for part-time workers.

- **48 months:** *Delaware* sets a 48-month lifetime limit. *Georgia* sets a 48-month lifetime limit for household heads and spouses; reduces benefits to others after 48 months.

(continued on the following page)

Box 1.1 **Welfare Time Limits: State Choices** (continued)

■ **60 months:** *Alabama, Alaska, Colorado, District of Columbia, Hawaii, Iowa, Kansas, Kentucky, Maine, Maryland, Minnesota, Mississippi, Montana, New Hampshire, New Jersey, North Dakota, Oklahoma, Pennsylvania, South Dakota, Washington, West Virginia, Wisconsin,* and *Wyoming* set unrestricted 60-month lifetime limits. *California* and *Rhode Island* reduce but do not terminate benefits after 60 months. *New York*'s Safety Net program helps families who lose benefits after 60 months. *Michigan* and *Vermont* set no time limits but require work after a specified period.

Every state plans to exempt some families (federal TANF dollars may be used to exempt up to 20 percent of the caseload from the 60-month time limit). Exemptions commonly cover families with an adult who has a disability, is over age 60, or is caring for a dependent with a disability; families experiencing domestic violence; and minor parents complying with school and living arrangement requirements.

The Center for Law and Social Policy and the Center on Budget and Policy Priorities provided help in assembling this list.

---

has made the time limit far more harsh by keeping the clock ticking even when families begin to work. The months those families continue to receive Medicaid are counted toward their state's 24-month lifetime limit, even though they are not receiving any cash assistance. A family who finds low-paid work and needs Medicaid coverage for two years will find itself ineligible for further aid if the parent should become unemployed. Advocates in Indiana are fighting the state over this interpretation of the law.

Work requirements. The 1996 federal welfare law requires that within 24 months of receiving TANF, parents or caregivers engage either in work (subsidized or unsubsidized) or in related activities such as job search, community service, on-the-job training, or a maximum 12 months of vocational training. Many forms of education or training do not count toward the law's first 20 hours per week of required work, and amendments to the law passed in the 1997 Balanced Budget Act made the education provisions even more restrictive. Whereas the original law limited vocational train-

ing to 20 percent of the entire adult caseload, now only 30 percent of those participating in work activities are eligible for such training. For many welfare recipients who had hoped their education or training would lead to better careers and long-term self-sufficiency, the restrictions mean setting aside their studies to take low-paying jobs.

The federal work participation requirement is 30 percent of all TANF single parents in Fiscal Year (FY) 1998, rising to 50 percent in FY 2002 and beyond. Seventy-five percent of two-parent families must have one parent engaged in work now, rising to 90 percent in FY 1999 and thereafter. It is expected that most states will meet the work participation rates for single-parent families, at least in the first year or two, but that states are likely to have trouble fulfilling the two-parent family requirements. States that fail to meet the participation rates will lose some of their federal TANF block grant dollars.

The federal Fair Labor Standards Act and other worker protection laws require that parents working off their grants (but not those pursuing education or training) must be paid at the equivalent of the minimum wage and must be protected against unsafe or discriminatory practices. Congressional efforts to deny these protections to TANF workers were unsuccessful in 1997, although they may resurface in 1998. If single-parent families do not receive enough in TANF (plus food stamps, at state option) to equal 30 hours at the minimum wage, states must either pay them more or reduce the number of hours they are required to work. If states reduce the required hours, these families will not count toward the federal work participation rates.

The Effects of Welfare Changes: Putting More Children at Risk

How has life changed for the millions of children affected by the 1996 welfare law? It is still too early to tell precisely, but the new rules for welfare recipients, immigrants, and children with disabilities put needy children in a more precarious position than ever.

The plight of families pushed off welfare. Placing work requirements on families without offering them the services they need to comply will force them off the caseload, imposing far greater hardship on children and families. As the most employable parents find jobs, those remaining in TANF are even more likely to suffer from debilitating problems.

Oregon, with a caseload drop of 54 percent between 1993 and 1997, now finds that a majority of families remaining in its TANF program are seriously troubled. Oregon estimates that 75 percent of its parents on welfare have mental health problems, 50 percent have substance abuse problems, and 50 percent are subject to violence. The state has been willing to provide appropriate services, and it counts mental health counseling, for example, as an allowable activity on the path to job readiness. Utah has taken a similar approach, conducting individualized assessments and creating self-sufficiency plans with parents. These plans may include activities such as literacy training, substance abuse treatment, or getting a driver's license

if they are seen as moving the individual toward successful job placement.

Parents who do find jobs are in most cases unable to secure incomes above the poverty level. Of the first 40 Virginia families hitting their two-year time limit on the receipt of cash assistance, 35 had jobs, but only eight were living above the poverty level. Nationwide about half the parents on welfare lack high school diplomas, and their income potential is not good. Two-thirds (64 percent) of all single mothers who have not finished high school live with their children below the poverty line, according to the Census Bureau. The future holds little promise of rising wages for parents leaving welfare. Brookings Institution economist Gary Burtless reports that young women who began the 1980s on welfare and later worked received real pay raises averaging only 6 cents per hour per year by 1990.

Comparing women of similar backgrounds over a 10-year period reveals some significant differences between those who receive welfare at some point and those who don't. In 1997 the Urban Institute analyzed data on women ages 18–27 from the National Longitudinal Survey of Youth and found that 45 percent of the welfare participants had not completed high school, compared with only 10 percent of women not on welfare. One-third of mothers who had received welfare had basic skills at the third-grade level; only 6 percent of nonrecipients had comparably low skills. Most significantly, only 24 percent of mothers who had received welfare at some point found jobs paying $8 an hour or more.

Difficulty in securing well-paying work is not the only problem facing families leaving welfare. The GAO study mentioned earlier found that those who lost cash aid tended also to lose food stamps and Medicaid, even though the great majority of families remained eligible for this support. In Wisconsin 84 percent of the families had received food stamps before termination; afterward only 56 percent continued to do so. Similarly, 100 percent of these Wisconsin families had received Medicaid before losing their cash aid; afterward that number fell to 53 percent.

Cutoffs of food stamps and Medicaid continue to accompany the loss of cash aid in other states as the 1996 federal law is implemented. Why the big drop-off? In part, families accustomed to getting cash aid, food stamps, and Medicaid as a package may not understand that they are still eligible. For some, going to the welfare office every three months to certify continuing eligibility is a difficult hoop to jump through. Parents who are working may be unable to get to welfare offices open only during regular business hours; others may find transportation expensive or unavailable. During the debate surrounding passage of the 1996 welfare law, proponents argued that although cash aid would be limited, families would be able to count on food stamps and Medicaid as their safety net. For significant numbers of families, the net is in tatters.

Immigrants. The 1996 federal welfare law denied Supplemental Security Income and food stamps to most legal immigrants until they become citizens, and gave states the option of continuing Medicaid and TANF for immigrants here legally at the time the law passed. Immigrants who entered the country later (after August 1996) were barred from receiving TANF or Medicaid for five years. States could opt to provide these benefits after five years, but they were also free to deny them permanently (even to those immigrants who had entered the country before the law was enacted).

By calling attention to the plight of elderly and disabled immigrants who had no hope of making up their lost SSI or food stamp income, advocates succeeded in reversing some of the cuts in 1997. Immigrants in the country legally as of August 1996 can now receive SSI if they were receiving it then or if they subsequently develop a disability. They remain ineligible for food stamps. Advocates pushing for legislation to change this have been encouraged by a partial restoration proposed in the President's FY 1999 budget. All states except Alabama have opted to continue TANF for legal immigrants. Twelve states (California, Florida, Illinois, Massachusetts, Maryland, Minnesota, Nebraska, New Jersey, New York, Rhode Island, Texas, and

Washington) are also providing aid in some form to at least some of the legal immigrants denied food stamps under federal law.

Children with disabilities. The 1996 federal law made it more difficult for poor children with disabilities to qualify for Supplemental Security Income. About 288,000 case reviews were required to determine whether children receiving SSI under the older standards would still qualify. As states have conducted these reviews under rules established by the Social Security Administration, they have denied assistance to large numbers of children. As of December 1997 about 263,000 cases (more than 90 percent) had been reviewed, resulting in the cutoff of benefits for more than half—about 135,000 children. The denial rate has varied widely among states, with nine states terminating assistance in 70 percent or more of the reviewed cases.

New applicants for SSI have even greater problems. Although the eligibility criteria emphasize matching a child's condition to those on an official medical list, the new law expressly allows the Social Security Administration to assess whether the limitations of a child's functioning are equivalent to conditions on the official list. The Clinton Administration was interpreting this provision so restrictively that between August 1996, when the law passed, and October 1997, only 32.2 percent of the children applying were approved. This was below the 42.8 approval rate in 1989, when an even more stringent eligibility standard was in effect. One indication of the overzealous restriction of benefits is that as of fall 1997, children in the first phase of appealing their denials succeeded 58 percent of the time. Prior to the new law, only about 10 percent of denials were reversed in the first stage of appeal.

In a victory for children with disabilities, Social Security Administration Commissioner Kenneth Apfel agreed to review the agency's implementation of the new law. He concluded in December 1997 that procedures were flawed, especially in mental retardation cases. The agency announced that it would review all of those denials, plus other cases with a high likelihood of error, including rejections of new applications. About 45,000 cases will be reviewed in all. In addition, families who may have been discouraged from appealing their child's denial will be given an extended period in which to do so. The Social Security Administration anticipates that of the 135,000 children who lost SSI, about 35,000 will have their benefits restored.

Inadequate Child Support

Census Bureau data for 1992 show that across the country, 11.5 million parents were raising children with an absent parent. Of those 11.5 million, only 54 percent had child support orders. Moreover, of the 5.3 million parents who had child support awarded and due, only *half* received the full amount due. About a quarter received partial payment, and a quarter received nothing at all.

That's a terrible record for children. And the problem cuts across race and income lines, affecting children in every community. Jointly funded federal-state child support agencies are supposed to help families collect child support—both families on welfare and other families who ask for help. In some states the system works well; in others, poorly. Nationally, though, the record is disheartening; some child support was collected in only 19 percent of all state agency cases in FY 1995 (the last year for which there are nationally reported data). Over five years this collection rate has remained virtually unchanged, although states have improved the rate at which they establish paternity—a vital first step for children born to unmarried parents.

Some additional help is on the way. In 1997 state legislatures dealt with child support changes required by the 1996 welfare law. They streamlined the process for establishing paternity and set up registries of newly hired employees to track down missing noncustodial parents and begin wage withholding quickly. They also devised new strategies to help collect support, such as revoking professional or driver's licenses and seizing bank accounts when child support is not paid. These are promising measures, modeled on successes in pioneering states.

At the same time, a number of states failed to meet an October 1, 1997 deadline to have automated systems up and running. Automation is important because it can help states stretch scarce resources and speed up the child support process. Most of the states that missed the deadline are close, but a few may be years away. Congress will be monitoring this problem carefully in the coming year. It is also expected to take up legislation that would reward states for better child support outcomes.

An Effective State Initiative: Making Work Pay in Illinois

One painful lesson of the welfare-to-work movement is that even full-time work at or near the minimum wage is not enough to pull families with children out of poverty. If the goal of ending poverty is to be achieved (especially when education and training are restricted), then parents' earnings must be supplemented from other sources. When child support and/or the Earned Income Tax Credit do not provide sufficient help, partial cash assistance benefits can be effective in boosting low wages.

Many states are making it easier for families with low earnings to receive small amounts of supplemental cash aid. But a dilemma has arisen in the new world of time limits. Families receiving even small sums use up a month of assistance, just as do those receiving full benefits. Parents may therefore be inclined *not* to combine welfare and work, even though the extra income could provide a margin of stability.

Illinois has found a creative solution, choosing to use state funds to offer an incentive for long-term employment. If a parent works at least 20 hours per week at pay low enough to qualify for partial assistance, the family's benefits are paid out of state dollars, which do not have to count toward the federal time limit.

Illinois combines this approach with its Work Pays program, which allows partial benefits until earnings reach the federal poverty line. The Work Pays program, the centerpiece of the state's welfare reform efforts, has dramatically increased the number of families combining welfare with work. In October 1993 a mere 6.9 percent of the caseload—14,144 families—had earnings; by August 1997 that number jumped to 39,795 families, or 25.4 percent of the caseload. Furthermore, 95 Illinois counties reported that at least 30 percent of their TANF families were working in 1997; not a single county had such a high proportion three years before. The state's willingness to provide a wage supplement based on each family's need and work effort, and not on an arbitrary time limit, seems to be putting more families on the track to employment and self-sufficiency.

Moving Forward: A 1998 Agenda for Action

A number of concrete steps can be taken to lift children out of poverty. Parents need the tools to get and keep jobs, and families need income supports when jobs do not pay enough to make ends meet. Even in a thriving economy, some families live in areas where work is not available and jobs must be created. Other parents simply cannot work, either temporarily or permanently, because of their disability or their child's. Not every family has the same needs, of course. Literacy training is a priority for some; others may need the chance to finish college. Many require subsidized child care; others have to find a way to get to work. For some, cash aid is essential to keep their children from destitution.

Eliminating child poverty is critical on grounds of humanity and compassion, but it is imperative, too, as an investment in our economic future. What actions can make a real difference in the lives of children and families?

■ Families need access to good jobs and the supports that make work possible. Federal and state governments should invest in child care and transportation so that parents can get to work and know that their children are safe and nurtured. Mothers, especially those escaping from abusive situations, may need counseling,

treatment for depression, or help in recovering from substance abuse before they can perform at work.

■ Parents need education and training as a means to compete for jobs with good pay. The federal government should give states the flexibility to count training or education as an allowable work activity, because every year of education improves the family's chance of rising out of poverty. Federal financial aid should expand on the work-study model to offer stipends to parents trying to upgrade their employment potential. Businesses should follow the recommendation of the National Association of Manufacturers and invest between 3 and 5 percent of payroll on employee training.

■ Children should be able to count on the support of both parents. States should eliminate the disincentives for marriage that linger from the old welfare system, dropping the rules that made it harder for two-parent families to qualify for aid. When parents cannot stay together, the absent parent should pay child support. States should act quickly to automate their child support enforcement systems, to register newly hired employees, and to use other enforcement tools to improve on the current dismal collection record.

■ States should pilot child support assurance programs. Under such programs, the state makes vigorous efforts to collect support from the absent parent. If no support payments can be obtained, however, the state pays a base amount per child that provides a sure source of income and, when combined with the custodial parent's earnings, offers families a far greater chance to escape from poverty.

■ The minimum wage should be raised until a full-time minimum wage job pays at least enough to support a family of three above the poverty line, as it did during most of the 1960s and 1970s.

■ States should enact their own Earned Income Tax Credits, as nine states already have. Massachusetts, Minnesota, New York, Vermont, and

Wisconsin have created refundable credits available to families even if their earnings are too low to owe taxes.

- The federal government should restore food stamps for legal immigrants, including hundreds of thousands of children, and should reverse the cutbacks that reduce food stamps for families with children and high housing costs.

- Cities, counties, businesses, and community institutions should create real jobs in areas with job shortages, taking advantage of existing tax incentives or wage subsidies when appropriate. Public jobs, with adequate pay and benefits, should meet community needs, including the need for housing rehabilitation, infrastructure repair, and services for children, youth, and the elderly.

- All employers, private and public, must do their part by paying family-supporting wages and benefits. A first step would be to endorse livable-wage campaigns calling for pay at least one-third higher than the minimum wage.

- Current unemployment compensation rules should be revised so that low-income workers with children are more likely to qualify for benefits. Today only about one in 10 single mothers with work experience who receive welfare ever qualifies for an unemployment check.

Ending child poverty in America requires an all-out campaign to help parents get and keep jobs that ensure a decent living. A national agenda to make work pay will enable working families to rise out of poverty and build better futures for their children.

Spotlight on Housing and Homelessness

Safe, decent housing is a cornerstone of a child's life. Having a place to call home and a feeling of belonging somewhere helps provide the security and stability that children need for healthy development and growth. Unfortunately, our nation is in the throes of a growing housing crisis that has profound implications for poor children.

The housing conditions of low-income families and children have worsened over the past 25 years for three key reasons: real average income for poor Americans has declined, rent increases have exceeded inflation, and the supply of affordable housing available to low-income families has shrunk. Rent burdens (the ratio of rent to income) for low-income families have increased so much that a majority now spend more than 40 percent of their income on rent. As a result, they often have inadequate funds to meet other pressing needs.

For too many poor families, adequate housing at any price is out of reach. A 1997 survey by the U.S. Conference of Mayors found that families with children represent 36 percent of those in homeless shelters. Many young families today are also finding that the American dream of homeownership is just that—a dream. In past generations, the GI Bill and other government housing programs helped young families buy homes or afford adequate shelter. Less assistance is available today, and children pay the price. Children who are homeless or constantly moving from one dilapidated place to another suffer numerous serious and long-lasting consequences: poor health, missed school, and emotional damage.

Growing hardship for low-income renters. In September 1997 Harvard's Joint Center for Housing Studies issued a new report warning that the housing crisis is rapidly worsening for low-income renters squeezed by government cutbacks. Welfare reform and retrenchment in government housing assistance have set up a "collision course for the nation's most disadvantaged families," the report states. "There are definitely a huge number of people that will have a hard time paying rent as a result of changes in welfare," says William Apgar, the former director of the center and now an official at the U.S. Department of Housing and Urban Development (HUD).

With rigid time limits on the provision of welfare benefits taking effect, hundreds of thousands of very low-income families will soon be ineligible for assistance. Although some former welfare recipients find employment, they typically make less than $10,000 per year and incur additional costs for child care and transportation to work. The majority of former welfare recipients continue to live below the official poverty line and have severe rent burdens. In addition, their jobs are often short-term, leaving them vulnerable to any slowdown in the economy.

According to HUD figures based on the Census Bureau's 1995 American Housing Survey data, more than 6.8 million renter households had severe housing problems in 1995. An estimated 2.7 million households with children experienced "worst-case" problems of overcrowding, deteriorated housing conditions, or heavy rent burdens (spending more than half their income on rent and utilities).

This feature was prepared in cooperation with Wayne Sherwood, housing researcher with Sherwood Research Associates and former research director of the Council of Large Public Housing Authorities.

The severe toll on children. Lack of adequate, affordable housing has adverse consequences for all poor Americans, but the impact is particularly harsh on children. Inability to afford housing is one reason poor families tend to move from place to place, forcing the children to change schools frequently. A new CDF report, *Poverty Matters,* cites studies showing that these children have lower math and reading scores and are much less likely to finish high school on time. *Poverty Matters* also reports findings that poor children often live in poor housing with faulty pipes and other water leakage problems, which can result in mold and roach infestations. These, in turn, cause many children to develop respiratory diseases like asthma, which are major reasons for missing school. Poor children also have more than triple the average risk of lead poisoning because of exposure to lead paint, a common problem in old housing. Lead poisoning causes neurological damage and has been linked to lower IQ and long-term behavioral problems.

The Doc4Kids Project at Boston Medical Center and Children's Hospital has compiled numerous examples of children whose health has been compromised by poor housing. The 1998 project report, *Not Safe at Home: How America's Housing Crisis Threatens the Health of Its Children,* documents cases of toddlers who develop life-threatening asthma because of cockroaches in summer or inadequate heat in winter and schoolchildren whose brains have been poisoned by lead. Such health damage can permanently cloud children's futures, increasing medical costs and impairing their ability to learn and work.

The impact on young families. Paying for housing is a particular strain for the 5.8 million families headed by a parent under the age of 30, who tend to have low earning power and high child care expenses. A 1997 CDF report, *Rescuing the American Dream*, noted that in 1993 more than 2 million (38 percent) of these young families exceeded federal affordability standards by spending more the 30 percent of their income on housing. A substantial number—900,000—spent more than 50 percent.

Those who aspire to homeownership are finding it harder and harder to attain. *Rescuing the American Dream* found that in March 1980 nearly one young family in two owned their own home; by March 1994 that proportion had dropped to only one in three. In the past, many young parents earned enough income to save up for a down payment or were helped on the path to homeownership by programs like the GI Bill. Today, with wages falling for young workers (see chapter 1), too many struggle simply to pay the rent.

Roughly 1.6 million young families cope with high housing costs by "doubling up" with grandparents or other relatives. Some have little choice; doubling up is sometimes the last step before landing in a homeless shelter. The crowded housing conditions that may arise when families try to share expenses can contribute to increases in respiratory infections, family conflicts, and other stresses.

Dwindling housing supply and more homelessness. A key finding of the Joint Center for Housing Studies 1997 report is that the recent revisions in welfare programs will lead to further erosion of the nation's stock of affordable rental housing. The new welfare rules will lower the incomes, and therefore the rent-paying ability, of the poorest people. Private landlords, in turn, reaping less revenue, will have fewer resources and less incentive to maintain low-cost rental units, leading to further loss and deterioration of such housing. Nonprofit housing providers, community development corporations, and even public housing agencies are hurt by this crunch. "This cycle of disinvestment will result in an acceleration of the already rapid disappearance of affordable, low-cost units from the inventory," the report says.

As low-cost housing becomes more scarce, more poor Americans are finding themselves out on the streets. In its 1997 survey of 29 cities, the U.S. Conference of Mayors found a 3 percent increase in requests for emergency shelter since 1996. This is a troubling statistic in the midst of economic growth and extremely low unemployment (below 5 percent). Furthermore, whereas single individuals accounted for most of the homeless in the past, the number of homeless families with children has steadily increased. It is a national disgrace that more and more children cannot count on a roof over their heads. Being homeless or living in a shelter is very hard on children. It breaks up families, disrupts schooling, and is associated with increases in child health problems and extreme emotional distress. No child should have to live so precariously.

Waning government help. What are federal, state, and local governments doing to respond to the crisis in affordable housing? Unfortunately, less and less. While federal tax benefits for middle- and upper-income housing continue to expand rapidly, federal outlays for low-income housing assistance are not growing enough to keep pace with inflation. In real dollar terms they are shrinking. The budgets for Fiscal Years (FYs) 1996, 1997, and 1998 included no funds for additional Section 8 rental assistance (rent subsidies for low-income tenants in privately owned housing). The number of public housing units has been shrinking as a result of demolitions, poor maintenance, and lack of modernization. It is also distressing that many housing authorities, feeling pinched by the federal funding crunch, plan to stop admitting very low-income people and start converting many of their developments into housing for families with incomes over $25,000, using scarce public housing dollars to subsidize their rents. Unless these trends are reversed, the next five years may bring further declines in housing for the families most in need. The good news is that the Administration has proposed new Section 8 funding in its FY 1999 budget.

Harmful legislation. Many changes made in the appropriations laws for FY 1996–FY 1998, as well as regulatory changes made by the Clinton Administration, have put families in worse straits.

- Congress suspended the federal requirement that local housing authorities target assistance to the neediest of the poor. Local authorities now have more latitude to set minimum rents that may be charged to even the most destitute. They also have broader discretion to rent more units to families who have higher incomes and need smaller subsidies (leaving fewer units available to poorer tenants). It makes sense to have more working families qualify for public and assisted housing, but many local agencies seem to be using the elimination of federal preferences to "skim the cream" from their waiting lists, picking only higher-income working families who appear unlikely to require counseling or specialized services. In so doing, they are closing the door on many who are homeless or in need of affordable, stable housing before they can seek, obtain, and hold jobs.

- The rent levels used to determine Section 8 subsidies have been reduced, raising the share of rent paid by some families and increasing the likelihood that Section 8 units will be overconcentrated in low-income neighborhoods.
- The long-standing requirement that a local housing authority must replace every unit of public housing lost through demolition or sale was suspended, creating a rush by housing agencies to tear down or sell off many properties. While one-for-one replacement of every unit lost is not always appropriate, in most communities it is desirable to replace the majority of lost units, because housing needs are still great.
- Funding is not being provided for replacements, yet HUD continues to push for even more public housing demolitions, thereby reducing the stock of affordable housing still further.

Some encouraging developments. Despite the troubling trends, there were some positive accomplishments and even a few signs of hope in 1997. Local housing and community development groups are building tens of thousands of new low-income units each year and in some cases helping to reclaim whole neighborhoods. They typically package federal financing—from, for example, the Community Development Block Grant, the federal Low Income Housing Tax Credit, and the HOME program—with funds from state and local governments, foundations, and private sources, including key groups like the Local Initiatives Support Corporation, the Enterprise Foundation, and the Neighborhood Reinvestment Corporation. Efforts were under way in late 1997 to expand Section 8 funding in the FY 1999 federal budget that could be used in conjunction with these new development initiatives.

A significant legislative achievement was that the Administration and Congress worked together to extend subsidies for the numerous Section 8 units for which funding was set to expire in FY 1998 or later. While this action will not increase the total number of Section 8 units funded, and the subsidy amount per unit will shrink somewhat in the future, at least the current Section 8 units will not lose their assistance.

A second achievement was a provision in the FY 1998 appropriations bill allowing HUD to restructure some Section 8 project-based assistance in a manner that will relieve some of the pressure on the HUD budget. It is not yet clear, however, how the Internal Revenue Service will treat these restructurings. If landlords participating in them receive relatively unfavorable tax treatment, many may opt out of the Section 8 program and raise their rents, which would force many low-income tenants to move out.

Although Congress failed to provide enough funding for low-income housing, it stopped short of passing legislation that would fundamentally undermine the entire housing program. Since early 1995, lawmakers have been considering proposals that would drastically change the nation's housing assistance programs and worsen the housing crisis for very low-income families. In 1997 this legislation failed to pass for the third year in a row. It is too early to assume the battle is over, however, as Congress will be reconsidering the matter in 1998.

The proposed legislation's most troublesome provisions would affect the future beneficiaries of public housing and Section 8 programs. Current recipients of such assistance earn, on average, only about 20 percent of the median income in the local area. The House measure would allow public housing authorities much wider latitude to primarily admit people earning between 50 and 80 percent of median income. Local agencies argue that they need some discretion to obtain higher rents to compensate for the loss of federal subsidies. Yet such action could deprive the neediest families of public housing or Section 8 assistance for years to come. For example, in a community where the median annual income is $35,000 (about the national average), a new applicant for public or assisted housing would need an income of more than $17,500, whereas the average income level of current tenants is only about $8,000 per year.

What needs to be done. What action can be taken in the coming year to help ensure decent, affordable housing for low-income families with children? Advocates can work to persuade Congress and the Administration to continue targeting the great majority of federal low-income housing assistance to those who need it most—households with very low income, particularly those with children. It is also vital to provide adequate funds to operate and modernize public housing and to expand Section 8 rental assistance to more families, especially because so many are living in poverty or leaving the welfare rolls. Low-income Americans need affordable housing if they are to go to work, hold permanent jobs, and "make work pay."

Another goal should be to prevent local housing agencies from giving preference exclusively to families with higher incomes. Although it is desirable to include more working families in these programs, denying assistance to the lowest-income families means abandoning some of our neediest parents and children, many of whom are homeless now.

Advocates can also be effective at the local level by researching the need for affordable housing and the impact of welfare reform in their community. Advocates should put together coalitions to work on these issues and call on local, state, and federal officials. Turning around the housing crisis will require not only a renewed commitment from the federal government to developing ample low-income housing, but also much more active involvement of state and local governments and the private sector. Failure to act jeopardizes the well-being and security of millions of poor children. A society that does not ensure adequate shelter for its most vulnerable members has failed to meet one of its most important challenges.

CHILD HEALTH

Adequate health care is essential for every child. Without it, children may suffer enormously, losing the chance for a healthy start in life and a productive future. Untreated medical conditions often worsen over time and can lead to permanent disabilities. In some cases, lack of medical care may cost children their very lives. Poor health can also jeopardize children's ability to succeed in school and in later jobs.

Yet more than 11 million American children lack health insurance today, and the percentage of children without health coverage has risen in recent years to the highest levels ever recorded by the U.S. Census Bureau. The vast majority of uninsured children, more than 90 percent, have parents who work. However, as more and more employers have made dependent health coverage more costly for employees or dropped it altogether, fewer families can afford private insurance. In the past year, extraordinary strides were made in expanding children's health insurance coverage through landmark legislation that may help up to 5 million uninsured children. Intensive efforts are required in all 50 states for children to benefit fully from this new law. States now have an unprecedented opportunity to make high-quality, affordable health care more widely available to uninsured children and to dramatically improve the health of millions.

Child Health: 1973 to 1998

Child health has improved in important ways over the past 25 years. For example, infant mortality and preventable childhood illnesses have declined substantially. Change has also swept the country's health care system, profoundly affecting access to health care for children. Notably, a nationwide shift to managed care delivery systems has altered the way many children receive health services. In addition, two dramatic and contradictory trends have emerged: a steep decline in employment-based coverage for children and significant increases in the number of children covered by Medicaid (health insurance coverage for low-income children and families, for elderly individuals, and for people with disabilities).

According to two different federal surveys, private coverage of American children (most of which is employment-related) dropped more than 7 percent between 1977 and 1987 and another 7 percent from 1987 to 1996. Meanwhile, the number of children covered by Medicaid rose from between 9 and 10 million in 1975 to 20 million in 1996. The decline in private coverage for children, however, has begun to overshadow the Medicaid expansions. As a result, the number and percentage of uninsured children have risen to historic levels.

Changes in Medicaid. In 1973 Medicaid coverage was largely tied to whether a family received cash assistance. In most states, children and pregnant women were denied Medicaid if their family income was too high to qualify for Aid to Families with Dependent Children (AFDC), even when that income was substantially below the federal poverty line.

Dramatic changes occurred in the mid-1980s. The federal government first permitted and then required states to extend Medicaid to large numbers of previously uninsured children and pregnant women from low-income, working families, and many states went beyond the minimum federal requirements. Medicaid eligibility was also expanded in many states to include numerous children with disabilities, including those from moderate-income families. Currently Medicaid covers one in four American children, including a large proportion of newborns and children with disabilities.

The benefits provided under Medicaid also expanded considerably (at least on paper) with the 1989 enactment of Early and Periodic Screening, Diagnosis, and Treatment (EPSDT) requirements that children covered by Medicaid must receive any medically necessary health care. The 1989 provisions require states to provide children with services that may not be covered for other age groups under state Medicaid programs.

The move to managed care. The country's basic health care delivery system has undergone fundamental change over the past 25 years. In the 1970s most Americans received health care through fee-for-service insurance. They could seek care from any provider, and insurers reimbursed for services provided. In recent years increasing numbers of families have been enrolled in managed care plans, which offer more limited choice of providers and often reimburse for set fees regardless of the services provided.

The era of managed care has brought new challenges. Instead of receiving care from solo or group physician practices or from nonprofit community hospitals, many families must now rely on for-profit corporate entities of increasing size. In the

Facts & Figures

- In 1996, 11.3 million children through age 18 had no health insurance—the highest number ever recorded by the Census Bureau. Seventy percent of all Americans added to the ranks of the uninsured that year were age 18 or younger.

- Ninety-two percent of uninsured children have at least one working parent; 66 percent have a parent who works full-time and year-round.

- In 1996 more than 40 percent of Medicaid beneficiaries were enrolled in managed care plans; as recently as 1991, fewer than 10 percent were enrolled.

- By 1996, 78 percent of all 2-year-olds were fully immunized, up from 55 percent in 1992.

- Infant mortality is at its lowest level ever (7.6 deaths per 1,000 live births in 1995). Although maternal and child health indicators have improved among Black children since 1991, their infant mortality rate (15.1 per 1,000) remains disturbingly high.

past, advocates for low-income children and children with disabilities worried that too few providers participated in Medicaid. The new concern is that Medicaid managed care may not always furnish accessible, high-quality care and may deny essential services and referrals.

Other developments. Shifting patterns of illness have also created new challenges, while new approaches have helped curb old problems. Infant mortality has declined radically and today is less than half the 1973 level. Still, the vast majority of industrialized countries have lower rates than the United States. Moreover, troubling racial disparities continue to characterize infant mortality rates and other key indicators of maternal and child health (see table 2.1 and later discussion). Teen birth rates, associated with low birthweight and similar problems, rose during the mid-1980s and early 1990s, but they have declined steadily in the past several years (see chapter 7).

Rates of vaccine-preventable childhood illnesses have fallen dramatically, thanks to new vaccines and greatly improved immunization rates since the early 1990s. This extraordinary improvement follows an immunization initiative begun by the Clinton Administration in 1993, which included the creation of the Vaccines for Children (VFC) program. VFC provides free vaccine to doctors immunizing uninsured children and children covered by Medicaid. Before the program was established, the price of all required vaccines for preschool children had risen from $28 in the early 1980s to $270 in 1994. VFC is now used by more than 80,000 providers in all 50 states, and the majority of states have committed their own funds to extend the program to additional children.

The national vaccination effort also expanded immunization clinic hours, created registries identifying children with incomplete immunizations, educated providers about missed opportunities for immunizations, and educated parents through

Table 2.1 **Maternal and Infant Health Indicators, by Race of Mother, 1995**

Indicator	All races	White	Black	Native American	Asian or Pacific Islander	Hispanic[a]
	Percentage of births					
Early prenatal care[b]	81.3%	83.6%	70.4%	66.7%	79.9%	70.8%
Late or no prenatal care[c]	4.2	3.5	7.6	9.5	4.3	7.4
Low birthweight[d]	7.3	6.2	13.1	6.6	6.9	6.3
Very low birthweight[e]	1.3	1.1	3.0	1.1	0.9	1.1
Births to teens	13.1	11.5	23.1	21.4	5.6	17.9
Births to unmarried mothers	32.2	25.3	69.9	57.2	16.3	40.8
Births to mothers who have not completed high school	22.6	21.6	28.7	33.0	16.1	52.1
	Deaths before age 1 per 1,000 births					
Infant mortality	7.6	6.3	15.1	—	—	6.1

— Data not available.
a. Persons of Hispanic origin may be of any race.
b. Care begun in the first three months of pregnancy.
c. Care begun in the last three months of pregnancy or not at all.
d. Less than 2,500 grams (5 lbs., 8 oz.).
e. Less than 1,500 grams (3 lbs., 4 oz.).
Source: U.S. Department of Health and Human Services, National Center for Health Statistics.

community-based, multilingual immunization campaigns. CDF–New York worked on one such local campaign, forming a public-private partnership with city and state agencies and Chase Manhattan Bank. The campaign involved public transportation ads; radio, television, and print public service announcements; telephone hotlines; and door-to-door canvassing to reach high-risk populations.

The nationwide immunization initiative has paid off with dramatically higher immunization rates. As recently as 1992, only 55 percent of 2-year-olds were fully immunized; by 1996, that number rose to 78 percent (see figure 2.1). Meanwhile, vaccine-preventable disease declined, with rates for six of eight such illnesses in children under age 5 reaching all-time lows in 1995 and 1996. Vaccine-preventable disease rates in 1996 were less than one-seventh their levels in the early and mid-1980s and one-third below their levels as recently as 1993. In 1995 and 1996 the rate of measles among children under age 5 fell to less than one case per 100,000, from an average of seven per 100,000 in 1980–88 and 44 cases per 100,000 during the 1989–91 measles epidemic. That epidemic involved 55,000 cases, 11,000 hospitalizations, and 130 deaths.

Sexually transmitted diseases that affected many young people in 1973 have also declined substantially. For example, the rate of gonorrhea among 15- to 19-year-olds in 1996 was half that in 1973. Likewise, the 1996 rate of syphilis in that age group was only one-third the 1973 rate.

Of course, HIV, the AIDS virus, was not known in humans in 1973. By September 1997 there were more than 25,000 cases of AIDS among teens and young adults under age 25, and over 7,000 newborn infants had been infected with the AIDS virus through transmission from their mothers. Fortunately, recent treatment of HIV-infected pregnant women with anti-AIDS medications has sharply reduced the number of newborns diagnosed with the AIDS virus.

Other childhood health problems have stagnated or worsened. The percentage of children born at low birthweight, for example, has shown little improvement since 1973 and has actually increased since 1986. Asthma, the most common chronic illness in children, has also become a more serious problem, causing hospitalization and significant absenteeism from school. The rate of asthma-related deaths among teens and young adults doubled from 1980 to 1993, and rates of

Figure 2.1 **More Children Immunized**

Immunization rates among infants and toddlers have risen sharply in recent years. In 1992 slightly more than half of the nation's 2-year-olds were fully immunized; by 1996 more than three-quarters were.

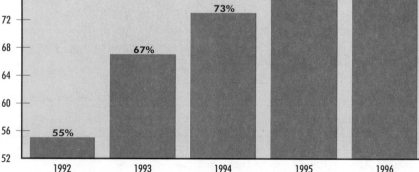

Percentage of 2-year-olds who were immunized[a]

a. Data are for children receiving four or more doses of either DPT or DT, three or more doses of poliovirus vaccine, and one or more doses of any measles-containing vaccine—all the vaccines recommended in 1992.
Source: U.S. Department of Health and Human Services, Centers for Disease Control and Prevention. Data for 1992–94 from National Health Interview Survey; 1995–96 data from National Immunization Survey.

hospitalization for asthma almost doubled among children under age 1. Although the reasons for this dramatic increase are not completely clear, poverty plays a role. Poor and minority children suffer from asthma disproportionately, and a number of studies have linked poor housing conditions to increased respiratory illness among poor children (see page 17).

Uninsured Children: An Urgent Problem

There is widespread agreement that health insurance coverage is vital to children's well-being and future success. Tragically, millions of children have no coverage whatsoever. The lack of health insurance for children is not only a grave problem but a growing one. According to the Census Bureau's March 1997 Current Population Survey, the number of children age 18 and under who are uninsured year-round reached more than 11 million in 1996—a record high. Of the 1.1 million Americans added to the ranks of the uninsured in 1996, about 800,000—70 percent—were children (see figure 2.2). The overwhelming majority of uninsured children came from working families: 92

percent had parents with jobs, and 66 percent had at least one parent working full-time all year long. However, as more and more employers have raised employee premiums for family coverage or dropped coverage altogether, and as more workers have shifted from full-time employment into contract, temporary, or part-time work without benefits, many working parents can no longer afford health insurance for the whole family. (For a ranking of the states with the most and the least health coverage for children, see table 2.2.)

New research confirms the risks children suffer when they lose health insurance. A July 1997 report from the National Center for Health Statistics shows that uninsured children are six times as likely as privately insured children to go without needed medical care, five times as likely to use the hospital emergency room as a regular source of health care, and four times as likely to have necessary health care delayed. Analysis of the report shows that one in four uninsured children either uses the hospital emergency room as a regular source of health care or has no regular source of care.

The 1996 annual report for Florida's Healthy Kids, a program that subsidizes health insurance

Figure 2.2 **Uninsured Children***

More than nine in ten uninsured children have working parents, and further cuts in employer health coverage are hurting children the most. Seven of every 10 Americans added to the ranks of the uninsured in 1996 were children.

Uninsured children and parental work status in 1996

At least one parent working 92.1%

No parent working 7.9%

The newly uninsured in 1996ᵃ

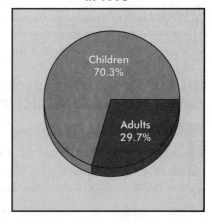

Children 70.3%

Adults 29.7%

*Data cover children through age 18.
a. Based on the total increase from 1995 to 1996 in the number of uninsured children and adults.
Source: U.S. Department of Commerce, Bureau of the Census, March 1996 and 1997 Current Population Surveys. Calculations by Children's Defense Fund.

Table 2.2 **Child Health Coverage: Best and Worst States***

Ten best states			Ten worst states		
Rank	State	Percentage of children uninsured	Rank	State	Percentage of children uninsured
1	Wisconsin	6.4%	51	Texas	24.1%
2	Hawaii	6.7	50	New Mexico	22.9
3	Vermont	7.0	49	Arizona	22.4
4	Minnesota	7.1	48	Oklahoma	20.8
5	North Dakota	7.9	47	Louisiana	20.3
6	Michigan	8.1	46	Arkansas	19.3
7	South Dakota	8.5	45	Nevada	19.1
8	Pennsylvania	9.3	44	California	18.7
8	Massachusetts	9.3	43	Mississippi	18.6
10	Nebraska	9.4	42	Florida	17.5

*Including the District of Columbia.
Source: U.S. Department of Commerce, Bureau of the Census, March Current Population Surveys for 1994–96. Calculations by Children's Defense Fund.

for children with family income up to 185 percent of the federal poverty level, corroborates these findings. The Florida report states that when parents got help in buying coverage for uninsured children, more children received health care in doctors' offices and fewer were treated in hospital emergency rooms. According to the report, children's emergency room visits dropped by 70 percent in the areas served by the program, saving state taxpayers and consumers $13 million in 1996.

CHIP: A Landmark Federal-State Partnership for Child Health

Tremendous help for uninsured children came in 1997 with enactment of the new State Children's Health Insurance Program (CHIP) as part of the Balanced Budget Act. A core of congressional leaders, including Senators Kennedy, Hatch, Chafee, and Rockefeller and Representatives Johnson, Matsui, and Dingell, championed the

program. The campaign for Child Health Now, a broad-based coalition of more than 250 organizations, garnered support for the measure, and it passed with strong bipartisan backing. On August 5, 1997, President Clinton signed the bill into law, approving the largest funding increase for children's health insurance coverage since the original enactment of Medicaid in 1965.

CHIP represents one of the most significant developments for children's health in decades. Effective October 1, 1997, it provides $48 billion over 10 years for children's health coverage. The program includes targeted Medicaid expansions and state grants of roughly $4 billion annually to cover uninsured children with family income above current Medicaid eligibility levels but too low to afford private health insurance. As many as 5 million uninsured children could benefit, depending on how states implement the new program. States need to move quickly so that children receive necessary health care as soon as possible (see box 2.1).

Box 2.1 **A State Advocate's Checklist for Implementing CHIP**

New federal funds for children's health coverage create an extraordinary opportunity for advocates and policy makers at the state level to give millions of uninsured children a healthy start in life. The new CHIP program leaves most critical decisions in the hands of states. For the initiative to achieve its promise, advocates in all 50 states must wage vigorous campaigns supporting the best possible health coverage for as many uninsured children as possible. Advocates should urge state and community decision makers to:

✔ **Give the federal government a state plan well in advance of July 1, 1998.** Plans must be approved by October 1, and the approval process could take months. States that fail to submit their proposals in time may have to turn over their 1998 federal grants to other states. The funds are available now; states should move quickly to serve children without delay.

✔ **Use the existing Medicaid (EPSDT) program, which was developed for children, rather than create a largely duplicative new program that may not meet children's needs.** Medicaid provides the benefits children need. And using this existing program, rather than creating a new program with a separate bureaucracy, means more money for children's health care and less for administrative costs.

✔ **Cover as many uninsured children as possible.** At a minimum, states should cover children with family income up to 200 percent of the federal poverty level ($26,660 for a family of three in 1997), because their parents are least able to afford private insurance that covers the entire family.

✔ **Ensure that fears of employers dropping coverage are not used as an excuse to leave children uninsured.** In states that have adopted generous public programs to cover uninsured children, officials report no resulting change in employer-sponsored family health coverage. Companies cut dependent benefits to save labor costs, whether the state does a lot or a little for uninsured children.

✔ **Use a family-friendly application process that cuts red tape.** Let families apply either by mail, at public and community health providers and organizations, or at the welfare office. Develop a simple one- or two-page application form that is easy for parents and community agencies to use and requires a minimum of supporting paperwork from parents.

States using separate state programs instead of Medicaid should take the following steps:

✔ **Keep costs affordable for low-wage, working parents.** According to CDF's analysis of Census Bureau data, the average family income of an uninsured child is $20,800 a year. For families at this income level, even a small payment for health insurance comes directly out of the family budget for other essentials, such as food and utilities. Minnesota thus limits premiums to $4 a month for low-income children. When states have asked low-wage, working parents to pay more, many children have remained without health care.

✔ **Provide comprehensive benefits for children.** Model benefits after Medicaid. Cover preventive care, including immunizations and well-child care through age 18. Tailor coverage to

Box 2.1 **A State Advocate's Checklist for Implementing CHIP** (continued)

children's needs; don't limit benefits to those offered by commercial insurance, which was developed for working adults. Such insurance often denies the speech and physical therapy that developmentally delayed children need to speak and walk, the eyeglasses and hearing aids that schoolchildren need to see the blackboard and hear their teachers, the ongoing mental health care needed by survivors of violence or child abuse, and treatment of dental problems.

✓ **Simplify Medicaid eligibility.** Under current Medicaid rules, many families will have their youngest children in Medicaid and their older children in a separate state program. To reach the commonsense goal of letting parents enroll their children in a single health plan and program, Medicaid eligibility must be simplified so that a child's age is not a factor. A family with a 4-year-old and a 14-year-old should not have to cope with multiple programs with different rules and procedures.

✓ **Use a single outreach and application process for both Medicaid and the separate state program.** Use the same organizations to educate the public about both programs. Have a single, common application form—don't ask families to fill out two different forms for two programs. And let families apply for both programs at the same places (including by mail). In short, make the system simple and seamless for families.

Key features. Key features of the State Children's Health Insurance Program include:

■ **A focus on uninsured children.** The core of the program is coverage for uninsured children. Ninety percent of a state's CHIP funds must be spent on health insurance for children; no more than 10 percent can be used for administrative costs, outreach, direct health services for children, or other purposes.

■ **State flexibility.** Each state can choose whether to participate in the new grant program and how to design its program. Participating states may use CHIP money to extend Medicaid benefits to more children, to create (or expand) a separate state program for children's health insurance, or to cover some uninsured children through Medicaid and others through a separate program. States may spend each year's funding allotment that same year or in the two following years. However, to receive first-year funding, a state must have its plan approved by the U.S. Department of Health and Human Services (HHS) before October 1,

1998. HHS has advised states that they should submit their plans no later than July 1 to receive timely consideration.

■ **Costs to the states.** To receive federal funds, a state must put up a matching amount. The state's contribution is relatively modest: 70 percent of its matching rate under Medicaid. Thus a state that pays 50 percent of general Medicaid costs would pay only 35 percent of the costs for newly insured children, whether they are covered through Medicaid expansion or a separate state program.

■ **A focus on low-wage, working families.** Generally, CHIP funds can be used to provide health coverage only to children with family income above the Medicaid ceiling but still too low to afford private family coverage—up to 200 percent of the federal poverty level ($26,660 a year for a family of three in 1997). However, there is an exception for states that, before the enactment of CHIP, provided Medicaid to children with family income above 150 percent of poverty ($19,995 for a family of three). In such states, new CHIP funds can cover children up to 50 percentage points above the old state eligibility level. Also, because states have leeway to define what is counted as income to determine eligibility, they may be able to design programs to cover even more uninsured children.

■ **A guarantee of certain benefits.** If a state decides simply to expand Medicaid to include more children, Medicaid's EPSDT program covers all medically necessary care. States that instead decide to create a separate state program must provide benefits at least equivalent to those in specified commercial insurance plans. The state may choose a different combination of services so long as the total value of all services is the same as or better than under one of these benchmark commercial plans. Advocates must work to ensure that the benefits included in separate state programs take into account the special health needs of children and are not simply modeled on commercial plans designed to meet the needs of working-age adults. (See figure 2.3 illustrating differences in the health problems of children and adults.)

■ **Limits on costs for families.** As a general rule, Medicaid bars states from imposing cost-sharing on low-income parents through copayments, premiums, or other fees for children's coverage and care. However, CHIP makes limited cost-sharing permissible in separate state programs. In such programs, families with income at or below 150 percent of the poverty level can be charged no more than the same small amounts for premiums, deductibles, copayments, and coinsurance that are permitted for adults under Medicaid. Families with income over 150 percent of poverty can be charged more, but total payments may not exceed 5 percent of family income. Regardless of the family's income level, well-baby care, well-child care, and immunizations are exempt from fees.

■ **Preservation of Medicaid coverage.** To receive grants under the new program, a state must maintain the Medicaid eligibility standards in effect for children in June 1997. A state that creates a new child health program must screen applicants for possible Medicaid coverage and enroll all eligible children in Medicaid.

Figure 2.3 Common Health Problems of Children and Working-Age Adults

Children and working-age adults have very different health care needs. Children are more susceptible to respiratory and ear infections, for example, but less prone to certain chronic conditions, such as arthritis and high blood pressure, that may require costly care.

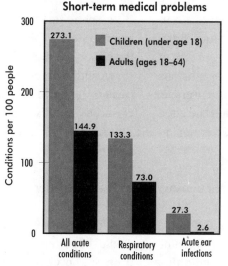

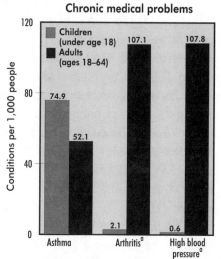

a. So few cases are reported among children that the estimated rates for children are not reliable.
Source: U.S. Department of Health and Human Services, National Center for Health Statistics, 1995 National Health Interview Survey. Calculations by Children's Defense Fund.

For example, under Connecticut's recently enacted statute, children with family income up to 185 percent of the federal poverty line ($24,661 for a family of three in 1997) qualify for Medicaid, and those with income between 185 and 300 percent of poverty ($39,990 for a family of three in 1997) qualify for a separate program. If a child with family income at 175 percent of poverty applies for the separate program, the child must be enrolled in Medicaid. Because the full range of Medicaid benefits is guaranteed, children are generally better protected by Medicaid.

Implementation of CHIP and related research. A number of states were quick to develop plans for implementing the State Children's Health Insurance Program. Indeed, even before its enactment, Arkansas, Indiana, Oklahoma, Rhode Island, South Carolina, Tennessee, and Virginia had all expanded Medicaid eligibility for children.

Advocates working with state officials to design state programs have worked through many different issues, ranging from funding the state match to basic program design. CDF's Web site (http://www.childrensdefense.org) provides an up-to-date report on the status of state plans and information on key implementation issues.

Several newly released studies address the charge that expansion of public health insurance programs "crowds out" other insurers from the market and leads to losses of employer-based coverage. For example, a 1997 Urban Institute study suggests that 40 percent of near-poor pregnant women reached by recent Medicaid expansions may otherwise have received employer coverage. That study, however, candidly admits that the cited declines in work-based coverage could be unrelated to Medicaid growth.

Indeed, other research published in 1997 refutes the notion of a cause-and-effect relationship between expanded public health insurance and reduced employer coverage. Two studies examined public health insurance programs for low-income children in Florida and Minnesota and found that only a tiny fraction (2 and 3 percent, respectively)

of new enrollees were previously covered through an employer. The Robert Wood Johnson Foundation's Alpha Center surveyed states that expanded children's health coverage and reported that state officials did not find significant "crowd-out."

New Federal Developments in Medicaid Coverage

The Balanced Budget Act of 1997 included other important Medicaid changes. The legislation gives state Medicaid programs the option of covering children for 12 consecutive months even if family income rises or children lose eligibility for other reasons. This allows states to promote continuity of care and meet children's health needs despite changes in family circumstances.

States also received the option to give children "presumptive eligibility," granting interim coverage before final eligibility has been determined, which can take months. If a preliminary investigation suggests that a child's family income is low enough to qualify for Medicaid, the child can be enrolled and begin receiving care immediately. By the end of the month after presumptive eligibility is granted, the family must apply for the child's ongoing Medicaid coverage. Whether or not the child is ultimately found eligible, the state reimburses providers for services furnished during the presumptive eligibility period, and the federal government matches state spending. Some of the costs are subtracted from a state's CHIP allocation, sometimes using the enhanced federal matching rate under CHIP.

Another important development in 1997 concerned the EPSDT Medicaid benefits package for children. In this case, the news is what did not happen. Advocates feared that Congress would resume the assault on EPSDT's guarantee of medically necessary treatment—an assault that began with the broader, unsuccessful push for Medicaid block grants in 1995 and 1996. Indeed, an early draft proposal from the Senate Finance Committee would have repealed this guarantee. Thanks to a prompt and vigorous response by a broad range of groups—including children's advocates, disability rights groups, health care providers, the education community, religious organizations, health care consumer groups, and others—this provision was deleted from the Finance Committee's final proposal. The budget bill ultimately included a provision requiring only that HHS study EPSDT.

New Developments in Managed Care

Research published in 1997 documents the continuing shift from traditional, fee-for-service health coverage into managed care programs. All but two states offer some type of Medicaid managed care, and these programs are rapidly growing to include more families (see figure 2.4). HHS reports that from January 1, 1993 to June 30, 1996, enrollment in Medicaid managed care programs increased by more than 170 percent. From 1995 to 1996 alone, enrollment jumped by over one-third. As of June 30, 1996, 40 percent of Medicaid beneficiaries—13.3 million in all—were in managed care plans. The vast majority were families with children. This increase is part of a broader move to managed care that also includes privately insured persons. The proportion of all Americans enrolled in some form of managed care rose from 36 percent as recently as 1992 to fully 60 percent in 1996.

Changes in Medicaid managed care laws. Before the 1997 Balanced Budget Act, federal law provided that Medicaid beneficiaries were free to choose their own health care providers (if the providers were willing to accept Medicaid's reimbursement, which in many states is very low, particularly for outpatient care). To require beneficiaries to enroll in managed care plans, states had to obtain a waiver of the law from the Health Care Financing Administration (HCFA), the federal agency that administers Medicaid. HCFA generally granted waiver requests but often imposed terms and conditions protecting quality or access to care. In addition, HCFA sometimes withheld approval of managed care waivers until states solved particularly serious problems, such as fraudulent marketing or grossly inadequate access to health care. Even in states with waivers, the "75/25 rule" typically required a managed care plan with Medicaid beneficiaries to have at least 25 percent of its enrollees privately insured.

Figure 2.4 **Growth of Medicaid Managed Care**

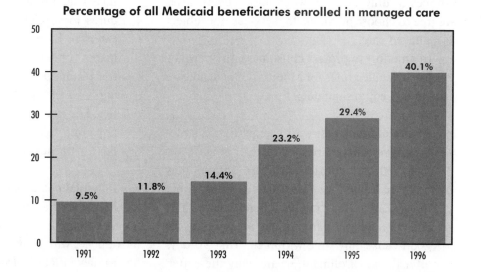

Enrollment in Medicaid managed care plans more than quadrupled from 1991 to 1996. Poor children and their parents constitute the vast majority of Medicaid beneficiaries in managed care.

Percentage of all Medicaid beneficiaries enrolled in managed care

- 1991: 9.5%
- 1992: 11.8%
- 1993: 14.4%
- 1994: 23.2%
- 1995: 29.4%
- 1996: 40.1%

Source: U.S. Department of Health and Human Services, Health Care Financing Administration.

The 1997 Balanced Budget Act made major changes in these rules—the most significant changes pertaining to managed care in Medicaid history. Medicaid managed care will now operate with much less oversight by HCFA and more state autonomy, although it will be governed by far more specific federal statutes. Whether children receive good care depends, now more than ever, on state officials and advocates.

Under the new law, states no longer need federal waivers to force most Medicaid beneficiaries to enroll in managed care, and the 75/25 rule is repealed. Waivers are still required, however, for children with disabilities, children in foster care or other out-of-home placements, children receiving adoption assistance under title IV-E of the Social Security Act, people eligible for both Medicaid and Medicare, and certain Native Americans.

Two types of managed care entities—managed care organizations (MCOs) and primary care case managers (PCCMs)—are permitted under the new law. MCOs provide a range of services from a closed network of providers in exchange for a set fee per beneficiary (a capitated payment). PCCMs locate, coordinate, and monitor an enrolled beneficiary's receipt of services and function as gatekeepers. A PCCM may be a physician, a physician group practice, a physician assistant, or a nurse practitioner. Both types of managed care entities may be responsible for either all Medicaid-covered services or only some, in which case beneficiaries are free to choose providers for services not subject to managed care.

In an effort to protect consumers, the new law sets forth detailed rules for Medicaid managed care programs. Features include:

■ **Choice of health plans.** As a general rule, states must give beneficiaries a choice of at least two managed care entities, although options may be more limited for some beneficiaries (those in rural areas, for example). Beneficiaries may change managed care entities at any time for good cause, any time within the first 90 days after initial enrollment, or annually thereafter. Beneficiaries who fail to choose a managed care entity are assigned one by the state, according to established criteria that take into account prior relationships with particular providers.

■ **Adequate access to care.** MCOs must demonstrate the capacity to serve expected enrollment by offering an appropriate range of services, access to preventive and primary care, and a sufficient number and mix of providers. In situations considered medical emergencies (in the judgment of an ordinary, prudent person, not a health professional), diagnosis and stabilizing treatment must be covered without requiring prior approval or limiting beneficiaries to a specified network of providers.

■ **Access to information.** Providers are required to give beneficiaries clear information on a variety of topics, including their rights and responsibilities, covered services, benefits available outside the managed care entity, costs, participating health care providers, service area, quality and performance indicators, and grievance and appeal procedures. In addition, MCOs generally may not impose "gag rules" that prevent network providers from discussing medical options with enrollees.

■ **Regulation and oversight**. By August 5, 1998, HCFA must issue quality assessment and improvement standards that states must follow. States likewise must establish and periodically review quality standards and monitoring procedures for MCOs. States must ensure annual, external, independent review of the care furnished under each MCO contract and make the results publicly available. Strict rules also apply to the marketing of managed care entities. For example, marketing materials must be approved by the states and may not contain false or misleading information.

Potential changes for private managed care. In 1997 state legislatures remained deeply involved in managed care issues. More than 1,000 bills were introduced, with more than 200 enacted. However, federal law (ERISA) forbids states from regulating managed care for employers who "self-insure"—that is, for those who assume the legal responsibility of paying for their workers' health care (although many such employers use insurance companies to administer health coverage). Forty percent of Americans with coverage through work have employers who self-insure. These workers and their families are not protected by state statutes regulating managed care; only the federal government can give them the protection of consumer safeguards.

Toward the end of 1997, several events foreshadowed a major congressional struggle in 1998 over managed care safeguards. In November 1997 the President's Advisory Commission on Consumer Protection and Quality in the Health Care Industry recommended enforceable, national standards to strengthen consumers' rights. The President called for federal legislation to implement these recommendations. However, while consumers and others were pushing for stronger patient protections, opposition began to form among some insurers, employers, and other interest groups. Newspapers reported meetings between such interest groups and the majority leadership in Congress to plan strategy for blocking enactment of managed care safeguards.

These events were accompanied by the introduction of major managed care legislation with considerable bipartisan cosponsorship in the House and Senate. More than 70 health care quality bills were introduced in Congress in 1997, and advocates of managed care reform promised vigorous action in 1998.

Progress in Maternal and Child Health

According to data released in 1997 by the National Center for Health Statistics (NCHS), fewer women died of complications during childbirth in 1995 than in 1994, a higher percentage of babies were born to mothers receiving early prenatal care, and fewer babies died before their first birthday. At the same time, however, the percentage of babies born at low birthweight (5.5 pounds or less) remained at its highest level in 20 years.

Other newly released data from NCHS show modest health gains for Black children and pregnant women in 1995. Infant mortality and low birthweight were down and prenatal care rates were up, continuing their improvement since 1990. This has been a welcome trend after nearly a decade of stagnant or worsening indicators in low birthweight and prenatal care during the 1980s. Improvement in Black infant mortality in particular accelerated after the Medicaid expansion in 1989, which was accompanied by a broad range of community-based efforts to reduce infant deaths among Blacks. The five years before 1989 saw only a 3.1 percent reduction in Black infant mortality, while the mortality rate dropped more than 16 percent between 1990 and 1995.

Following are some key statistics. The appendices present additional data on rates of early prenatal care, low birthweight, and infant mortality.

■ The overall infant mortality rate has been falling for decades, reaching a record low in 1995 (the latest year for which final data are available). In that year, 29,583 babies died before their first birthday, putting the rate at 7.6 deaths per 1,000 live births—far below the infant mortality rate of 17.7 two decades earlier (see table 2.3). Put differently, had infant mortality remained at its 1973 level in 1995, nearly 40,000 more American babies would have died before their first birthday.

■ Although infant mortality declined among White, Black, and Hispanic infants in 1995, a disproportionate number of Black babies died. In 1995 the mortality rate for Black infants was 15.1 per 1,000 live births—more than twice that for Whites (6.3 per 1,000 live births). Hispanics had an even lower rate (6.1 per 1,000 live births), although the rates for different groups of Hispanics vary widely.

■ In 1995, 81.3 percent of babies were born to mothers who received early prenatal care, up from 80.2 percent in 1994.

Good news is also emerging in the battle against childhood AIDS. Between 1992 and 1996

Table 2.3 **Progress Toward the Surgeon General's Goals for Selected Maternal and Infant Health Indicators**

Indicator and race or ethnicity	1991 rate	1995 rate	2000 goal	Projected 2000 rate[a]	Projected year goal reached[a]
Infant mortality (deaths before age 1 per 1,000 live births)					
Overall	8.9	7.6	7.0	6.0	1997
Black	17.6	15.1	11.0	12.0	2002
Early prenatal care[b] (percentage of all births)					
Overall	76.2%	81.3%	90.0%	87.7%	2002
Black	61.9	70.4	90.0	81.0	2005
Hispanic	61.0	70.8	90.0	83.1	2003
Low birthweight[c] (percentage of all births)					
Overall	7.1%	7.3%	5.0%	7.6%	Never
Black	13.6	13.1	9.0	12.5	2028

Note: For Hispanics, the Surgeon General articulated a distinct goal only for early prenatal care.
a. Projections assume a continuation of 1991–95 trends.
b. Care begun in the first three months of pregnancy.
c. Less than 2,500 grams (5lbs., 8 oz.).
Source: U.S. Department of Health and Human Services, National Center for Health Statistics. Calculations by Children's Defense Fund.

the number of newborns contracting the disease from their mothers dropped 43 percent, according to NCHS. This dramatic improvement resulted from providing the drug zidovudine (AZT) to infected mothers as part of prenatal care.

Effective State, Local, and Private Initiatives

Pennsylvania: CHIP implementation advocacy. Soon after passage of the State Children's Health Insurance Program, children's advocates in Pennsylvania convinced their governor to claim every penny of Pennsylvania's allocation of federal CHIP funds for FY 1998. In 1992 advocates had played a key role in creating a state-sponsored insurance program for low- and moderate-income children.

Since then, despite waiting lists, state officials had been very slow to extend coverage to more children, and changes in legislative and gubernatorial leadership left the program with uncertain political support.

In fall 1997, when CHIP made substantial federal funding available to Pennsylvania to improve children's health coverage, it was not clear that state leaders would take full advantage of these new resources. Children's advocates worked tirelessly with the media, legislators, and gubernatorial staff to urge signficant expansion of Pennsylvania's existing program. They drove home a simple and clear message: Pennsylvania should draw down all available federal money to cover uninsured children in working families, settling the details later. As a result, on September 30 the governor committed to using all federal funds. In October he submitted a preliminary plan to HCFA and announced that Pennsylvania's state health insurance program would immediately open enrollment to children on its waiting lists. The governor also publicly committed to a process for developing an expanded state plan to allocate the balance of the state's federal funds beginning July 1, 1998 (the first day of the next Pennsylvania budget year).

"We now have more work to do to keep the pressure on and make the changes in [our state program] and Medicaid that we need in Pennsylvania," commented Joan Benso, executive director of the Pennsylvania Partnerships for Children. "But at least we're off to a good start."

Positive initiatives by managed care plans. A number of successful strategies to improve children's health have been undertaken by managed care organizations. HealthPartners in Minnesota has produced a 14-minute videotape called "Food for Thought," which stresses the importance of early stimulation for infants' brain development and gives parents concrete tips on interacting with their babies. Every family with an infant born in a HealthPartners clinic receives the video and a picture book before the child's first birthday. HealthPartners has also released the video for free mass distribution throughout the Minneapolis–St. Paul area, using public libraries, video stores, child care providers, community clinics, and other organizations.

The Columbus Health Plan and Dayton Area Health Plan (DAHP) of Ohio emphasize well-child care by urging parents and physicians to make sure that all enrolled children have a health check by their birthday each year. If a child has not seen a physician by then, nurses follow up with home visits. The DAHP program also provides health checks at local schools when students miss their doctors' appointments.

The state of Maryland is likewise working with schools to meet the health care needs of young people. Under Maryland's HealthChoice Program, Medicaid MCOs are required to contract with all school-based health centers and to reimburse their services at the established Medicaid rate. In many

other parts of the country, teens enrolled in managed care often lose access to school-based services, or their school-based providers lose access to reimbursement.

An Oregon MCO, Kaiser Permanente Interstate West of Portland, has developed a comprehensive teen pregnancy clinic that provides social work, health education, medical care, counseling, and follow-up until after the baby is born. The program also includes adolescent-only birthing classes and mentors who support pregnant teens during labor.

Moving Forward: A 1998 Agenda for Action

The top priority for child health advocates in 1998 must be the successful implementation of the new CHIP program at the state and federal levels. Box 2.1 describes some of the key issues on which to focus as states gear up to extend health coverage to uninsured children in working families. CHIP offers a tremendous opportunity to provide health care to millions of uninsured children, but it will take hard work to make this happen in every state.

Other issues, of course, remain important, including:

◼ **Increasing Medicaid coverage of uninsured children.** Millions of uninsured children qualify for Medicaid but have not been enrolled. States should vigorously promote the program through celebrity advertising campaigns, posters at sporting events, and other creative outreach efforts using schools, child care and nutrition agencies, child support agencies, public and community health providers, civic organizations, recreation programs, and the like. In addition, states should make applying for Medicaid family-friendly, with short and simple forms, options to apply by mail, and a minimum of red tape. States should also make sure that eligible families losing cash assistance under the 1996 welfare law (see chapter 1) do not lose Medicaid coverage.

■ **Improving Medicaid managed care**. The federal government should ensure that the Balanced Budget Act provisions that apply to Medicaid managed care are implemented in ways that promote the best possible care for families. States should hold managed care plans accountable for providing high-quality, accessible services appropriate to the unique health requirements of children and teens, including those with special needs. States should supplement regulatory safeguards with incentives for managed care plans to provide good care. For example, to reward a managed care organization with a superior track record of providing well-child visits and immunizations, a state could assign it a significantly larger share of the Medicaid families who, after receiving ample notice and opportunity to act, fail to choose a health plan themselves.

■ **Strengthening protections for children in private managed care plans**. Both Congress and state legislatures should enact enforceable standards to ensure that private managed care organizations provide consumers with good information and accessible, high-quality care that addresses the unique health care needs of children and teens.

■ **Encouraging voluntary efforts by managed care plans**. All managed care plans—those serving Medicaid and CHIP children as well as those covering only privately insured children—must make a concerted effort to give better care to children and teens. This means ensuring good access to the full range of necessary services for young people, ranging from well-child care and home health visits to ongoing benefits for children with special health care needs.

■ **Improving maternal and child health**. Federal, state, local, and private entities must continue their efforts to increase immunizations, reduce infant mortality, and address other pressing health problems of children and teens, such as asthma and sexually transmitted diseases (including AIDS). Special attention must be given to children with disabilities and to low-income and minority children, who are disproportionately likely to suffer poor health. As states increase children's health coverage through the new CHIP program, they must expand coverage for pregnant women as well.

■ **Maintaining employer health coverage**. Employers should stop eliminating coverage for children from their employees' health benefits or paying a smaller and smaller share of premiums for family health coverage. When more health insurance costs are shifted to workers, more children and families become uninsured. Campaigns directed at improving wages and other employer support for families should encourage the public and private sectors to consider companies' health coverage when selecting contractors and vendors. Contracts should be restricted to companies that pay a substantial proportion of their workers' family insurance costs, provide comprehensive health insurance benefits, and limit out-of-pocket costs for employees and their families.

CHILD CARE

Good-quality child care and early education programs are essential for millions of American families. Thirteen million preschool children—including 6 million infants and toddlers—spend all or part of their day being cared for by someone other than their parents. In addition, millions of school-age children need supervision during the hours when their parents are at work and their schools are closed. Many parents, however, are hard pressed to find affordable, reliable child care that gives them peace of mind about their children while they work.

The number of parents for whom adequate child care is a constant concern has grown dramatically over the past 25 years. In 1973 approximately 30 percent of mothers with children under age 6 were in the work force, as were more than 50 percent of mothers of school-age children. By 1997 these percentages had grown to 65 percent and 77 percent, respectively (see table 3.1). As recent changes in the welfare laws compel recipients of government assistance to work, the numbers will keep climbing. In addition, because income is declining for young families (see chapter 1), many simply cannot make ends meet unless both parents

work. About half of America's families with young children earn less than $35,000 per year, and the Families and Work Institute reports that the majority of working women provide half or more of their household income. More than ever, American families desperately need child care that is affordable and of high quality.

Child Care: 1973 to 1998

Families in 1973 found little help from either the government or the private sector as they searched for child care that would enable them to work and ensure their children's safety and well-being. President Nixon had just vetoed the 1971 Comprehensive Child Development Act, which would have provided $2 billion to help states and local communities expand and improve families' access to quality child care. Head Start, now a widely acclaimed early childhood development program, was a relatively new initiative serving 379,000 low-income children—many in summer programs only. The federal government provided only limited funds for child care services, primarily for families receiving welfare.

Table 3.1 **Labor Force Participation of Women with Children Under Age 6, Selected Years**

Year	All women in the labor force		Married women in the labor force	
	Number	**Percent**	**Number**	**Percent**
1950	—	—	1,399,000	11.9%
1955	—	—	2,012,000	16.2
1960	—	—	2,474,000	18.6
1965	—	—	3,117,000	23.2
1970	—	—	3,914,000	30.3
1975	—	—	4,518,000	36.7
1980	6,538,000	46.8%	5,227,000	45.1
1985	8,215,000	53.5	6,406,000	53.4
1990	9,397,000	58.2	7,247,000	58.9
1997	10,610,000	65.0	7,582,000	63.6

— Data not available.
Source: U.S. Department of Labor, Bureau of Labor Statistics.

Past problems. In 1972 *Windows on Day Care*, a study by the National Council of Jewish Women (NCJW), exposed the glaring inadequacies of the nation's child care system. The study, based on observations of programs and interviews with families across the country, revealed problems that are strikingly familiar today: substandard care, insufficient supply (particularly for infants, toddlers, and school-age children), and a lack of funds to help families pay for care.

NCJW members visited 431 child care centers enrolling nearly 24,000 children. They found that only 1 percent of the for-profit centers and 9 percent of the nonprofit centers provided what NCJW members regarded as truly developmental care, including educational, health, nutritional, and, where needed, social services. A significant proportion of programs were of poor quality and should have been closed.

A 1971 *Washington Post* article likewise described poor conditions at a center in Washington, D.C.:

In one corner of the large, neat, and very bare room, 21 children, ages 3 to 6 years old, and two adults sit, watching "Captain Kangaroo" on a small-screen black-and-white television perched far above their heads on a room divider. About half the children seem attentive, a handful are squinting or glassy-eyed, and five have their heads down on the table either resting or sleeping. . . . There is no talk, either during commercials or after the program ends.

According to the reporter, there were few books in the center, no educational toys, and little if anything to stimulate creative play.

Windows on Day Care also documented a serious shortage of child care for two large groups—children under age 3 (infants and toddlers) and those of school age. One of the most distressing findings of the report "was the almost total absence of quality care for infants and toddlers outside the home." Similarly, interviewees in almost every community spoke of "a large need for before- and after-school care . . . about which very little, if anything, was being done." Mother after mother reported that there was no care of any kind available for after-school hours.

Low wages for child care providers were another problem in the 1970s. In 1977 almost two out of three caregivers had annual earnings below the poverty line for a family of four.

Current issues. Although more resources are now available to families, many of the problems highlighted in *Windows on Day Care* in 1972 remain just as challenging today. National studies continue to reveal alarming deficiencies in the quality of care in many communities. According to *Cost, Quality, and Child Outcomes in Child Care Centers*, a 1995 study conducted by researchers at the University of Colorado at Denver, the University of California at Los Angeles, the University of North Carolina at Chapel Hill, and Yale University, six out of seven child care centers provide care that is mediocre to poor. One in eight might actually be jeopardizing children's safety and development. Equally disturbing problems in home-based care were documented by Ellen Galinsky and others in a 1994 report for the Families and Work Institute. According to their *Study of Children in Family Child Care and Relative Care: Highlights of Findings*, one in three settings provided care that could conceivably hinder a child's development.

Low wages continue to be the norm for child care providers, just as they were 25 years ago. Child care teachers and providers today earn less per year than the average bus driver ($20,150) or garbage collector ($18,100). Staff employed in child care centers typically earn about $12,000 per year (only slightly above minimum wage) and receive no benefits or paid leave. As a result, turnover among child care providers is high, shattering the stable relationship that infants and children need to feel safe and secure.

In addition, many states have woefully inadequate health and safety standards for child care. Staff education and training are among the most critical elements in improving children's experiences in child care. Yet 39 states and the District of Columbia do not require prior training for providers who look after children in their homes, and 32 states do not demand prior training for teachers in child care centers (see figures 3.1 and 3.2). In contrast, becoming a licensed haircutter or manicurist typically requires about 1,500 hours of training at an accredited school.

Even the standards that are in place are often poorly enforced because of a growing number of child care facilities coupled with insufficient inspection staff. A 1994 Inspector General's report on licensed child care centers in five states found

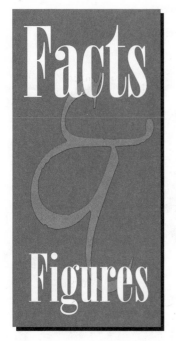

- Every day, 13 million children—including 6 million infants and toddlers—are in child care.

- Two-thirds of mothers of young children work outside the home—many out of economic necessity. Fifty-five percent of working women provide half or more of their family's income.

- Half of American parents with young children earn less than $35,000 per year, and two parents working full-time at minimum wage earn only $21,400 per year. Yet child care can easily cost $4,000 to $10,000 for a single child.

- Forty percent of infant and toddler rooms in centers provide care that could jeopardize children's safety and development.

- Thirty-two states require no prior training for child care teachers. They are among the lowest-paid workers in America, earning only $12,058 per year, on average, and receiving no benefits or paid leave.

- Juvenile crime peaks between 3 and 7 p.m., when nearly 5 million children are left home alone after school.

unsafe and unsanitary conditions in a significant number. Moreover, relatively few child care centers meet the higher standards required for accreditation. In 1997, for example, only 6 percent of all child care centers were accredited by the National Association for the Education of Young Children.

A 1996 report by the Carnegie Corporation, *Years of Promise: A Comprehensive Strategy for America's Children,* states that child care and early education services "have so long been neglected that they now constitute some of the worst services for children in Western society." The report observes that the care most children receive not only can "threaten their immediate health and safety, but also can compromise their long-term development." Kindergarten teachers estimate that one in three children enters the classroom unprepared to meet the challenges of school.

Families with children under 3 continue to face especially daunting obstacles to finding safe and supportive child care. Both the supply and the quality have been found wanting. A 1995 Urban Institute study of child care needs found shortages of infant care in the majority of the cities examined. The *Cost, Quality, and Child Outcomes* study

revealed that 40 percent of the rooms serving infants and toddlers in child care centers provided such poor care as to jeopardize children's heath, safety, and development.

The need for before- and after-school care has barely been addressed. The U.S. Census Bureau estimates that nearly 5 million children are left unsupervised by an adult after school each week. The consequences are grim; according to the U.S. Department of Justice, juvenile crime peaks between 3 and 7 p.m. A study by Kathleen Dwyer and others, published in the September 1989 issue of *Pediatrics,* found that eighth-graders who were left home alone after school reported greater use of cigarettes, alcohol, and marijuana than those in adult-supervised settings. The lack of good after-school options is especially acute in low-income neighborhoods. In 1993 only one-third of schools in such neighborhoods offered before- and after-school programs.

Finally, many low-income working families have little hope of receiving help to pay for child care. In 1997 New Jersey, for example, reported that as many as 15,000 children were on waiting lists for child care subsidies, and Texas had a waiting list of 37,000 families (see table 3.2). New York

Figure 3.1 **Training Requirements for Teachers in Child Care Centers**

Thirty-two states do not require teachers in child care centers to have completed any training prior to serving children.

States that require no prior training, 1997

Source: Center for Career Development in Early Care and Education.

state can provide child care subsidies to only one in 10 eligible children. According to the Census Bureau, poor families earning less than $14,400 in 1993 spent 25 percent of their income on child care. The annual cost of center-based care for one child in an urban area can range from $5,000 to $12,000 for infants and $4,000 to $8,000 for pre-schoolers (see table 3.3). Moreover, the average American family has two children.

About one-quarter of employed mothers with children under 6 care for their children while they work, or rely on their spouses to do so (see figure 3.3). Another quarter leave their children with other relatives. But these are not always options, and low-income families who need outside child care face extraordinary pressures. Many are forced to make choices between placing their children in potentially harmful care settings or leaving their jobs and turning to welfare. The 1996 welfare law, which imposes work requirements on recipients and limits the amount of time they can get public assistance, intensifies the need to make child care affordable for parents in low-wage jobs. These families must have reliable child care whether they are moving off welfare or struggling to avoid dependence on it.

More resources. Over the past 25 years some additional help for families has been provided. In the late 1980s a major initiative, the Act for Better Child Care, moved through Congress with biparti-san support. That legislation, which established what is today the Child Care and Development Block Grant (CCDBG), now provides a significant portion of the federal resources for child care. Largely through the CCDBG program, the federal government currently invests $3 billion a year on child care needs, and the states supply additional funds. The money goes to help low-income families pay for child care, to support resource and referral programs that help families find care, to train providers, to monitor child care programs, and to expand the supply of care.

In addition, families recoup some of their out-lays for child care through the Dependent Care Tax Credit, which costs the federal treasury $2.8 billion a year. Approximately half the states likewise offer state tax credits or deductions for families with child care expenses. Close to 800,000 children now participate in Head Start—more than twice as many as in 1973. Almost $300 million is invested in the Early Head Start Program, providing comprehensive child care and family support services to fami-

Figure 3.2 **Training Requirements for Family Child Care Providers**

Thirty-nine states and the District of Columbia do not require family child care providers to have completed any training prior to serving children.

States that require no prior training, 1997

Source: Center for Career Development in Early Care and Education.

lies with infants and toddlers. States spend about $1 billion on prekindergarten initiatives for 3- and 4-year-olds. Finally, more than 2.5 million children in child care centers, Head Start, and neighborhood family child care homes receive nutritious meals and snacks through the Child and Adult Care Food Program (see chapter 4).

Although greater resources are devoted to child care today, the number of children needing care is also much greater. As a result, the gap between the supply of adequate, affordable care and the demand for it remains as wide today as it was 25 years ago.

Federal Action in 1997

In 1997 several events brought home the importance of good child care and the serious shortcomings in America's present approach. The "I Am Your Child" campaign, a far-reaching public education initiative, emphasized the need for better care for babies and toddlers by focusing attention on the critical brain development that takes place during the first three years of life. *Kids These Days*, a report on a survey by the Public Agenda Foundation, revealed deep and widespread concern about today's children. A majority of respondents, how-

ever, believed that after-school programs would be a very effective way to help children. Finally, in October the White House Conference on Child Care cast a national spotlight on the myriad challenges of child care.

Members of Congress responded to the growing concern about child care by introducing an array of bills that would increase federal funds to help families with the costs of child care, strengthen the quality of child care, create better options for families with infants and young children, expand before- and after-school programs, and create incentives for businesses to become involved in child care. Although no action was taken on any of these proposals in 1997, Congress seems likely to devote much more attention to child care this year.

The Administration is also making child care a priority for 1998. In his State of the Union address in January, President Clinton proposed a variety of new federal subsidies and tax breaks to ease the burdens of child care for working families. The President's new proposal amounts to almost a $22 billion investment in child care and Head Start and provides a solid and significant foundation for congressional action.

Uneven Progress by States

Changes in the welfare system that require millions of women on welfare to work are causing an enormous surge in the demand for child care. How are states responding?

In 1997 every state should have been able to improve its policies and increase its investment in child care. State economies were strong, and welfare caseloads were shrinking. Furthermore, states received approximately $600 million in new federal child care money (if they provided matching funds), and they were allowed to use a portion of their new federal welfare grants under the Temporary Assistance for Needy Families (TANF) program for child care.

Setbacks. Given these favorable conditions, it is disheartening that a number of states took steps

Table 3.2 **Waiting Lists for Child Care Subsidies, Selected States, 1997**

State	Number	
Alabama	8,000	children
Florida	21,000	children
Georgia	12,000	children
Kentucky	6,000	children
Massachusetts	12,500	families
New Jersey	15,000	children
North Carolina	11,500	children
Pennsylvania	6,000	families
Texas	37,000	families
Virginia	10,000	families

Source: Helen Blank and Gina Adams, *State Developments in Child Care and Early Education 1997* (Children's Defense Fund, December 1997); CDF survey.

backward. For example, half the states no longer guarantee child care assistance to welfare families. Fourteen states reduced eligibility for child care assistance, and one in five states increased or plans to increase copayments for low-income parents. Four states froze or reduced reimbursement rates to providers. Minnesota took a giant step in the wrong direction by passing legislation that undermines efforts to ensure the health and safety of children enrolled in family child care homes. Providers may now care for a total of five children without being licensed, and those wishing to seek a license will actually be prohibited from doing so. Michigan lowered the minimum age at which relatives and at-home providers can receive public funds, allowing adolescents as young as 16 to take on the significant responsibility of child care for up to 10 hours each day.

Financial help for needy parents. Several states, however, recognized the importance of providing child care assistance to low-income families, regardless of whether they are receiving TANF. Although these states have not made such assistance a legal entitlement for all families below a certain income level, state officials believe they have appropriated or otherwise secured enough funds to help every family currently eligible for child care subsidies.

For example, Illinois increased state funding by $100 million, making it possible to provide child care assistance to all families earning less than 50 percent of the state median income (roughly $22,000 for a family of three in 1997). The state of Washington transferred $152 million from TANF to the CCDBG to help families earning up to 175 percent of the federal poverty level. Wisconsin is using $80.1 million transferred from TANF to provide child care assistance to working families with income below 165 percent of the poverty level.

Although these are important steps to address child care needs, some aspects of the initiatives raise serious policy concerns. For example, Wisconsin families are given a financial incentive to opt for less expensive child care with providers who have no training, making it more difficult for financially strapped families to choose higher quality

Table 3.3 **Average Annual Child Care Cost at Centers, Selected Cities, 1997**

City	Infant (12-month-old)	Preschooler (4-year-old)
Boston	$12,300	$7,900
Minneapolis	$ 9,400	$6,700
Seattle	$ 8,800	$6,100
Hartford, Conn.	$ 7,200	$5,700
Wake County, N.C. (including Raleigh)	$ 5,800	$5,000
Denver	$ 5,100	$4,600
Tucson, Ariz.	$ 5,100	$4,100

Source: Joint survey of local resource and referral agencies by the Children's Defense Fund and the National Association of Child Care Resources and Referral Agencies.

care. The state also has a "light touch" policy directing welfare caseworkers to inform welfare recipients only of services they ask for or need. Washington state has lowered the rates it pays providers who serve children receiving public child care funds. Consequently, many providers may limit the spaces open to poor children, charge parents additional fees, or even leave the child care business, all of which reduce parents' options. Illinois has raised families' fees in order to help finance child care assistance. High fees make it possible for state governments to provide aid to more families, but they can severely strain a low-income family's budget.

Over the next several years, as work requirements for TANF families increase, all states will face greater demand for child care and growing needs for funding. As a result, even larger investments in child care will be necessary to enable parents to find and keep jobs and to protect children's safety and development.

Prekindergarten programs. Responding to heightened interest in ensuring that children enter school ready to learn, states continue to support prekindergarten programs, either by investing in state initiatives or by supplementing the federal Head Start program with state dollars. In 1997 three states—Connecticut, New Jersey, and New York—took strides forward by developing new plans for prekindergarteners. Connecticut will support full-day, full-year programs for children whose parents work outside the home. In New Jersey, by the 2001–02 school year, 125 school districts serving large numbers of low-income children will be required to offer full-day kindergarten for all 5-year-olds and prekindergarten for 4-year-olds. New York approved a universal program that is expected to grow to $500 million by 2001–02. Meanwhile, Ohio estimates that by using state and federal funds, it will be able to provide Head Start to 84 percent of the state's eligible children in 1998.

Recent Research Findings

Reports issued in 1997 highlight the paucity of child care options available to families. The General Accounting Office released *Implications of Increased Work Participation for Child Care*, a study of four sites (Baltimore, Chicago, and two largely rural counties—Benton and Linn—in Oregon). In all four areas, the current supply of child care is inadequate to serve children in certain age groups, particularly children from low-income

families. For example, Chicago was expected to meet just 14 percent of the demand for infant care at the end of 1997. By 2002 the demand for infant care could exceed the existing supply by almost 24,000 spaces. The study identified other problems, too, that could affect low-income families' access to care, including its steep cost, the limited availability of both high-quality care and nonstandard-hour care, and limited or unaffordable transportation.

Another study, *"Back to School" Is Not for Everybody* by the National Law Center on Homelessness and Poverty, reported that homeless children in particular are underserved by preschool programs. Staff in almost 50 percent of the family shelters surveyed said that few, if any, eligible homeless children attend preschool. Staff in 70 percent of the shelters indicated that current federal, state, and local funding is inadequate to meet the preschool needs of these children.

Other research suggests that preschool is far less accessible to low-income families than to those with higher income. A 1997 study by the National Education Goals Panel found that about 55 percent of all 3- to 5-year-olds participated in preschool programs in 1996. However, families earn-

Figure 3.3 **Who's Watching the Children?**

Of the children younger than 5 with employed mothers in 1994, nearly half were cared for in child care centers or family child care homes.

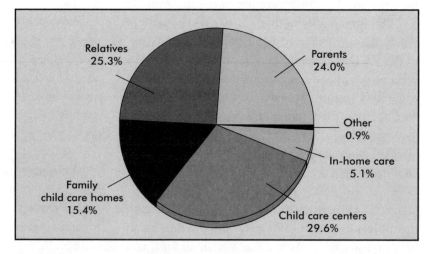

Child care arrangements used for preschoolers whose mothers were employed, 1994

Relatives 25.3%
Parents 24.0%
Other 0.9%
In-home care 5.1%
Child care centers 29.6%
Family child care homes 15.4%

Source: U.S. Department of Commerce, Bureau of the Census. Calculations by Children's Defense Fund.

ing more than $75,000 enrolled their children at nearly twice the rate of families with income of $10,000 a year or less.

Similar findings are presented in *An Unfair Head Start: California Families Face Gaps in Preschool and Child Care Availability*, a 1997 report by the PACE Center at the University of California at Berkeley, the California Child Care Resource and Referral Network, and the University of Chicago. According to the report, children's opportunity to attend preschool or child care programs in California depends largely on family income and where they live. In some counties, notably Los Angeles, parents in affluent areas are twice as likely to find a child care or preschool slot as parents in poor areas.

Effective State and Local Initiatives

Several states are taking innovative steps to meet the growing need for child care. As mentioned, a number are helping more families pay for child care by guaranteeing child care assistance to all working families below a certain income level. States are also pursuing creative approaches to improving the quality of care.

Investing in caregivers in North Carolina. North Carolina's Teacher Education and Compensation Helps (T.E.A.C.H.) Early Childhood Project recognizes that adequate training and compensation for teachers are essential ingredients for raising the quality of care. The program offers scholarships to help defray tuition and other costs for child care teachers, center directors, and family child care providers pursuing child care credentials or degrees in child development. Some scholarships also include paid leave time. What is most unusual about T.E.A.C.H. is that participants receive wage increases or bonuses when they complete an agreed number of course hours.

More than 5,000 providers in the state have gone through the program. On average, participants working toward associate degrees in 1997 completed 18 credit hours and received a 10 percent increase in wages. Fewer than 10 percent left their jobs during the year, compared with 42 per-

cent of child care staff statewide. Such low turnover is remarkable and enormously beneficial to children.

Funding for T.E.A.C.H. comes from foundations, corporate contributions, the Child Care and Development Block Grant, and state funds. Program participants and their sponsoring child care centers also pay a portion of the cost. T.E.A.C.H. has already spread to Colorado, Florida, Georgia, Illinois, and New York.

Targeting young children in Oklahoma. Oklahoma has recognized the importance of providing comprehensive services to infants and toddlers. With $1 million transferred from its TANF block grant, the state plans to support an Early Head Start program that follows the federal Early Head Start standards. Other TANF funds will be used to make more families eligible for child care assistance, reduce families' copayments, hire additional staff to inspect child care programs, and provide higher reimbursement rates to programs that offer better care.

After-school care in Georgia. Georgia is investing in after-school child care through the 3:00 Project. A component of the Georgia School-Age Care Initiative, the program began with a $125,000 public investment in 1994 to support programs for middle-school children at 17 sites. Program evaluations showing improvement in students' grades, attendance, and behavior convinced the legislature to authorize and appropriate an additional $1 million in 1997 for a statewide after-school program for middle-school students. State funds have also leveraged $172,000 from private and corporate foundations and more than $800,000 in direct, in-kind support to expand and improve after-school opportunities. The importance of safe and supportive settings for children has been highlighted by the governor's proposal to increase funds for after-school and summer reading programs to $10 million in 1998.

A community venture in New York. In the state of New York the Rochester–Monroe County Early

Childhood Development (ECD) Initiative aims to broaden the commitment to and responsibility for early childhood education. Participants, who work as volunteers, include representatives from the United Way, the city and county governments, the Chamber of Commerce, the Catholic diocese of Rochester, and local foundations. Every year they review local needs, gaps in service, and available resources and then collaborate on solutions. Public and private dollars go toward three broad efforts: (1) making child care more affordable and available by supporting more child care subsidies and higher reimbursement rates for providers; (2) expanding supply by creating new child care facilities, family learning and resource centers, and a home instruction program for preschool students; and (3) improving quality through the accreditation of more child care centers and family child care homes, educational scholarships for staff, a public awareness campaign about the importance of good early childhood education, and new associations to bring the arts into child development programs and science and technology into the preschool curriculum.

Recently, the ECD initiative took on a new task to help Rochester effectively use its share of state funds for New York's prekindergarten program. The participants in the initiative convened a committee to develop an initial prekindergarten plan for the school district. Because the district faces a shortage of classroom space but wants to reduce class size, the committee recommended using space that the ECD initiative previously helped develop in community child care and Head Start facilities. The committee also proposed a partnership with the school district that would give the initiative a pivotal role in launching and running the prekindergarten program.

Corporate involvement in Texas. In Fort Worth, Texas, 10 companies have made a three-year commitment to the Corporate Champions program. Companies have not only donated funds totaling $360,000 but have also pledged the involvement of a high-level executive. The money supports equipment grants for child care centers, scholarships for family child care providers working toward accredi-

tation, resource and referral services for member companies' employees, training for child care workers, work-family seminars, and the development and distribution of materials promoting high-quality child care and family-friendly work policies.

Moving Forward: A 1998 Agenda for Action

Three ongoing developments provide a powerful impetus for action on child care issues: escalating work requirements for families on welfare, increasing awareness of the importance of the first three years of life, and growing concern about school-age children left home alone. In 1998 we must move forward with new strategies and investments ensuring that parents have reliable child care, that infants and toddlers get the nurturing and stimulation they need for future learning, that older children have after-school activities that keep them out of trouble and help them succeed in school, and that parents who wish to stay home during their children's early years have the opportunity and support to do so.

We can meet these goals only through partnerships that draw together resources from the public and private sectors. In 1998 a broad-based coalition will be working at all levels—federal, state, and local—to expand the child care options of American families.

At the federal level, advocates should:

- Lobby for a guaranteed $20 billion to the states over five years to strengthen the quality of child care for all families and make child care more affordable. Improving the quality and availability of care for children under 3 and children of school age should be a special priority, given the alarming gaps in the quality and supply of care for these groups.
- Campaign to reauthorize Head Start with more funds targeted to infants and toddlers and additional funds to move Head Start toward serving all eligible children who need it.
- Support an extension of the Family and Medical Leave Act to cover all employers with 25 or

more workers. The act guarantees up to 12 weeks of unpaid leave to employees with a new child or a serious illness in the family, but it currently applies only to private employers with 50 or more workers and to all public employers.

■ Support paid parental leave through family leave insurance or other means to help parents stay home with their children during the critical early months of life.

■ Support changes in the Child and Adult Care Food Program that would make it easier for schools to participate and allow more school-age children (up to age 18) to be served. Provide funds for meals and snacks at for-profit child care centers serving low-income children, and increase funding for family child care providers.

At the state level, advocates should:

■ Encourage states to expand their investments in child care assistance to help more families afford care. In addition, states should guarantee child care assistance to all low-income working families.

■ Call for child care policies that ensure a true choice of good providers for families receiving child care assistance. Such policies might stipulate reimbursement rates for providers that are based on current market-rate costs, higher reimbursement rates for accredited programs, and reasonable fees for families.

■ Work to strengthen state licensing standards and enforcement so that parents can be confident their children are in safe and supportive child care settings.

■ Ensure that resource and referral programs are available in communities to help families find child care that meets their needs.

■ Urge lawmakers to provide resources to local communities for initiatives to improve the quality and expand the supply of child care.

■ Expand training and career opportunities in child care and link increased education and training to increased compensation. Support or replicate programs (like North Carolina's T.E.A.C.H., described earlier) that motivate and reward caregivers who seek professional development.

■ Support initiatives to expand and improve child care for infants and toddlers, such as family child care networks, better training for caregivers, and higher reimbursement rates for infant care.

■ Press for the funding of high-quality prekindergarten programs that offer comprehensive services and operate on a full-day, full-year basis.

■ Support creative before-school, after-school, and summer programs for both elementary and middle-school students.

At the community level, advocates should:

■ Build the local supply of high-quality child care to give families more and better options. Encourage religious institutions, schools, and other community organizations to make child care and after-school programs a top priority, mobilizing funds, volunteers, space, and other resources.

■ Encourage local government leaders to play a greater role in improving the quality, affordability, and supply of child care and school-age programs.

■ Encourage employers to contribute to community child care funds that help families pay for child care and bolster the quality of care in the community.

■ Urge businesses to establish family-friendly policies (such as flex-time and compressed work weeks), help employees find and pay for quality child care, and operate child care centers on-site or nearby. Not only do such efforts benefit families, but with unemployment at its lowest point since the mid-1970s, they make good business sense as a means of attracting and retaining workers.

Spotlight on Education

A solid education is a key to success for every child. It opens the door to good job opportunities and is the surest route out of poverty for poor children. Today's college graduates can expect to earn twice the wages of high school graduates and nearly triple the wages of a high school dropout. Sadly, many young people leave school early or without acquiring essential skills and knowledge. America's educational system is failing to prepare millions of our children for the future, particularly those with the greatest needs in the poorest communities in America.

Expanded opportunities for some. In the past 25 years America's educational system has undergone many changes, and by several measures, progress has taken place. For some children, access to education has dramatically improved. A 1974 CDF report, *Children Out of School in America*, documented the plight of more than 2 million children not enrolled in schools, including hundreds of thousands of children with disabilities. The following year, Congress addressed the exclusion of these children with the Education for All Handicapped Children Act (the forerunner of today's Individuals with Disabilities Education Act, which was reauthorized with strong bipartisan support in 1997). The 1975 law greatly expanded educational opportunities for children with disabilities, marking one of the most significant changes in education in the past 25 years.

Children Out of School in America also focused on children excluded by language—"non-English-speaking children who sit uncomprehendingly in classrooms conducted in English"— and urged more resources for bilingual-bicultural programs. The Supreme Court, in its 1974 decision in *Lau v. Nichols,* ruled that public schools must provide appropriate services to children with limited proficiency in English, thereby helping expand educational opportunities for millions more children who had been denied them.

Academic advances have also occurred. National Assessment of Educational Progress (NAEP) reports show modest but real gains in the reading and mathematics performance of U.S. students from 1973 to 1996. Additionally, the gaps between Whites and Blacks in reading and math achievement and high school graduation rates narrowed. In 1973, 80.2 percent of all students had completed high school, but the figure for Whites, 84.0 percent, was much higher than that for Blacks, 64.1 percent. By 1995 the overall percentage of young adults with a high school diploma or an equivalency certificate had increased to 86.9 percent, and the differential between White and Black students had shrunk from about 20 percentage points to less than 6 (92.5 percent of White students and 86.8 percent of Black students were graduates). High school completion rates for Hispanic students, however, have changed little in 25 years and continue to lag far behind those for Blacks and Whites, with only 52.3 percent of Hispanics in 1973 and 57.2 percent in 1995 receiving a high school diploma or equivalency certificate.

Progress halted. There are disturbing signs that progress has not been sustained. Almost all of the improvement in educational performance and high school completion occurred in the 1970s and 1980s. In the 1990s the racial gap in academic achievement is either staying the same or widening, depending on grade and subject area. According to NAEP data, the gap in reading scores between 17-year-old Black and White students was reduced by more than half between 1971 and 1988. Had progress continued at the same pace throughout the 1990s, the scores for the two groups would have equalized in 1998. Unfortunately, gains leveled off, and as the end of the decade approaches, the reading score gap remains about where it was at the beginning.

Similarly, the National Education Goals Report released in 1997 indicates essentially no change in the number of high school graduates between 1990 and 1996. Each school day more than 2,700 students drop out.

Although more young people of all racial, ethnic, and economic backgrounds attend college today, only one in three high school graduates completes a college degree (compared with about one in four in 1973). That leaves two-thirds of high school graduates without the education necessary for the majority of new jobs in the next century. Children from low-income families in particular often lack the means and the encouragement to pursue higher education. The most recent data from the U.S. Department of Education (DOE) indicate that only about one-third of youths from low-income families are in college in the October following high school graduation, compared with more than 80 percent from high-income families. The DOE also reported that in 1996 the percentage of White high school graduates who completed a four-year college degree was double that of Blacks and Hispanics.

Just as a college degree is becoming more critical to obtaining a well-paying job, higher education costs have escalated, soaring beyond the reach of many low-income students. According to the Education Trust, average tuition and fees at public two-year colleges, the least expensive higher education option, have more than tripled since 1980. Costs at four-year public colleges have risen to more than three and a half times their 1980 levels. Meanwhile, student financial assistance has shifted from grants to loans. In 1979 the maximum federal Pell grant to low-income students covered 77 percent of the average cost of attending public college; in 1993, only 35 percent. In 1998, as Congress considers reauthorization of the Higher Education Act, it will have an important opportunity to make higher education more attainable for all students.

Despite repeated commissions, studies, and reports, efforts to improve America's schools seem to have stalled. In 1990 President Bush and the 50 governors established education goals for the year 2000. The 1997 report of the National Education Goals Panel, however, showed slim progress in six areas, deterioration in seven, and no change in seven others. In 1997 President Clinton and Congress struggled over the mechanism for establishing national standardized tests to measure academic achievement but paid little attention to ensuring that students actually learn.

Shortchanging poor and minority children. While the nation's overall educational outlook is cause for concern, the plight of poor children and minority children is even bleaker. As disparities in school performance appear to be growing again, some suggest that nonschool problems such as poverty, family turmoil, violent neighborhoods, and drug abuse explain the lagging performance of disadvantaged children. These conditions do take a heavy toll. Two recent CDF publications, *Poverty Matters* and *Wasting America's Future*, document how poverty robs poor children of educational opportunities. Good schools, however, can help children transcend difficult circumstances.

(continued on the following page)

A critical factor in success or failure is the willingness of cities, states, and the nation to invest in decent schooling for all children. From the 1960s into the mid-1980s, there was focused national attention on the need for greater equity in education. Policy makers, educators, and child advocates shared a commitment to ensuring that low-income children, children with disabilities, and minority children had access to high-quality education. This commitment was evident in the creation and growth of programs such as Head Start, Title I compensatory education, bilingual education, and migrant education programs. Although inequities and other problems persisted, the marshaling of public energy and resources began to produce demonstrable results. The number of poor and minority children who mastered basic skills increased, while academic achievement gaps narrowed. In the past few years, interest in ensuring that all children have a sound education appears to have waned, and a wide gap in resources separates wealthy and poor school districts.

The 1997 DOE *Report on the Condition of Education* found that schools with the highest proportion of poor children have markedly fewer resources than schools serving affluent students. The nation's richest school districts spend 56 percent more per student than do the poorest. Even when those figures are adjusted to take into account regional differences in the cost of living and the additional resources devoted to students who need special education, bilingual, and compensatory education services, the wealthier schools spend 36 percent more per pupil than the poorest schools.

Schools serving large numbers of poor children have fewer books and supplies and teachers with less training. According to the 1997 *Condition of Education* report, more than 70 percent of the teachers in schools with a high concentration of low-income students lacked some necessary materials for their classes, and only 53 percent of these schools had Internet access, compared with 88 percent of more affluent schools. Twice as many students in poor schools were taught by math teachers without a specialty in math or math education. And teacher salaries in the 1993–94 school year averaged 28 percent more in the relatively affluent schools ($45,547 versus $35,496 in lower-income schools).

Many schools are in disrepair, but those in the poorest communities are in the most dire shape. In 1995 the General Accounting Office (GAO) reported that elementary and secondary schools needed about $112 billion in repairs and upgrades. By GAO's estimates, about 14 million students attend schools requiring extensive repair work or replacement. A second GAO report in 1995 concluded that "most schools are unprepared for the 21st Century" and that schools in central cities and those with over 50 percent minority enrollment "are more likely than others to have insufficient technology and unsatisfactory environmental conditions."

The DOE has identified a growing body of research linking achievement and behavior to students' physical surroundings. These studies found poorer academic performance associated with such conditions as overcrowded buildings, substandard science facilities, faulty air conditioning, and external noise.

What needs to be done. America faces an immediate challenge to improve the overall quality of education. Equally critical is the need for a renewed commitment to educational equity. Political and civic leaders, educators, and ordinary citizens must join forces to ensure that our schools provide educational opportunities for all children, not just a privileged few.

Throughout our history, public education has been a stepping stone to satisfying work and a way out of the most impoverished environments. Despite the current debates over alternative schools, charter schools, and vouchers for private education, the majority of America's children will continue to be enrolled in public schools. We need to make sure that these provide the rich learning opportunities that serve as a gateway to a better future for all children.

Federal leadership and support are important, but state and local governments have primary responsibility and provide the vast majority of resources for educating America's children. The federal government, in fact, contributes only about 9 percent of all spending on education. Communities throughout America have the greatest stake in making schools responsive to the needs of their children; they must help lead the effort for reform.

The critical elements for educational improvement are clear: high standards, well-trained teachers, adequate resources, and challenging curricula. In addition, children must enter school ready to learn. To make sure they do, we need to invest adequate resources in child care and early education programs like Head Start. Many of the reform movements today—the drives for educational standards, school restructuring, better teacher preparation—focus on one ingredient for success or another. But reform must be comprehensive, sustained, and intensive to produce results.

David Hornbeck, Philadelphia's superintendent of schools and president of CDF's board of directors, has outlined specific steps to improve learning: (1) define what children need to know; (2) develop "smart" tests to measure progress; (3) create strong accountability systems for teachers, administrators, and students; (4) give teachers, principals, and parents the major role in deciding what should happen in schools; (5) provide new kinds of training for educators; (6) provide early childhood development programs to help get children ready to learn; (7) harness technology to kindle learning; (8) use resources wisely; and (9) provide equitable access to resources. Most important for success, according to Dr. Hornbeck, is having strong expectations that all children can excel in school.

If we fail to demand the best from our schools, we fail in one of our principal obligations to our children. A sound education can immeasurably enhance career success, financial security, and personal growth. Moreover, America's economic and social progress depends on a literate, skilled population with the ability to reason clearly, solve problems, and apply and advance knowledge. We must therefore do the utmost to improve teaching and foster learning in all schools, for all children.

CHILD NUTRITION

Many American parents face an ongoing struggle to stock their pantries with healthful foods and feed their families balanced meals. Each year millions of American children experience hunger or lack proper nourishment. This is inexcusable in a nation that has bounteous agricultural resources and produces enormous quantities of food and in an age when the benefits of proper diet and nutrition are widely known. For decades the federal government has supported a variety of measures, including food stamps, child nutrition programs, and meal subsidies, to help ensure that low-income families have enough to eat. The 1996 welfare law, however, has wrought drastic changes in food assistance programs, with devastating consequences for many needy children, particularly those from legal immigrant families.

Child Nutrition: 1973 to 1998

A historical overview. In the 1970s major expansions of nutrition programs were under way. The current food stamp program, which dates back to the 1960s, and the National School Lunch Pro-

gram, started in 1946, grew steadily during this period, and two new child nutrition programs grew as well. The special Supplemental Food Program for Women, Infants, and Children (WIC) was established in 1972. The National School Breakfast Program, begun as a pilot project in 1966, was permanently authorized in 1975.

Over the past 25 years all of these programs have expanded to serve more low-income individuals and families. The year 1996, however, marked a turning point. Nutrition programs fell under a sustained attack and were reduced substantially.

Recent blows to low-income families. The 1996 welfare law targeted food assistance programs for the deepest cutbacks in their history (see figure 4.1). The food stamp program, the nation's most far-reaching program to bolster child and adult nutrition, is bearing the brunt of these cuts. It is absorbing more than half of *all* the spending reductions made by the law, amounting to well over $20 billion in cuts over six years. As a result, food purchasing power has shrunk for all low-income families who use food stamps to help feed their children. Poor legal immigrant children have been

This chapter was prepared in cooperation with Robert Greenstein, executive director of the Center on Budget and Policy Priorities.

affected most severely; for most of them, food stamps have been terminated altogether. In addition, children who are citizens but whose parents are legal immigrants have seen their families' food supplies sharply reduced because only these children, and not the whole family, can now receive food stamp benefits.

The welfare law also altered several other child nutrition programs. Of greatest significance, it substantially restructured and reduced federal resources for the family child care component of the Child and Adult Care Food Program (CACFP). Although these changes have only recently taken effect and data on their impact are not yet available, a sizable number of family child care providers may drop out of the program. In addition, the 1996 welfare law ended federal outreach grants to states to promote expansion of the school breakfast program and the Summer Food Service Program (SFSP).

Congress has also ended a two-decade period of increases for WIC, one of the most effective of all federal programs. The General Accounting Office estimates that each $1 spent on WIC food and nutrition counseling for pregnant women averts $3.50 in medical costs, income support, and special education expenditures for low-birthweight infants. Fund-

ing for Fiscal Years (FYs) 1997 and 1998 maintains WIC participation at its current level of 7.4 million women, infants, and children, but no further growth can be accommodated. Congress rejected Administration requests for both years to continue expanding the program to reach more of those eligible for it. This marks the first time since WIC's inception that Congress has halted its growth.

A welcome development. Despite the generally grim outlook for nutrition programs that benefit children, there was positive action on one front in 1997. In June Congress passed legislation giving states the option of retaining food stamps—at state cost—for some or all legal immigrant households who became ineligible for federally funded food stamps under the welfare law. As of late 1997, 11 states had acted to continue benefits for at least some of these families.

Food Stamp Reductions

Only about 2 percent of the spending reductions in the food stamp program come from provisions to reduce fraud and abuse, impose tougher penalties on recipients who violate pro-

Figure 4.1 **Food Assistance Cuts**

The 1996 welfare law, as modified by the 1997 Balanced Budget Act, cuts well over $20 billion from the food stamp program over six years. Another $2.9 billion is being cut from other nutritional assistance for children.

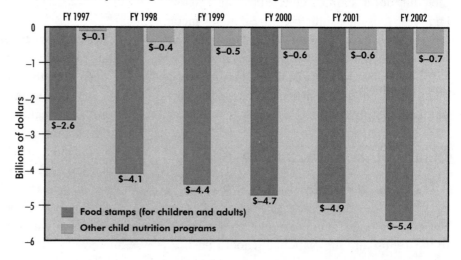

Federal spending reductions resulting from the 1996 welfare law

Source: Center on Budget and Policy Priorities, based on Congressional Budget Office estimates.

gram requirements, and reduce administrative costs. The vast majority of savings arise instead from across-the-board benefit cuts for all recipients—including families with children, the working poor, the elderly, and people with disabilities—and from a series of benefit cuts that target particular groups of low-income households.

Between September 1996 and September 1997, the number of individuals receiving food stamp assistance plummeted by an astounding 3.9 million (see figure 4.2). This is far more than can be explained by improvement in the economy and the expected effects of the 1996 welfare law. In addition, a survey by the U.S. Conference of Mayors finds that requests for emergency food assistance have risen sharply. Despite the economy's growth and the low unemployment rate, requests for aid were up by an average of 16 percent in 1997 in the 29 cities surveyed, with the majority of these requests coming from families with children. This increase appears directly related to the sharp shrinkage in food stamp assistance. More troubling, most of the data in the mayors' study are for the period *before* most of those legal immigrants who were terminated from food stamps in large numbers lost their benefits. The study also found that 19 percent of the requests for food are estimated to have gone unmet, with 71 percent of the cities reporting that some of those in need may have to be turned away because of a lack of resources.

Effects on children. Two-thirds of the spending cuts for food stamps affect families with children, including poor working families as well as those receiving welfare benefits. In FY 1998, according to the Center on Budget and Policy Priorities, more than 5 million families with children will lose an average of $36 a month in food stamp benefits. Because such families averaged only $600 a month in gross income in 1995—just 54 percent of the poverty line—this represents a substantial loss. Moreover, benefit reductions will deepen over time, giving families slightly less food purchasing power with each passing year.

The costs to children go beyond economic ones. Myriad studies have shown that children who are afflicted with even mild forms of undernutrition—a type of malnutrition caused by limited food supply—suffer adverse health and learning effects. These include iron deficiency anemia (which is associated with impaired cognitive development),

Figure 4.2 **Fewer Food Stamp Recipients**

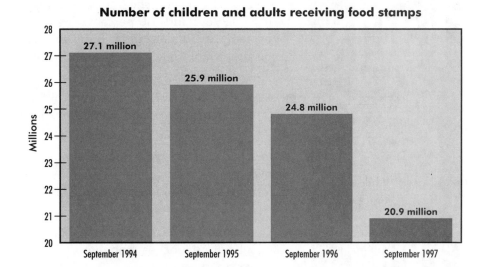

The number of food stamp recipients (the majority of whom are children) plunged sharply after passage of the 1996 welfare law.

Number of children and adults receiving food stamps

27.1 million
25.9 million
24.8 million
20.9 million

Millions

September 1994 September 1995 September 1996 September 1997

Source: U.S. Department of Agriculture, Food and Consumer Service.

fatigue, trouble concentrating in school, and stunted growth.

No relief for families with high living expenses. In 1997 the Clinton Administration proposed three measures to blunt the pain of food stamp cuts for families with children. One of these would have benefited poor families with children and high housing costs (those who spend more than half their income on rent and receive no government housing assistance). Under the food stamp rules, a portion of the money that some of these families must spend for rent is inappropriately counted as being available to purchase food. As a result, the food stamps these families receive fall short of what they actually need, and many have trouble paying their rent and utility bills and also feeding their children. The Administration's proposal would have meant larger food stamp benefits for families in this predicament, putting them on a par with elderly individuals and those with disabilities who have high housing costs and have long received augmented food assistance. Congress, however, refused to adopt this proposal.

Congress also rejected a measure intended to soften the blow of the 1996 welfare law on parents who need cars to commute to work. The law sets a *permanent* ceiling of $4,650 on the market value of a car that is exempt from the food stamp program's stringent limits on assets. This frozen limit is only 3 percent higher than the cap initially set in 1977. Since then, however, used car prices have nearly tripled, increasing 170 percent. As automobile costs rise with inflation in the years ahead, growing numbers of poor families who must drive to work, especially those in rural areas and parents commuting to suburban jobs from inner cities, may become ineligible for food stamps.

The welfare law also freezes the standard deduction for food stamp recipients—the amount subtracted from the income of most food stamp households for the purpose of calculating benefit levels. The Administration proposed a change in the rules so that the deduction would eventually keep pace with the cost of living, as it had in the past. Again, however, Congress rejected the plan, and a permanent freeze remains in effect. As inflation raises the cost of food and other necessities and the standard deduction stays constant, these families will find it a little tougher each year to adequately feed their children and themselves and cover other expenses.

- Of the 13.2 million children who received monthly food stamps in FY 1996, nearly 80 percent were under the age of 12, and 37 percent were under age 5. Thirty-seven percent were Black, 36 percent were White, and 21 percent were Hispanic.

- More than 5 million families with children will lose an average of $36 each month in food stamp benefits during FY 1998.

- In 29 cities nationwide, requests for emergency food aid jumped an average of 16 percent in 1997. Most of the requests came from families with children, and nearly one in five went unmet.

- During the 1997 school year, 26.9 million children received free or subsidized lunches, and almost 7.1 million received a daily breakfast at school.

At the same time, Congress did work out a compromise on an Administration proposal to modify one of the two most severe food stamp provisions in the welfare law—the limitation of food stamps to three months out of every three years for jobless adults ages 18 to 50 who are not raising minor children. The compromise, however, provides substantially less relief in this area than the Administration had sought.

The Plight of Immigrant Children

Federal food stamp benefits have vanished for nearly all legal immigrant children. The only exceptions are children who are refugees or asylees who have been in the United States for less than five years, children whose parents have been employed in the United States for 40 calendar quarters, and children of veterans or active-duty members of the U.S. armed forces. However, the overwhelming majority of poor legal immigrant children—some 200,000—have lost their food stamps. An additional 600,000 children who are U.S. citizens have suffered indirectly; food assistance for their households has dropped dramatically because one or more family members, usually the children's parents, are legal immigrants pushed out of the food stamp program.

With food assistance to immigrant families sharply curtailed or eliminated, it is unclear how these children will receive adequate nutrition. Moreover, legal immigrant children who entered the United States on or after August 22, 1996 (the date the welfare law was signed) will be ineligible for at least five years both for federally funded cash assistance under the new welfare block grant and for Medicaid (except for emergency medical services).

State action to fill the gaps. As already noted, states can choose to use their own money to maintain food stamp assistance for legal immigrants, including children, who no longer qualify for federal food stamp aid. Eleven states so far are funding food stamps for some categories of legal immigrants in some or all counties; in addition, Minne-

sota is providing cash in lieu of food stamps. Ten of these 12 states—California, Illinois, Maryland, Massachusetts, Minnesota, Nebraska, New Jersey, New York, Rhode Island, and Washington—cover some or all legal immigrant children who would qualify for federal food stamps were it not for their immigrant status. (In New York, provision of food stamp assistance to legal immigrants is a local option.)

Under 200,000 legal immigrants—less than 25 percent of those who lost food stamps because of the welfare law—are now receiving state-funded food assistance instead. This means 70 to 75 percent remain unaided. Furthermore, two of the states with the largest number of immigrants, Florida and Texas, have reinstated food stamp assistance only for legal immigrants who are elderly or have disabilities. *Children* in these states who are legal immigrants remain ineligible. So do children in a number of other states with large immigrant populations: Arizona, Michigan, New Mexico, Ohio, Pennsylvania, and Wisconsin have so far been unwilling to provide food stamp assistance to legal immigrants at state cost.

When Congress voted in June 1997 to give states the option of funding food stamps for legal immigrants, a number of state legislatures were already out of session. These states will be able to consider this option when their legislatures meet in 1998.

Other nutritional aid temporarily secure. Undocumented immigrant children and pregnant women, as well as some legal immigrant children, face additional threats under the welfare law. The law allows but does not require states to terminate the eligibility of these individuals for WIC, CACFP, and SFSP.

These child nutrition programs historically have been among the few types of programs open to undocumented immigrant children. As of late 1997, no state had acted to bar these children from WIC, CACFP, or SFSP. States generally have realized that doing so would be cumbersome administratively and could lead to significant costs later on. For example, if undocumented pregnant women are denied WIC benefits, their newborns are more likely to be of low birthweight. These infants will be American citizens because they are born on U.S. soil, and they will consequently be entitled to Medicaid coverage if they are poor or near-poor. Medicaid coverage for low-birthweight infants is costly, and states bear a sizable share of Medicaid costs. Thus a state decision to exclude undocumented immigrants from WIC, which is fully funded by the federal government, would probably mean higher Medicaid expenses for the state, along with increases in low-birthweight births, childhood anemia, and even infant mortality.

State Procedures: An Obstacle to Food Stamp Assistance?

As noted earlier, the number of food stamp participants plummeted by 3.9 million in the past year, an unprecedented decline. Improvement in the economy accounts for some of this drop, and some is attributable to the welfare law, which makes legal immigrants and certain other individuals and households ineligible for food stamps. The data strongly suggest an additional contributing factor: a decline in the proportion of children eligible for food stamps whose parents actually apply for and receive them.

It is not clear why the food stamp participation rate is falling among eligible children. The drop-off is probably due in part to families being inappropriately removed from the food stamp program when they lose cash assistance. Under the Food Stamp Act, families who leave the welfare rolls because they have exceeded the state's welfare income limit or because they have hit a time limit on cash assistance may *not* simply be terminated from food stamps. In such cases, the families are supposed to continue receiving food stamps unless the state agency finds them ineligible for food stamps as well. However, it appears that in some areas, these families may be losing food stamp assistance when they leave the welfare rolls.

In addition, some states are diverting large numbers of families from their welfare programs by various means. For example, some states require a month or more of job search before the families can apply for cash assistance. Others give families a one-time payment, such as a lump sum to fix an old car so a parent can find or keep a job, in lieu of monthly public assistance payments. These procedures seem to be discouraging some low-income families from applying not only for cash assistance but also for food stamps. Some who are still eligible for, and in need of, food stamps may mistakenly believe they will be turned away.

Reductions in the Family Child Care Component of CACFP

Federally funded school breakfasts and lunches, WIC, the summer food program, and CACFP have been a bulwark against child hunger and malnutrition for school-age children, infants, and preschoolers. However, the welfare law reduces these child nutrition programs by $2.9 billion between 1997 and 2002.

More than 85 percent of these reductions come in CACFP, which primarily helps pay for meals provided to children in child care centers and family child care homes. Most of the CACFP cuts result from reduced federal support for meals served in family child care homes that are not located in low-income areas or operated by low-income providers.

Before the welfare law was enacted, the family child care component of CACFP did not make income a consideration in its benefit structure. It offered the same meal reimbursement rates for all children, regardless of family income (although those rates were somewhat lower than what CACFP paid child care *centers* for meals for low-income children). Approximately one-third of CACFP spending for family child care went toward meals for low-income children (those whose family earnings fell below 185 percent of the poverty line). Two-thirds supported meals served to children from households at higher income levels, but providers had to meet state licensing requirements. This encouraged many small family child care providers to become licensed, thus helping to expand the supply and quality of child care.

Under the welfare law the rules and meal reimbursement rates in effect before July 1, 1997 apply only to family child care homes located in low-income areas or operated by low-income providers. For other homes, the law reduced aggregate meal reimbursements by about one-half, on the presumption that these homes serve children whose families are not low-income and have less need. The providers in these homes can arrange for a means test for the children in their care; only then can they receive substantially higher reimbursement rates for meals fed to children who have family incomes below 185 percent of the poverty line.

Key questions remain as to whether large numbers of family child care homes outside low-income areas or not operated by low-income providers will drop out of the program (or, in the case of new homes, not seek to enter it), and to what extent low-income children and families will be affected. The meal reimbursement rates for these homes have been reduced substantially.

Many child advocates fear that the changes to CACFP will drive a substantial number of homes out of the program. Data are not yet available to determine to what extent this may be occurring. If many homes do withdraw and new ones do not join, the impact on children could be substantial. In addition to serving as an incentive for providers to become licensed, CACFP is one of the major sources of training and support for family child care providers.

How states implement the changes may affect the extent to which homes drop out of the program. Family child care homes outside low-income areas are supposed to be allowed to use simple methods to show that some of their children are below 185 percent of the poverty line, without having to collect income forms from parents. States need to explain these rules clearly to family child care providers and sponsors.

Subsidized Meal Programs

Data from the U.S. Department of Agriculture (USDA) show that while 6.2 million recipients lost food stamps between 1994 and 1997 (a 23 percent drop), participation in other major child nutrition programs increased (see figure 4.3). The school breakfast program showed the

Figure 4.3 **Participation in Food Programs**

While the food stamp program has shrunk drastically, subsidized meal programs are serving more children than ever before.

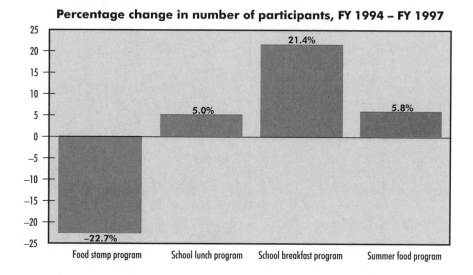

Percentage change in number of participants, FY 1994 – FY 1997

Food stamp program: −22.7%
School lunch program: 5.0%
School breakfast program: 21.4%
Summer food program: 5.8%

Source: U.S. Department of Agriculture, Food and Consumer Service.

most spectacular growth, reaching 21 percent more children by 1997, or 1.2 million more children on an average day. The summer food program reached 6 percent more children, or 125,000 more on an average day.

Stability in the summer food program. The SFSP provides lunches and other meals to children in low-income areas during the summer, when school-based programs are not available and family food budgets are squeezed harder as a result. SFSP meals are also a central component of the full-day recreational and academic programs run by various groups, including Freedom Schools, a program of CDF's Black Community Crusade for Children. Such programs keep children in poor communities safe and engaged in positive activities during their out-of-school months.

The 1996 welfare law reduced reimbursement rates for meals served through SFSP. However, summer food providers still receive 16–17 cents more per lunch than schools and child care centers receive for lunches they serve free to poor children under the school lunch program. Thus far, the lower reimbursements do not seem to have prompted significant numbers of providers to drop out of the program. In fact, instead of contracting as many had feared, the program expanded in 1997. The number of SFSP meals served rose by 8.3 million, or 7 percent—about the same rate of growth as in the previous year when the meal reimbursement rates were higher. It appears that many state agencies and nonprofit organizations, anticipating a decline in participation as a result of the welfare law changes, intensified their efforts and recruited more summer food sites into the program in 1997.

Expansion funding ended for school breakfast and summer food programs. The welfare law also ended the provision of about $5 million a year to states for various outreach initiatives to expand the school breakfast program and the SFSP. Since expansion funds were first provided in 1990, they helped to finance tremendous growth in the school breakfast program. In 1977 only slightly more than 20,000 schools participated; by 1987 that figure had risen to 37,000; today nearly 70,000 schools operate the program. Nearly three out of every four children attending a school with a lunch program can also receive breakfast at school (see figure 4.4). Access is even greater among low-income children: more than four-fifths attend a school with a breakfast program.

Figure 4.4 **More School Meals**

Growth in the school breakfast program has meant that almost three-fourths of children eligible for school lunches can now start their day with a nutritious meal as well.

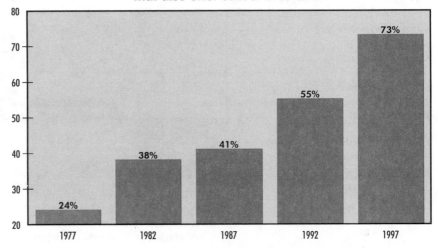

Percentage of schools offering lunch that also offer school breakfast

Year	Percentage
1977	24%
1982	38%
1987	41%
1992	55%
1997	73%

Source: U.S. Department of Agriculture, Food and Consumer Service.

School lunch program holding steady. The past year was a relatively quiet one for the school lunch program. The welfare law made no significant changes in the program, and it continues to grow, largely in tandem with the growth in school enrollment. USDA data show that between FY 1994 and FY 1997, school lunch participation rose 5 percent, to serve 1.3 million more children on an average day.

Moving Forward: A 1998 Agenda for Action

A number of opportunities to help children receive more adequate food and nutritional assistance should present themselves in 1998. The federal government will consider reinstating food stamp eligibility for some categories of poor legal immigrants, including families with children. This is a badly needed step. In addition, states across the country, many of which are flush with budget surpluses, can fill further gaps by reinstating food stamp aid to more legal immigrants. Some improvements in child nutrition programs also are likely to be considered at the federal level, when Congress reauthorizes the programs in 1998.

Priorities for 1998 include:

■ **Enacting federal legislation to restore food stamps for legal immigrants.** The Clinton Administration has proposed in its FY 1999 budget to reinstate food stamp eligibility for several categories of low-income legal immigrants, including families with children who would be eligible for food stamps were it not for their immigrant status. The national anti-hunger organizations and the national organizations that help immigrants have made passage of the Administration's proposals their highest priority for this year. The proposals would restore $2.4 billion in food stamp assistance for legal immigrants over the next five years. Securing enactment will be an uphill battle, and it is possible that Congress could restore food stamps for certain categories of legal immigrants who are elderly or disabled but fail to help legal immigrant children. Advocates need to press for the restoration of benefits for needy immigrant families with children.

■ **Enacting state legislation to restore food stamps to legal immigrants.** Action by states to help meet the needs of poor legal immigrants is also important if the federal government fails to act. States such as Florida and Texas that have agreed to fund food stamp benefits only for legal immigrants who are elderly or have disabilities should be urged to extend this protection to children and, if possible, their parents. States that have not yet acted should be prodded to provide some relief. When states pay for food stamp assistance for legal immigrant children or for legal immigrant families with children, the funds count toward a state's maintenance-of-effort requirement under the Temporary Assistance for Needy Families (TANF) block grant. This gives states an additional incentive to provide food stamps to legal immigrant children.

■ **Rectifying problems in state food stamp procedures.** A coordinated effort is needed to monitor state procedures for providing food stamp assistance to families moving off welfare or being diverted when they seek to enroll. Children's advocacy groups and state advocates for low-income groups should work in concert with USDA to keep poor families from missing out on the opportunity to apply for food assistance or improperly losing food stamps when they stop receiving cash welfare benefits. A number of states may need to modify their administrative systems to eliminate such problems.

■ **Revising federal reimbursement policies for meals served to children in child care settings.** As changes in the welfare system and other developments push more low-income mothers into the labor force, more families need after-school or before-school child care. Two shortcomings in federal nutrition programs should be remedied. First, they are set up in a way that may discourage some schools from applying for reimbursement for meals they serve in after-school child care programs, thereby reducing the supply of such programs. Second, meal reimbursement is not available for children over age 12 in after-school care settings. This is a concern in impoverished communities where programs to keep teens off the streets are especially needed. Federal action is warranted both to make meal reimbursement easier for after-school child care programs in schools and to extend reimbursement benefits to after-school programs serving at-risk adolescents in low-income areas. In addition, CACFP should be amended to allow for-profit child care centers serving low-income children to more easily participate.

■ **Monitoring and strengthening the family child care component of CACFP.** It will be important to track the effects of the welfare law on the number of family child care homes in CACFP and the consequences for all children. Changes in CACFP should be sought to correct any adverse effects of the 1996 law. If providers are dropping out at a rapid rate, states and nonprofit organizations need to encourage them to remain in the program and help them maximize funding with the least administrative burden. In any case, given existing shortages in the supply of child care, efforts are needed to bring more family child care homes into the program. Unlicensed providers in low-income areas should be encouraged to take advantage of the federal funds available to help them upgrade their facilities so they can become licensed and take part in CACFP.

■ **Providing more school lunches.** A significant number of children eligible for free school lunches are not certified for these meals because their parents have not submitted application forms. Some parents do not understand the form, and others may lose it or forget to complete it. Federal law provides a way around this problem by allowing school districts to use a mechanism called direct certification. First,

data on food stamp participation are matched with data on children enrolled for free school meals. All students whose families receive food stamps can then be certified as eligible for free meals, unless the child's parent objects. Direct certification is in use in many school districts and usually results in a marked increase in the number of poor children receiving free meals. Advocates should press school officials in all districts with large numbers of low-income students to follow this approach.

■ **Expanding the school breakfast and summer food programs.** The dramatic growth of the school breakfast program in recent years should not lead to complacency among child advocates. Communities should continue working to bring this program to schools in low- or moderate-income areas that may not yet be offering breakfasts to needy children. Likewise, states and communities should continue expanding SFSP, which can help keep children in low-income communities involved in positive activities during summer months when schools are closed.

■ **Expanding WIC.** Again in 1998, as it does every year, Congress will set the WIC funding level for the next fiscal year. In so doing, it will determine whether WIC will grow and reach more eligible children, nursing mothers, and pregnant women, contract and serve fewer, or provide benefits to about the same number. With the federal budget headed toward balance and possibly surplus, Congress should resume progress toward the long-standing bipartisan goal of serving all of the low-income women, infants, and children eligible for this beneficial program. The Clinton Administration has proposed an increase of $157 million in WIC funding for FY 1999. This would enable the program to keep pace with food price inflation and expand from the 7.4 million women, infants, and children served each month to 7.5 million.

CHILDREN AND FAMILIES IN CRISIS

For every child, the path to adulthood has some rough patches and hurdles. Most children manage to steer clear of serious trouble with help from families, friends, sympathetic teachers, clergy, or other caring adults. Sadly, some children confront overwhelming obstacles they cannot overcome without special help. Too many are the victims of abuse or neglect or are left to drift for years in the foster care system. More than half a million children are estimated to be in foster care today, a 25 percent increase from 1990. Estimates of the number of children abused or neglected each year range as high as nearly 3 million.

The past 25 years have brought increased capacity to better meet the needs of the most vulnerable children—those who are abused or neglected, homeless, or have serious emotional disturbances—and to support their families. But progress has been curtailed by growing problems such as drugs and domestic violence. The intractability of such problems, combined with heavier demand for services and a lack of adequate resources, has left many child welfare systems beleaguered and children and families unserved. Much more vigorous efforts are needed to keep children safe and help families in crisis.

Child Welfare: 1973 to 1998

More resources to meet children's needs. A national framework for protecting children, aimed at promoting permanence and more appropriate care for those in need, has emerged over the past 25 years. Although federal support for child welfare services and foster care existed much earlier, the passage of the Child Abuse Prevention and Treatment Act (CAPTA) in 1974 marked a significant development. CAPTA heightened public awareness of child abuse and neglect, which had been brought to light in the early 1960s by Dr. Henry Kempe's identification of the "battered child syndrome." CAPTA required states to establish systems for reporting child abuse and neglect, provide appropriate representation and protection for children in court proceedings, and put other safeguards in place. CAPTA also created a child abuse prevention and treatment demonstration program. Four years later, CAPTA was amended to include the first federal effort designed specifically to encourage the adoption of children with special needs—the Adoption Opportunities Act of 1978.

Other legislation was enacted in the 1970s to protect the rights of particular groups of children. Most notably, Congress passed the Juvenile Justice and Delinquency Prevention Act, the Indian Child Welfare Act, the Developmentally Disabled Assistance and Bill of Rights Act, and the Education for All Handicapped Children Act. The 1974 enactment of the Title XX Social Services Program sparked hope of new services to prevent child abuse and neglect, but these hopes diminished in 1981 when Title XX funding was reduced and the program was made into a block grant. Today, funding for Title XX is at its lowest level since the program's inception.

Building upon these earlier measures, the Adoption Assistance and Child Welfare Act in 1980 attempted to restructure the federal government's role in protecting children and to encourage similar state efforts. The act's comprehensive approach to reform emphasized the need to (1) keep children from being unnecessarily placed in foster care, as well as the need to get them out; (2) link basic protections for children and parents to state funding; (3) provide help in finding permanent homes for children free for adoption; and (4) monitor state progress in protecting children. Although implementation was hindered by efforts in the early 1980s to repeal or weaken the act, it stimulated the development of prevention and reunification services in some states and dramatically increased the adoption chances of children with special needs. The number of children who found permanent adoptive homes with federal assistance grew from an average of 165 a month in 1981 to more than 112,000 a month by 1997.

Later federal legislative reforms prompted further state action. States undertook initiatives to help older youths in foster care prepare to live independently, promoted new methods of service delivery for children with serious emotional disturbances, and worked with communities to expand services that help families prevent or defuse problems. In addition, some states and communities, often with foundation leadership and support, developed programs to promote adoption, permanency planning, specialized foster homes, family preservation, family support, and, more recently, community partnerships for protecting children.

Courts also have made state policies and practices more responsive to children's needs. In the

Facts & Figures

- In 1996, 3.1 million children were reported abused or neglected, and the reports were substantiated for at least 969,000.

- Eighty percent of the child welfare cases served in 1994 involved allegations of abuse or neglect, compared with 45 percent in 1977.

- An estimated 40 to 80 percent of the families who become child protective service cases have problems with alcohol or drugs.

- Approximately 502,000 children were in foster care at the end of 1996—about 25 percent more than in 1990.

- In 1996, 2.14 million children lived in households headed by a relative with no parent present. A majority of these children—1.43 million—lived with grandparents.

past 25 years court orders or consent decrees in 22 states have addressed the inappropriate care of children and prompted changes. In individual legal cases involving neglect, termination of parental rights, and adoption, courts have defined the rights of parents and children and have pressured public agencies to recognize these rights.

New problems. The children who enter the child welfare system today bring more acute problems. A sizable percentage come from families with substance abuse problems, many are believed to be victims of or witnesses to domestic violence, and AIDS affects the families of a considerable number. The 1997 *National Study of Protective, Preventive and Reunification Services Delivered to Children and Their Families* reported striking changes in the population being served by child welfare agencies between 1977 and 1994. Although about the same number of children were in foster care, there was a 60 percent decline in the number of children receiving in-home services (see figure 5.1). The study also found that 80 percent of the child welfare cases served in 1994 involved allegations of abuse and neglect, compared with 45 percent in 1977. It is no coincidence that reports of

child abuse and neglect have risen steadily since 1976, shooting up more than 90 percent between 1981 and 1986 and increasing 45 percent between 1987 and 1996.

Clearly the child welfare system is not equipped to handle these problems alone. Many child welfare agencies are overwhelmed, operating in a constant crisis mode that jeopardizes their ability to address the individual needs of the children and families who seek help. As the intensity of children's problems has increased, the agencies have been forced to focus on basic child protection services, rather than on a broader range of services for families in need. The challenge is likely to be even more formidable in coming years. Child protection officials predict greater stresses on families and greater demand for child welfare services as families lose cash aid, food assistance, and other benefits as a result of the 1996 welfare law.

Need for interagency and community participation. In the 1970s and early 1980s, solutions to children's and families' problems were defined narrowly and directed to different agencies acting independently of each other. Although practitioners knew that the child welfare, juvenile jus-

Figure 5.1 **Children Served by the Child Welfare System**

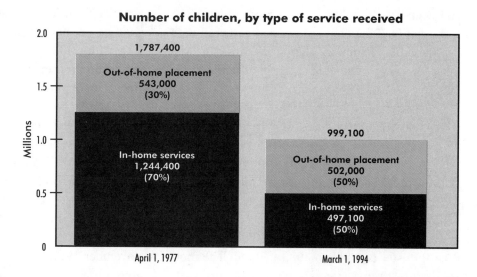

As children victimized by abuse and neglect have come to make up a larger share of agency caseloads, agencies have been able to serve far fewer children.

Number of children, by type of service received

1,787,400
Out-of-home placement
543,000
(30%)

In-home services
1,244,400
(70%)

April 1, 1977

999,100
Out-of-home placement
502,000
(50%)

In-home services
497,100
(50%)

March 1, 1994

Source: U.S. Department of Health and Human Services, *National Study of Protective, Preventive and Reunification Services Delivered to Children and Their Families: Final Report* (1997).

tice, and mental health systems were struggling to care for many of the same children, federal and state policies seldom promoted interagency approaches, nor was community participation emphasized. Service systems did not comprehensively address the needs of individual children and families.

The Child and Adolescent Service System Program (CASSP), begun in 1983 with a $1.5 million budget, was the first initiative focused exclusively on improving the coordination of service agencies for children and teens with serious emotional disturbances. As funding grew, services expanded, but the principle of partnering with agencies, parents, and others working for children remained key. The 1993 Family Preservation and Support Services Program also required states to bring together these kinds of partners to identify existing supports and needs for children and families and to plan for the use of new resources.

Families in Crisis: The Scope of the Problem Today

A survey of state child protection agencies in 1996 by the National Committee to Prevent Child Abuse reported 969,000 children abused and neglected. However, some experts believe that as many as three times that number need help. Indeed, 3.1 million children were reported abused and neglected to public child protection agencies, and a national incidence study that gathered data from additional sources suggested that actual victims may have numbered 2.8 million children in 1993.

The American Public Welfare Association estimates that 502,000 children were in foster care on an average day in 1996—about 25 percent more than in 1990. Although a current national profile of these children does not exist, an interesting picture emerges from the 1997 Multistate Foster Care Data Archive's examination of placement patterns in six states (accounting for about half of all children in foster care) from 1983 to 1994. The most recent growth in foster care placements primarily involved children placed with relatives. The study

also found infants and young children entering foster care in greater numbers than any other age group and remaining in care longer than older children.

Of particular concern are children who become long-term clients of the child welfare system. Most reunification of children with their families occurs within two years of a child's entry into foster care, but more than one-third spend much longer periods in care (see figure 5.2). Reentry into care is a problem too. Of the children who entered care in 1988, about 20 percent returned within five years.

Children with serious emotional problems, whose special needs too often go unmet and who may be at great risk of entering foster care, are another concern. The Center for Mental Health Services in the U.S. Department of Health and Human Services (HHS) announced in 1997 that between 3.5 million and 4 million children ages 9–17 have a serious emotional disturbance. The center also reported that emotional problems are especially prevalent among poor children. It has published estimates of the number of children with emotional disturbances in each state, based partly on the child poverty rate in the state.

Promoting Adoption and Other Permanency Options

In 1997 considerable attention was paid to providing permanent families for children, particularly the 100,000 children living in foster homes and group care settings who cannot return safely to their birth families.

Federal and state action. Last year the HHS secretary, responding to a December 1996 presidential directive, announced a plan to double the numbers of adoptions and other permanent placements for foster children by 2002. Congress also took action with passage of the Adoption and Safe Families Act. Signed into law by the President in November 1997, the act includes numerous provisions developed with bipartisan support that are intended to promote adoptions for children waiting in foster care. Some provisions are intended to accelerate decisions about children's permanent care and expedite proceedings to terminate parental rights (a necessary precursor to adoption). The legislation also gives states fiscal incentives to move children into adoptive families. For example, states that increase the number of adoptions of foster children (in a given year over a base year) will be rewarded financially, with higher payments for certain children. The standard payment will be $4,000 per child, but states will receive $6,000 per child for adoptions of children with special needs (children with physical, mental, or emotional problems, children who are adopted together with their siblings, and children who, because of age, race, or ethnicity, could not be adopted without assistance).

A number of these reforms build on changes already under way in states. During 1997 the General Accounting Office, the American Bar Association's Center on Children and the Law, and the New England Association of Child Welfare Commissioners and Directors all highlighted positive state activities. These include efforts to expedite permanency hearings, streamline termination of parental rights proceedings, increase adoptions, de-

velop new service strategies to promote the stable reunification of families, and train staff to plan for reunification while concurrently developing an alternative permanency plan for each child. State courts meanwhile are moving children more promptly through the judicial system, often with the help of the State Court Improvement Program reauthorized by Congress as part of the Adoption and Safe Families Act.

Expediting permanency decisions. New York City's past experience in placing children in adoptive homes illustrates the bureaucratic barriers to adoption. Dr. Trudy Festinger of the Shirley M. Ehrenkranz School of Social Work at New York University reviewed the records of children in out-of-home care who were adopted in 1995, most with state financial support. The children's median age at adoption was 7.3 years old, although their median age at the time they were placed with their adoptive family was 2. In 85 percent of the cases, the parental rights of at least one parent had to be terminated first in court, a process that is too frequently dragged out. Even after parental rights were terminated, delays continued. Although New York law permits the filing of an adoption petition

---

Figure 5.2 **What Becomes of Children in Foster Care? A Look at Six States***

Although most children in foster care in these six states returned to their families within two years, and about one-sixth were eventually adopted, another one-sixth remained in some form of public care for at least six years.

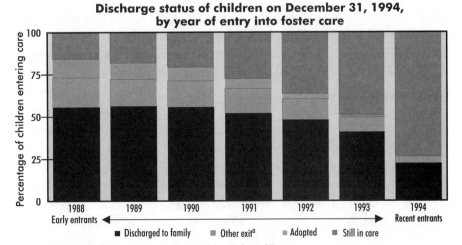

Discharge status of children on December 31, 1994, by year of entry into foster care

Percentage of children entering care

■ Discharged to family   ■ Other exit[a]   ■ Adopted   ■ Still in care

*California, Illinois, Michigan, Missouri, New York, and Texas.
a. Includes children who reach the age of majority while still in care, runaways, children who attain independence, those moved to juvenile detention or other public facilities, and some for whom the discharge destination is unknown or unspecified.
Source: Fred H. Wulczyn, Allen W. Harden, and Robert M. George, *Foster Care Dynamics 1983–1994: An Update from the Multistate Foster Care Data Archive* (Chapin Hall Center for Children at the University of Chicago, 1997).

when a termination is pending or completed, the median duration between termination of parental rights and final adoption was more than a year and a half.

In response to such findings, New York City officials, with prodding from adoption advocates and others, undertook several initiatives to expedite and increase adoptions. The strategies included giving foster care agencies fiscal incentives to increase adoptions, finalizing adoptions for the large number of children whose cases were stuck in the courts, and intensifying efforts to recruit adoptive families. These activities were strengthened through collaboration with New York's Families for Kids initiative, supported by the W.K. Kellogg Foundation. As a result, the number of foster children adopted in the city increased 74 percent between Fiscal Years 1994 and 1997.

Other states and communities are also working to expedite permanency decisions. For example, the Massachusetts Department of Social Services launched Assignment Adoption in 1993. The previous year, only 599 of the almost 5,000 children whose case plans called for adoption were adopted, after an average wait of four years from the time adoption became their case plan goal. The Assignment Adoption project involves aggressive recruitment of adoptive families, enhanced staffing, legislative changes, and intensive partnerships with the courts. Adoptions in Massachusetts have now increased considerably. In 1997, for the fourth year in a row, more than 1,000 foster children were adopted.

Children in Kinship Care

When abuse or neglect occurs or when financial pressures, health problems, mental illness, immaturity, or other troubles leave parents unable to care for their children, family members often step in. Data from the National Survey of Families and Households (reported by Esme Fuller Thomson, Meredith Minkler, and others in the June 1997 issue of *The Gerontologist*) reveal that more than 10 percent of grandparents at some point assume primary responsibility for rais-

ing a grandchild for six months or more, most often during infancy or preschool years. The Census Bureau reported that in 1996, 2.14 million children lived in households headed by a relative with no parent present; two-thirds lived with grandparents (see figure 5.3). These arrangements are often referred to as "kinship" care.

Most kin caregivers never have contact with the formal child protection or foster care systems. Many have never received public assistance. For those who do, however, 1997 brought uncertainty and prospective changes in state support for relatives caring for children without their parents present.

The new rules for recipients of Temporary Assistance for Needy Families (TANF) create new challenges for kin caregivers. Although state rules vary, generally when a nonparental relative and child both receive benefits, the relative is subject to the customary work requirements and time limits for receiving aid (see chapter 1). Alternatively, the grant may be for the child only, not the relative caregiver. But limited assistance may make it difficult for some relatives to continue caring for the child. Instead, they may have to look to foster care.

Nationally, HHS estimates that about one-third of all children in foster care are in kinship care arrangements. In California almost half of the approximately 100,000 foster children are living with relatives.

More support to kin. Some states, such as California, Missouri, and South Dakota, are considering new approaches to supporting relative caregivers. To provide kin caregivers in California with more assistance, the caregivers, child advocates, county welfare departments, and state leaders together addressed safety, support, and permanence issues for children in kin placements. A statewide Kinship Care Task Force, convened by the California Partnership for Children, issued a report titled *Kinship Care in California: The Challenges and Opportunities Facing Relatives and the Children Placed in Their Care*. And the legislature enacted three bills in 1997, establishing services for kinship caregivers in pilot counties, allowing access to child abuse information when assessing relative placements, and making adoption laws friendlier to relative caregivers.

Other states are also seeking the best and most appropriate ways to make placement with relatives a viable alternative to long-term foster care. Maryland, for example, received HHS approval in 1997 for a five-year demonstration program that will offer relative caregivers ongoing financial assistance. The state will make a $300 per month guardianship payment for children who have spent at least six months in a foster home with a kin (or non-kin) provider with whom they have a strong attachment, if returning to their birth parents and adoption have both been ruled out. The state proposes to place at least 300 children in guardianship each year and to guard against families moving inappropriately from the TANF program to the child welfare system.

The Children's Bureau in the Administration for Children, Youth and Families in HHS also awarded about 20 grants in 1997 to state and local child welfare agencies, some private providers, and universities. The grants will be used to train staff in assessing and supporting relative caregivers, to

train caregivers and offer them special services, and to explore adoption by caregivers.

The Brookdale Foundation is offering support to a broader group of relative caregivers, including those without contact with the formal child welfare system, through its Relatives as Parents Program. In 1997 the foundation awarded grants to 15 community-based organizations and five state agencies to develop assistance to grandparents and other relatives who have assumed parenting responsibilities. State initiatives must include a statewide organization of local programs, an interagency task force to collaborate on behalf of grandparent caregivers, and the establishment of new relative support groups.

Community Partnerships to Protect Children

The past year brought renewed support for community efforts to keep children safe from abuse and neglect. A July 1997 General Accounting Office report, *Child Protective Services: Complex Challenges Require New Strategies*, recommended that the secretary of HHS target future child protection funding to localities exploring col-

Figure 5.3 **Children in Relatives' Care**

The number of children living with relatives and no parent in the home grew 59 percent between 1989 and 1996. The number of these children living with grandparents increased 62 percent during the same period.

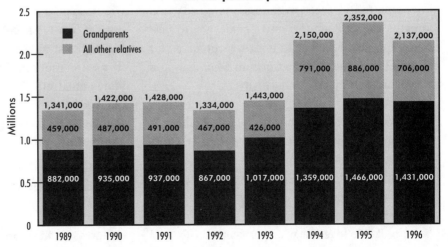

Number of children being raised by relatives with no parent present

Source: U.S. Department of Commerce, Bureau of the Census, March Current Population Surveys for 1989–96.

laboration among community agencies and to the development of specific techniques to promote community-based child protection services.

Support for the concept of community partnerships to deal with child abuse and neglect also came from other sources. A 1997 paper issued by the Executive Session on Child Protection at Harvard University's Kennedy School, *Child Protection: Building Community Partnerships—Getting from Here to There*, outlines a new vision for protecting children and seven steps for communities to take to move toward this vision (see box 5.1). The goal is to encourage family members, informal support networks, community organizations, and teams of multiple service agencies to collaborate with child protective services and local law enforcement agencies. Under the new community partnership, the child protection agency maintains a central but less autonomous role, helping to catalyze, organize, and lead other partners in activities to keep children safe.

Partnerships developed in response to the Promoting Safe and Stable Families Program. Establishing partnerships has been an important part of the work undertaken by states over the past four years to implement the Promoting Safe and Stable Families Program (formerly the Family Preservation and Support Services Program). Preliminary reports from 1997 surveys indicate that this program has helped bring together groups at the state and community levels to assess the needs and strengths of communities and decide where new dollars can best be spent to improve outcomes for children. Implementation efforts in Michigan and Florida are particularly noteworthy:

■ With federal and extra state funds, Michigan's Strong Families/Safe Children Program established coordinating councils in all 83 counties. Councils include consumers, seniors, community and religious representatives, prosecutors, judges, and personnel from various agencies who decide together what services to offer and what changes to make. They have a mandate to track and report their progress in achieving at

least four goals: increasing immunizations, decreasing the number and duration of out-of-home care placements, increasing adoptions, and expanding services to relatives acting as surrogate parents.

■ Community-wide involvement is also the cornerstone of Florida's family support and family preservation programs and practices. Community facilitators in each service district, in collaboration with any established councils or coalitions, help design plans to meet local needs. "Asset-based mapping" identifies existing community strengths and resources and helps determine how to best use new resources.

Partnerships for mental health. Local systems of care established with funding from the federal Children's Mental Health Services Grant Program are another example of community partnerships. The goal is to ensure that children with serious emotional disturbances and their families receive the help they need. The systems of care link various child-serving agencies and draw in parents and other family members to create a range of services individually tailored to children.

Efforts are being made to transfer the principles of partnership to early childhood development programs. The value of partnership is described in a 1997 publication of the National Center for Children in Poverty and the American Orthopsychiatric Association, *Lessons from the Field: Head Start Mental Health Strategies to Meet Changing Needs*. It highlights strategies used by Head Start programs to assure the healthy emotional development of young children. These strategies include emphasizing staff training, finding new ways of engaging families, and building stronger connections to the community.

Needs of Special Populations

Another concern in 1997 was the need to increase and improve services for two groups of children particularly likely to end up in the child protection system—children from families

> Box 5.1 **Steps to Promote Community Partnerships for Child Protection**
>
> The following steps can help communities broaden responsibility for child protection to better keep children safe.
>
> 1. Agree that the child protective services agency alone cannot protect children and that change must include partnerships.
>
> 2. Start partnerships that include parents as well as other agencies and organizations that serve children.
>
> 3. Create different responses tailored to families' varied needs for child protection.
>
> 4. Develop comprehensive neighborhood-based supports and services that include both formal and informal supports, and reorganize services to be more accessible.
>
> 5. Transform the public child protection agency so that it can assess families' needs more comprehensively, engage families and informal support networks, and form teams across agencies and with community representatives.
>
> 6. Shift intake and follow-up care for lower-risk families to the community-based system. This will enable them to receive earlier attention, while freeing child protection agencies to concentrate on families with the most serious problems.
>
> 7. Institute a system of governance and accountability in which responsibility for protecting children is shared by multiple agencies and community organizations.
>
> Adapted from *Child Protection: Building Community Partnerships—Getting from Here to There*, by Frank Farrow with the Executive Session on Child Protection (John F. Kennedy School of Government, Harvard University, Cambridge, Mass., 1997).

with substance abuse or domestic violence problems. These families may also have some of the greatest barriers to employment and be left behind as states implement the work requirements in the 1996 welfare law.

Children from families with substance abuse problems. An estimated 40 to 80 percent of the families that become child protective service cases have problems with alcohol and other drugs. About three-quarters of the states surveyed in 1997 by the National Committee to Prevent Child Abuse named substance abuse as one of the top two problems exhibited by families reported for child maltreatment. In a 1997 study of state child welfare agencies, the Child Welfare League of America found that at least half the placements of children in foster care were due in part to parental alcohol

or drug abuse. Agencies also reported that they could help fewer than one-third of the families with substance abuse problems.

Substance abuse is assumed to particularly contribute to the increase in the number of very young children entering foster care. The Multistate Foster Care Data Archive reported in 1997 that children entering care at the age of 1 outnumber other entrants by more than three to one, and infants have the longest stays in care.

Dr. Richard Barth, director of the Child Welfare Research Center and Abandoned Infants Assistance Resource Center at the University of California at Berkeley, testified before Congress in 1997 about the risks of simply removing newborns from substance-abusing mothers without treating the mothers. He pointed out that unless the parent's addiction is addressed, subsequent children are likely to be born substance-exposed. Barth cited a study of California foster care cases where parental substance abuse was suspected: of 1,576 newborns brought into care in 1995, 60 percent already had at least one sibling in the foster care system; about 25 percent had three or more.

In a 1997 paper for the Executive Session on Child Protection, Sid Gardner and Nancy Young at Children and Family Futures in Irvine, California, also documented the importance of providing services to mothers with substance abuse problems. They cited data indicating that a small number of women who abused alcohol or other drugs while pregnant accounted for 41 percent of child protective service referrals and out-of-home placements in the state of Washington. Gardner and Young described staff training, case assessment, and service initiatives in Delaware, Washington, and Sacramento County, California, aimed at building bridges between child protective service agencies and substance abuse treatment providers.

Children exposed to domestic violence. Children in families where domestic violence occurs are at significant risk of being abused. A 1995 review of domestic violence research cited by the American Humane Association revealed that between one-third to one-half of children exposed to domestic violence are direct victims. Many more—up to 87 percent by some reports—witness the abuse.

Child protection agencies are now giving more attention to these problems. Community partners in Cedar Rapids, Iowa, identified distinct overlaps between incidents of child and spousal abuse, which helped the community refocus its energies on this area. The Family Violence Prevention Fund in San Francisco has developed a training curriculum for child protection staff and is working with child protection agencies, domestic violence advocates, and shelter programs to encourage increased collaboration. Massachusetts, Michigan, and Washington state train child protection workers to recognize and address domestic violence; they also sensitize the staff of domestic violence shelters to children's needs.

Focusing on Outcomes

Although improvements are being made, the failings of the systems set up to protect children remain deeply troubling. These concerns have focused attention on holding child protection agencies more accountable for what happens to the children and families they serve.

The new Adoption and Safe Families Act requires the secretary of HHS, in consultation with public officials and child welfare advocates, to establish outcome measures for assessing how well states protect children and a system for rating state performance on these outcomes. An annual progress report is required beginning May 1, 1999, in which the secretary must inform Congress how each state is doing and how it might improve. HHS also must develop a performance-based incentive system for providing federal child welfare payments to states.

This "outcome-based" accountability is also a part of the reforms sought as state child welfare agencies begin to apply the principles of managed care, or privatization, to their work. The Child Welfare League of America found that 31 of the 50 state child welfare agencies surveyed in 1997 are incorporating at least some of these principles into the current management, financing, or delivery of at least some of their child welfare services. This may mean, for example, "capitated" payments, whereby the state prepays a fixed amount per child for a range of services and the managing agency then is responsible for providing the needed services, either directly or through subcontractors. The agency may retain unspent portions of these capitated payments, but it also must absorb excess costs.

Kansas, which has probably gone furthest in privatizing its services, is holding providers accountable for achieving specific outcomes in family preservation, foster family and group care, and adoption. The contract agencies are paid a set dollar amount per child or per family, tied to their achieving certain outcomes for their caseloads.

Most states are beginning more slowly with pilot programs that include some managed care.

HHS is funding such demonstration projects in Michigan, New York, North Carolina, Ohio, and Oregon. The Protect Ohio project, for example, which will involve no more than 20 counties initially, uses funds currently invested in foster care to develop community-based services to keep children safer and help families resolve problems. As foster care costs decline because of the availability of more preventive services, counties will be able to reinvest these dollars in other child welfare services. The project will be evaluated on the basis of improved outcomes for children and families.

Although privatization and managed care in child welfare are appealing in theory, too often they are proposed simply as part of a larger plan to contain costs. The resources to achieve outcomes and measure progress are not provided. The challenge in any outcome-based system is to define the desired outcomes, find ways to achieve them, and establish ways to measure and track progress consistently across agencies, across cases within the same agency, and over time. In Kansas, for example, the lack of a comprehensive data system is one of the barriers to effective privatization of its activities.

An Exciting Local Initiative

After a full year of planning, Louisville, Kentucky, launched its Community Partnership for Protecting Children in 1997. With funding from the Edna McConnell Clark Foundation and technical assistance from the Washington, D.C.-based Center for the Study of Social Policy, Louisville is starting to shift responsibility for child protection from a single public agency to a partnership of agencies, community centers, schools, neighborhoods, and families.

Kentucky and Louisville had already experimented with many reforms in the areas of family support, child welfare, and children's mental health services. In the early 1990s a statewide education initiative required the creation of family resource centers for elementary school students and youth service centers for high school students in most school districts. The Jefferson County Family Court sought creative new ways to mediate cases and secure appropriate services for families in need. At the same time, Louisville developed the concept of "A Neighborhood Place," where services for children and families would be centralized in one place in some of the city's most vulnerable neighborhoods. Managed with help from parents and community members, these sites bring together staff and services from various public agencies, including health and human services, mental health, social insurance, child protection, employment, education, and law enforcement.

In September 1995 Kentucky Youth Advocates (KYA) chronicled the child protection crisis in a report titled *Above and Beyond*. It described hundreds of calls to a statewide hotline KYA set up after the death of a child under agency supervision, and made a strong case that child welfare workers were overburdened and unable to keep children safe. Funds for better training and more staff resulted, and publicity about the hotline findings also helped mobilize the community to act.

The Community Partnership for Protecting Children grew both out of Louisville's earlier reform efforts and out of the community's desire to take charge and find better ways to safeguard children from abuse and neglect. The project exemplifies the importance of commitment, communication, and time in building true partnerships to protect children. Its activities have focused on Neighborhood Place Ujima, housed in a multiservice center.

A major challenge during the planning stage was overcoming the mistrust among people in the neighborhood, the child protective services agency, and other government agencies. Trust developed as participants created a common vision and agenda and clarified their respective roles, responsibilities, and authority. Participants now see the partnership as "a covenant of arms linking everyone together in the belief that childhood is a sacred time and that safety is the promise our community makes to its children and families." The planning phase also involved much struggle to set objectives for partnership activity and benchmarks for evaluating progress. The partners eventually agreed to three desired outcomes: reductions in child abuse and neglect, less repeat abuse and neglect, and fewer serious injuries to children.

The strategies now being undertaken to improve safety for children include a new "family solutions" approach for those working with families. Parents get help identifying triggering events that place their children at risk, and they learn new skills for better responding to these triggers. Family-group decisionmaking broadens the support network for some families in trouble. Informal neighborhood helpers work with other individuals, agencies, and community groups. A community-wide service network and a system of staff training will address families' individual needs for substance abuse services. At the same time, work groups cochaired by community leaders and agency representatives are examining the current child protection agency response to families in crisis. They are also pursuing new approaches to ensuring child safety and developing a decision-making mechanism that respects the different roles and responsibilities of the various partners. Communications and evaluation efforts are under way as well.

Moving Forward: A 1998 Agenda for Action

Keeping children safe depends on keeping them in nurturing families and communities. That will require action at the local, state, and national levels and partnerships among all those with a stake in protecting children—parents and other relatives, foster families and adoptive families, public and private child-serving agencies, community and business leaders, religious organizations, educators, and child advocates. It requires that we look holistically at what is jeopardizing families' abilities to protect their children, and at who can help to prevent those problems and build on families' strengths. No single agency alone can assume responsibility for keeping children safe. Nor is there any single solution for keeping a child in a permanent family.

During 1998 advocates at the state and local levels must:

■ **Constantly seek better strategies to promote safety and permanence for children.** Collect and establish baseline data so that the impact of the new Adoption and Safe Families Act can be assessed after a year and over the longer term. Identify effective strategies, focusing on what works best to treat children as individuals with unique circumstances and needs. Work to extend successful strategies to other communities and states, and explore new approaches. Evaluate the adequacy of existing resources and the extent to which they are being used efficiently; identify the gaps and craft the best case for new investments. Push for systemic reforms as well as services to reach more children and families.

■ **Pay attention to special problems that threaten children's safety.** Alcohol and drug abuse, domestic violence, and the mental health problems of parents can all endanger children. To ensure that families' needs are appropriately assessed and addressed, encourage collaboration between child welfare agencies and those that treat substance abuse, mental illness, and domestic violence. Include welfare and employment and training agencies too, since these same problems often pose serious barriers to employment for families required to work under the 1996 welfare law. Help the public to better understand the connections. Treating families' problems and keeping parents on the employment track can keep them moving toward economic and social stability and prevent them from needing to seek help from the child welfare system.

■ **Forge partnerships.** Learn more about the community partnerships in Louisville and elsewhere, and consider how you might foster collaboration with the child protection agency in your community. Build on the work already done in some states to reach across agencies and into communities to implement the Promoting Safe and Stable Families Program and the Children's Mental Health Services Grant Program. Link efforts to prevent family violence to broader anti-crime initiatives. Be sure to tap both formal and informal supports to prevent family violence.

- **Support care by kin.** Garner community support for the increasing numbers of grandparents and other relatives who are becoming surrogate parents. Work to change state or federal policies that threaten relatives' ability to safely care for children, rather than waiting until these children are forced to move to foster care with strangers.

- **Develop new resources**. Engage businesses, religious organizations, and other community groups to contribute dollars, space, or volunteers to establish family resource centers in every neighborhood, whether at schools or other sites. Encourage local health, child welfare, and education agencies to jointly create home visiting programs to guide the parents of infants and young children in caring for their children appropriately. The benefits will be twofold: more children will receive the nurturing they need to thrive, and more child abuse and neglect will be averted.

CHILDREN, VIOLENCE, AND CRIME

Violence involving children—as victims or as perpetrators—is intolerable. By virtually every indicator, however, violence by and against youths is going down dramatically. According to data released in 1997, fewer young people are dying from gunfire, fewer are being murdered, and fewer are being arrested for violent crime. Community efforts involving a range of carefully crafted prevention programs, along with targeted law enforcement activities, are helping keep many children safe and out of trouble. These efforts are making the public safer too. Unfortunately, national leadership is heading in a different direction, forsaking investment in crime prevention and gun safety in favor of harsher, punitive measures for all juvenile offenders.

Criminal activity of any kind demands swift, firm punishment, but deterring young people from criminal behavior is far wiser and more cost-effective. Our children need balanced public policies designed to reduce and prevent violence and shield them from harm.

Children, Violence, and Crime: 1973 to 1998

Over the past 25 years, the menace of guns has increasingly threatened children. In addition, families' work patterns have changed, and children now have more unsupervised time than they did a generation ago. However, some of the concerns about youth and violence today—such as appropriate treatment of children who break the law—are issues that policy makers also confronted in the 1970s.

Children in adult jails. Twenty-five years ago, children who committed crimes—and even those picked up for running away from home or skipping school—were tossed into adult jails. Many suffered abuse. Enlightened leaders, however, recognized that children needed protection and deserved a chance to grow into productive members of society.

By 1973 Congress was moving toward passage of the Juvenile Justice and Delinquency Prevention

Act of 1974. This landmark legislation took a giant step forward in seeking to keep children away from adults in jails and prisons and to remove "status offenders" (runaways, truants, and others whose actions would not be criminal if they were adults) from the criminal justice system. The 1974 act required states to separate children from adults as a condition of receiving federal funds for their juvenile justice systems.

The law was passed because of a deep national concern about what happens to children when they are locked up, especially with adult criminals. The Children's Defense Fund helped spotlight the issue by filing a number of lawsuits in the early 1970s involving children in adult jails. In 1973 CDF President Marian Wright Edelman and Judge Justine Wise Polier, head of CDF's juvenile justice project, testified before the Senate Judiciary Committee drafting the juvenile justice reform act. Judge Polier warned the committee that failure to institute reforms would mean giving up on thousands of children, denying them services, and thrusting them back into the criminal courts, jails, and prisons of America. CDF later published *Children in Adult Jails*, documenting many of the tragedies—sexual assaults, physical abuse, suicides—that

had occurred when children were confined with adult criminals.

In 1998 Congress is poised to pass legislation that would turn back the clock and allow children once again to be incarcerated with adults, without adequate safeguards for their well-being. The proposed measures also would more often put runaways and truants in jails rather than community facilities. Certainly, strong measures are needed to deal with the small percentage of young people who commit violent crimes—0.5 percent of all youths ages 10–17, according to the Office of Juvenile Justice and Delinquency Prevention (OJJDP). However, subjecting them to abusive conditions in adult jails is not the answer, nor should that be the fate of the nonviolent youths who constitute the vast majority of juvenile offenders.

The gun epidemic. Beginning in the late 1980s, guns in the hands of children and those who would harm children became far too prevalent. Children themselves too often have been the victims of gun violence. In 1973 an average of nine children died from gunfire each day; by 1983 the number had fallen to eight per day. Over the next decade, how-

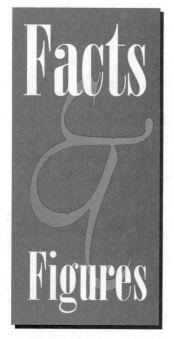

- An average of 14 children die *each day* from gunfire in America—approximately one every 100 minutes.

- In 1994 there were nearly 200 million firearms in American homes—almost one for every adult and child.

- Violent crime by young people peaks between 3 and 7 p.m.

- Children in adult prisons are eight times more likely to commit suicide, five times more likely to be sexually assaulted, and two times more likely to be assaulted by staff than are children in juvenile facilities.

- Each new juvenile correction facility typically costs $102,000 per bed to build. The average after-school program, by contrast, costs approximately $3,000 per child.

ever, the number nearly doubled, so that in 1994 an average of 16 children were dying daily. The next year finally brought a reversal to this deadly trend; in 1995 gun deaths dropped for the first time in 11 years, to a still staggering 14 children dying each day from gunfire. That meant that almost every 100 minutes, on average, a bullet claimed the life of a child.

As the explosion in crack cocaine trafficking wreaked havoc in many urban communities, children increasingly reported a need to carry a gun for protection. They also found guns easier to obtain. Not surprisingly, gun murders by children rose sharply (until recently). Data from OJJDP show that between 1985 and 1994 such killings quadrupled, from more than 500 to more than 2,000. Meanwhile, the number of murders by children *without* guns held steady at about 500 annually.

National response to this death toll has been minimal, and little has changed in our approach to regulating guns since 1973. According to a 1997 U.S. Department of Justice study, there were nearly 200 million firearms in American homes in 1994—almost one for every adult and child. The good news is that the overall percentage of homes with firearms has declined slightly since the 1970s; it is now about 35 percent.

Two measures—the 1993 Brady Act requiring waiting periods and criminal background checks for handgun purchasers, and the 1994 Assault Weapons Ban outlawing many nonsporting automatic weapons—have moved gun regulation in a commonsense direction. Unfortunately, many other national initiatives to keep children safe have not been enacted. These include bans on cheap, poorly made, nonsporting handguns popular with young people ("junk guns"); limits on the number of handgun purchases allowed in a given period ("one handgun a month") in order to stop bulk purchasers who resell guns illegally to children; and requirements for child safety locks and other consumer protections. Although progress in gun safety has been made at the state and local levels (see later discussion), guns remain an enormous threat to children.

Empty after-school hours. Another major change for children in the past 25 years is the amount of time they are left on their own, away from parents and other caring adults. According to the Bureau of Labor Statistics, in 1973 half of the mothers of school-age children were in the work force; today 77 percent are. More children now live in households where all the adults work outside the home. Many children spend less time with their parents and are often unsupervised for hours each day before their parents return from work. In total, nearly 5 million school-age children are left home alone each week.

Some children are fortunate to have attentive caregivers, after-school lessons or sports, extracurricular clubs, and other positive options to fill their out-of-school hours. Many use television and other media to fill the gap (see box 6.1). Others turn to riskier behavior: juvenile violent crime rates peak between 3 and 7 p.m. More positive opportunities for youth are needed to keep them safe and on track.

Declines in Violence by and Against Children

One of the most welcome pieces of news in 1997 was the report that gun deaths of children had decreased in 1995. In that year, according to the National Center for Health Statistics, such deaths dropped for the first time in a decade, and by nearly 10 percent—from 5,820 the previous year to 5,277 (see table 6.1). Reductions in gun deaths among Black males (which had skyrocketed in recent years) drove the decline, falling more than 20 percent. The National Center for Health Statistics also reported a lower incidence of killings of youths by *all* causes in 1995, building on a slight dip the previous year (see figure 6.1).

Juvenile crime also decreased. New OJJDP data released in 1997 show that arrest rates of young people for violent crimes (murder, rape, robbery, aggravated assault) fell in 1996 for the second year in a row—a total drop of more than 12 percent (see figure 6.2). Juvenile homicide arrest rates dropped for the third straight year since

Box 6.1 **Children and the Media**

Children today are exposed to alarming amounts of violence and other inappropriate material in television, movies, and popular music. They are also vulnerable to exploitation on the Internet. While the mass media and computers can be marvelous tools for education and enjoyment, they can also pose dangers to children.

Children and television violence. Two major developments in 1997 could herald better-quality, less violent television for families—but only if parents hold the television industry accountable. First, voluntary TV ratings that debuted in October provide both an on-screen age-advisory and information about program content. A TV-Y7-FV rating, for example, indicates fantasy violence in children's programming and recommends that viewers be at least 7 years old, and a TV-14-V denotes violence in general programming suitable for an audience over 14. The content information was added only after sustained pressure from parents and child and family advocates. Advocates demanded the use of the V and FV codes, in particular, because of the hundreds of studies that link the viewing of violence to increased aggression, heightened fear, and reduced sympathy for others' pain and suffering.

Despite this step forward, questions remain. Will all networks use the new ratings? (NBC and BET still do not.) Will objective criteria be developed to help networks apply the same standards in rating similar programs? Will parents use the rating system—and the V-chip, expected in TV sets sold in 1998 and later—to turn off violent and otherwise objectionable content? Advocates will keep monitoring the implementation of the new ratings and will work with parents and the industry to fine-tune them to meet families' needs.

A second development was the September 1 launch of the E/I rating, indicating educational or informative programs for children, and the new Federal Communications Commission (FCC) requirement that stations air at least three hours per week of such programs. It is hoped that stations will respond with better (including nonviolent and noncommercial) shows for children, and that families will eagerly and easily find them. The fall 1997 season contained some promising programming, and with positive feedback from parents and continued FCC oversight, improvement may be ongoing.

Children's safety on-line. The first summit on children and the Internet was held in December 1997, bringing together political leaders, industry executives, and child and family advocates. The summit focused on safety, particularly children coming into contact with pedophiles and pornography on the Internet. Participants discussed some of the potential protections that are emerging: filters available from software or Internet service providers, ratings of sites, and selected sites set aside for children. Many who want to safeguard children see such tools as an important supplement to legislative regulation—especially given that the Supreme Court struck down, on First Amendment grounds, the indecency provisions in the Communications Decency Act of 1995.

Pressure remains on the public and private sectors to develop solutions that keep children safe in cyberspace. Future Internet summits will focus on other critical issues, including universal access for all children, good content for children, privacy concerns, and on-line commercial marketing to children. Families can find information about Web sites for children and parents through the Parent's Resource Network on CDF's home page: www.childrensdefense.org.

Table 6.1 **Firearm Deaths of Children and Teens, by Cause**

Year	Homicide[a]	Suicide	Accident	Unknown	Total
1979	1,644	1,220	722	112	3,698
1980	1,730	1,212	686	105	3,733
1981	1,647	1,211	602	113	3,573
1982	1,484	1,207	549	77	3,317
1983	1,231	1,149	511	60	2,951
1984	1,274	1,112	552	77	3,015
1985	1,339	1,256	517	72	3,184
1986	1,529	1,292	469	72	3,362
1987	1,582	1,280	466	80	3,408
1988	1,961	1,386	543	91	3,981
1989	2,384	1,379	563	71	4,397
1990	2,858	1,474	538	71	4,941
1991	3,264	1,436	549	95	5,344
1992	3,351	1,426	500	90	5,367
1993	3,647	1,460	526	104	5,737
1994	3,608	1,565	510	137	5,820
1995	3,272	1,450	440	115	5,277

a. Includes firearm deaths by legal intervention (such as by law enforcement officials).
Source: U.S. Department of Health and Human Services, National Center for Health Statistics, Division of Vital Statistics. Calculations for 1979–93 by NCHS, Office of Analysis, Epidemiology and Health Promotion. Calculations for 1994 and 1995 by Children's Defense Fund.

1993, plummeting 31 percent. These declines were especially pronounced for Black children. Arrest rates of Black children for homicide dropped 24 percent from 1994 to 1995; arrest rates of White children fell 8 percent. Also heartening were large declines in arrests for violent crime among juveniles ages 13–15, suggesting less violent behavior among young teenagers.

The 1997 National Crime Victimization Survey confirmed the OJJDP findings of a decline in violence by children. According to the survey, victims reported 25 percent fewer violent crimes committed by juveniles between 1994 and 1995. The survey also indicated some improvement in the victimization rate of young teens. Crime against 12- to 15-year-olds decreased from a rate of 118.4 per 1,000 in 1993 to 113.0 per 1,000 in 1994. However, crime against older teens ages 16–19 rose by a comparable amount, with victimization rates climbing from 114.2 per 1,000 to 120.5 per 1,000—the highest of any age group.

Protecting Children from Guns

In 1997 political leaders, child advocates, and families across the nation heralded the decline in gun deaths of children. There was less cause for celebration on the policy-making front. At the national level, congressional gridlock prevented the enactment of any new gun safety initiatives. And in July 1997 the Supreme Court (relying on the Tenth, not the Second Amendment) struck down part of the Brady Act requirement for background checks of gun purchasers, on the grounds that it placed an unconstitutional mandate on states. The requirement for a waiting period remains constitutional and in effect, however, and a majority of states and localities are continuing to do background checks voluntarily during the waiting period, according to Handgun Control, Inc.

The Clinton Administration has also pursued some modest measures. Initial reports on the Bureau of Alcohol, Tobacco and Firearms' Project LEAD, which tracks guns recovered from youths at crime scenes in selected cities, indicate that it has succeeded in identifying and shutting down illegal sources of guns for children. The project has now expanded from 17 cities to 27. The Administration also required licensed gun dealers to post warnings against illegally furnishing guns to children and brokered a voluntary agreement with most major handgun manufacturers to provide child safety locks with all new handguns sold. These are positive steps, but they fall far short of the comprehensive safety regulations needed to protect children from guns.

At the state and local levels, advocates working for gun safety initiatives met with some success in 1997. In California more than 32 jurisdictions have now passed gun regulations, including bans on "junk guns." (Unfortunately, a state bill to do the same was vetoed by the governor.) A consumer protection effort in Massachusetts resulted in requirements that child safety locks be provided with every new handgun. Chicago passed a similar ordinance, and advocates throughout Illinois won passage of a statewide gun-tracing initiative to identify the sources of guns recovered from crimes. In

Washington state, however, a "Safety First" ballot initiative that would have required child safety locks and licensing of gun owners was defeated, largely because of a heavily funded, last-minute campaign against it by the National Rifle Association.

The Move Toward Stiffer Penalties for Juveniles

Just as violence by and against young people seems to be steadily waning, Congress is moving forward with new punitive measures aimed at responding to the higher violent juvenile crime rates between 1987 and 1994. The emphasis of the new initiatives is on punishment and prisons. One such bill, H.R. 3, passed the House of Representatives in 1997. A corresponding Senate measure, S. 10, was still pending in early 1998. It would allow states to put more children in adult jails and prisons without critical protections from assault and suicide, and it would reduce the confidentiality of juveniles' records. A second House bill, H.R. 1818, that has also passed already, would largely preserve core protections for children in jail and provide modest prevention investments. However,

Figure 6.1 **Homicides of Teens**

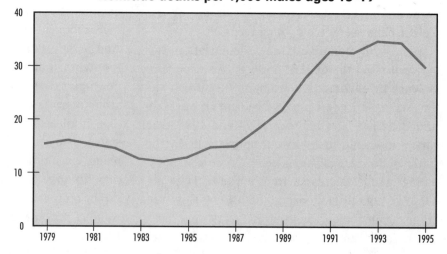

Fewer youths were murdered in 1996, a relief after the sharp increase in teen homicides that began in the late 1980s. Gun deaths drove this increase, rising 153 percent between 1985 and 1995, while all other murders rose only 9 percent.

Homicide deaths per 1,000 males ages 15–19

Source: U.S. Department of Health and Human Services, National Center for Health Statistics.

it would not overcome the provisions of H.R. 3 and S. 10 that present grave risks to children.

How the proposed legislation would affect children. Although the Senate measure would provide new funds for juvenile courts, it would encourage the transfer of more children to adult criminal courts. Even more troubling, it would allow states to put more children in jails and prisons with adult offenders and weaken the laws protecting them from adult contact and abuse. It would also allow states to hold runaways in jail for up to 14 days, and truants for up to three days. Any status offender could be held for 24 hours in an *adult* jail. This could actually stretch to a longer period because weekends and holidays are excluded.

Housing children in jails and prisons with adults puts them at greater risk for suicide, rape, assault, and murder. Children in adult facilities are eight times more likely to commit suicide, five times more likely to be sexually assaulted, and two times more likely to be beaten by staff than are youth in juvenile facilities, according to research published in the February 1989 issue of *Juvenile and Family Court Journal.* The physical danger to children incarcerated with adults is also evident

from the track record in Kentucky, which declined federal funds rather than comply with the provisions of the 1974 law requiring removal of children from adult jails. According to a study by Kentucky Youth Advocates, *Violent Incidents Against Juveniles in Kentucky Adult Jails, 1974-1992,* over this 13-year period there were four suicides and one attempted suicide by Kentucky children in adult jails.

Not only are children in adult facilities at increased risk of harm, but their chances for rehabilitation are markedly reduced because they are exposed to precisely the wrong role models and receive *no* education, counseling, or other services. The National Coalition of State Juvenile Justice Advisory Groups reviewed a number of studies and found that children put in adult facilities have higher recidivism rates than those handled in juvenile systems for the same offense. Rather than learn ways to become productive citizens, they encounter more experienced criminals and are more likely to return to their communities with an even greater propensity to engage in criminal activity.

Another provision of the Senate legislation would mandate state changes in recordkeeping practices that would make juvenile records more

Figure 6.2 **Juvenile Arrests**

Fewer youths were arrested for violent crimes in 1996, the second year of decline after a decade of steep increase. The drop was most pronounced for juveniles ages 13–15, and for the crime of murder.

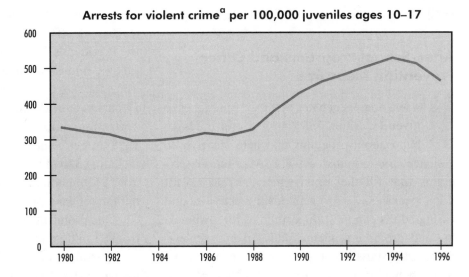

Arrests for violent crime^a per 100,000 juveniles ages 10–17

a. Murder, rape, robbery, and aggravated assault.
Source: Office of Juvenile Justice and Delinquency Prevention.

widely available. The excessively broad language would appear to require all juvenile records, including arrest records, to be made available not only to law enforcement personnel but also to schools, including postsecondary schools and colleges. Such extensive dissemination of juvenile records could have devastating effects on young people's future employment and educational opportunities. Moreover, it would go far beyond what is necessary to protect communities from violent offenders.

An untargeted and unbalanced approach. According to the FBI, only a small percentage (5 percent) of juvenile offenders are responsible for the serious, violent acts that endanger our communities and families. S. 10, however, would treat *all* offenders like the 5 percent, exposing them all to adult jails and prisons and unjustifiable record sharing.

Also important, the Senate bill and one of the House bills (H.R. 3) fail to set aside any money for crime prevention activities. The other House bill (H.R. 1818) proposes prevention funding that is minimal and could be vulnerable in the appropriations process. Rather than guaranteeing more resources to support effective prevention efforts and strengthen law enforcement aimed at stopping youth violence and crime, these measures—H.R. 3 and S. 10 in particular—misguidedly focus on incarceration and punishment for all juvenile offenders.

After-School Programs and Other Prevention Measures

While Congress debates punitive approaches to juvenile crime, information continues to build about programs that help stem youth violence and criminal activity. After-school programs that fill the hours when juvenile violent crime peaks (3–7 p.m.) with positive activities and caring adults can limit opportunities for lawbreaking and promote academic and personal achievement. Other targeted programs can also curb delinquent behavior. Researchers at the University of Maryland surveyed recent evaluations of preven-

tion programs in a 1997 study called *Preventing Crime*. They found that the keys to success were targeting funds to the most violent communities, coordinating efforts with law enforcement agencies and other community entities, and continuously evaluating programs on their results.

A new study by the American Youth Policy Forum, *Some Things Do Make a Difference for Youth*, catalogs some of the strategies that have succeeded in keeping children and communities safe. These include mentoring programs like Big Brothers and Big Sisters, which operates nationwide, and high school graduation incentives for at-risk youth, such as those provided by the Quantum Opportunities Project in five communities—Milwaukee, Oklahoma City, Philadelphia, Saginaw (Michigan), and San Antonio. Providing authentic job and community service opportunities is another successful strategy; YouthBuild, which operates at over 100 sites across the country, takes this approach.

The clear conclusion is that prevention programs work. Indeed, a recent survey of 780 police chiefs by Northeastern University found that nine out of 10 police chiefs, as well as other community leaders, support prevention programs as an effective way to fight crime. Nevertheless, the 1998 federal budget largely ignores prevention efforts. None of a new $250 million juvenile accountability block grant in the Department of Justice can be spent on prevention; the funds are reserved solely for activities related to incarceration and law enforcement efforts. Moreover, Congress stripped the President's Ounce of Prevention Council of its funding and eliminated money that had been set aside for Community Schools, a program of the Department of Health and Human Services to support after-school safe havens. Modest funds for 1998 were provided for some prevention programs, including $20 million for local delinquency prevention, $12 million for mentoring programs, and $12 million for gang prevention.

One promising note was a substantial increase, from $1 million in 1997 to $40 million in 1998, for a Department of Education after-school initiative known as 21st Century Community Learning Centers. The Clinton Administration has proposed an additional increase to $200 million in Fiscal Year 1999. This initiative will give grants to local middle and elementary schools in rural and urban areas to provide after-school opportunities, including education and recreation. Nonetheless, much more is needed to sustain this and other after-school and summer programs held at both schools and community-based organizations.

Effective Local Initiatives

A number of localities are pursuing balanced approaches to youth violence that are keeping their communities and their children safer. These approaches merit study and emulation.

Boston: Collaborating to save children's lives. Boston's comprehensive violence prevention plan has had extraordinary success. This broad-based community effort resulted in a 65 percent drop in arrests of juveniles for violent crimes between 1993 and 1995. Furthermore, not a single child died from gunfire between July 1995 and December 1997 (when a 16-year-old was shot and killed).

Boston's program involves all segments of the community in keeping young people safe. Police, probation officers, judges, and federal and state prosecutors collaborate across jurisdictional lines to focus on "hot spots" of guns and violence. With funding provided in part by federal prevention dollars, youth workers keep schools open after-hours and staff community centers to provide young people with mentoring, tutoring, counseling, and other positive activities. Businesses offer summer job opportunities. Religious organizations, including the ecumenical 10 Point Coalition, sponsor programs whereby congregations "adopt" young gang members or support neighborhood crime watches. In these myriad ways, the community lets children at risk know they are cared for and there are consequences for their actions. As a result, all the people of Boston are safer.

Nashville: Handling probation and truancy in innovative ways. Through the leadership of Juvenile Court Judge Andy Shookhoff, the Davidson County Juvenile Court is working hard to protect the safety of children and the Nashville community. One focus has been probation, the first sanction for many juvenile delinquents. Over the past few years the court has opened 25 neighborhood probation offices in housing developments, schools, and community centers. Because the offices are centrally located, the probation officers become part of the community, making them more accessible and more effective. They are able not only to reach out to the children whose cases they monitor, but also to join a community-wide effort to keep children from getting in trouble in the first place. Furthermore, the neighborhood probation offices are multipurpose resources: they serve as "suspension schools" where suspended students do supervised school work instead of watching TV at home or roaming the streets, and they offer tutoring, mentoring, computer labs, incentive programs, after-school activities, and parenting classes.

Another feature of Nashville's program is the Immediate Response Early Truancy Program. Every morning of every school day, court staff receive from 22 elementary and middle schools a list of children who are not in school. A staff member then goes to the home of each student to investigate. If there is no good reason for the absence, the child is taken to school and the parent is taken to court. Truancy at such a young age is often a result of problems at home, in many cases related to parental drug or alcohol use, mental illness, or child neglect and abuse. Addressing these problems early helps reduce the likelihood of later school dropout, substance abuse, teen pregnancy, and juvenile crime and violence.

Nashville, like many other cities across the nation, has learned the value of partnership. Government officials have increased their collaboration with community agencies and their involvement with volunteers. By working with programs and service providers already established within the community, Davidson County Juvenile Court is creating a unified web to protect all children.

Allegheny County, Pennsylvania: Emphasizing both law enforcement and crime prevention. The city of Pittsburgh and Allegheny County have succeeded in reducing youth violence by fostering collaboration among law enforcement officials and engaging all segments of the community in crime prevention efforts. One part of Allegheny's approach has been to convene a group of Law Enforcement Agency Directors (LEAD)—two dozen local, state, and federal law enforcement leaders who share information and collaborate. LEAD's six task forces, including a gun task force that focuses in part on those selling guns to young people, have been key to improving community safety.

A second thrust involves a Youth Crime Prevention Council, initiated and chaired by the U.S. Attorney. Council members include the mayor of Pittsburgh, the county commissioner, a corporate leader, the local Catholic diocese's bishop, a foundation chair, the local Urban League chair, and two dozen other representatives from the community. The council, which focuses on implementing prevention programs, has increased the number of trained volunteer mentors, started sports leagues serving 3,200 youths each year in 12 communities, placed nearly 2,500 high school students in jobs in the private and nonprofit sectors, and established four new family support centers.

Allegheny County has found that sustained coordination among different agencies maximizes the impact of individual efforts to keep children and communities safe. Arrests of young people for violent crime in the county plunged 30 percent between 1994 and 1995, compared with a statewide decline of 9 percent.

Moving Forward: A 1998 Agenda for Action

The recent drop in violence by and against young people is an encouraging development. Nonetheless, far too many American children still crowd the justice system rather than the school system, and far too many others are haunted by fear and victimization.

How can we rescue our young people from the threat—and the reality—of violence and crime? Communication is vital: advocates for youths and young people themselves must voice their concerns and put forward solutions at every opportunity. Collaboration is also key. Partnerships should be built across jurisdictions and job functions, and all segments of the community should be included. Political and civic leaders, police, prosecutors, judges, youth workers, businesses, foundations, schools, churches, and hospitals, as well as parents and young people, all have a stake in keeping children and the public safe, and all can make valuable contributions.

In the coming year advocates should:

- **Emphasize prevention.** Those who know that prevention works—through activities such as mentoring, after-school and summer programs, community policing, and intensive probation—must send the message over and over to policy makers and the public that prevention is the smart way to reduce violence by and against children. New spokespeople in the community, especially police, corrections workers, and judges, need to come forward. Greater efforts must be made to articulate the effectiveness—and the cost-effectiveness—of prevention. The National Council of State Legislators estimates that a new juvenile prison bed costs $102,000, compared with $3,000 for an after-school slot. Advocates should continue to pound home the point, so that political leaders never find it easy to cut funding for prevention efforts.
- **Develop opportunities for young people in their out-of-school hours.** Children and families in 1998 need new supports to reflect the changes in the work world since 1973. After-school activities—at schools, churches, YMCAs, and other community-based organizations—must be made available. Communities must seek and create more opportunities to link children with caring adults and positive activities, including mentoring programs and jobs.
- **Replicate successful programs.** The success stories in Boston, Nashville, and Allegheny County need to be replicated. Advocates should share information about what works to

reduce juvenile crime, and public and private funders should help adapt promising approaches to local needs.

■ **Work for gun control.** Advocates must continue to stress the clear connections between guns and deadly violence by and against children. No child should be able to obtain a gun at home or in the community. Laws to regulate guns are urgently needed, and advocates of such measures must not be silenced by the powerful pro-gun lobby.

■ **Oppose incarcerating children with adults and criminalizing status offenders.** Children should not be locked up with adults. Runaways and truants do not belong behind bars at all. Although secure jails and prisons are needed for the most violent offenders, states and localities should be encouraged to provide community facilities with services to deal with the problems facing most children who are arrested.

As a nation, we need to strengthen our efforts to keep children safe from violence and prevent children from falling into lives of crime and destructive behavior. We must not simply wait for tragedy and then either bury our children or lock them away in places where they themselves will become the prey of adult criminals. Prevention, commonsense gun safety, and rehabilitation keep children and communities safe, and these principles should guide the crime fighting efforts of our nation, states, and communities.

Spotlight on Employment Opportunities for Youth

In 1997 the national unemployment rate dropped to less than 5 percent, but the unemployment rate for teenagers was three times as high. Those with jobs typically receive meager earnings and few opportunities to move up the economic ladder. As a result, too many young people see little reward for avoiding high-risk behaviors that lead to criminal activity, drug abuse, and teen pregnancies.

Unfortunately, for the past 25 years the employment and economic prospects of teenagers and young adults have steadily worsened. Changes in our economy have made it increasingly difficult for young people with little education or training to gain a foothold in the labor market. At the same time, the economic return for their labor has diminished. Part of the solution to the problems engulfing so many teenagers and young adults lies in job opportunities that will help them break free of their bleak environments. The transition into adulthood is trying enough; without hope, it is fraught with even greater perils. Young Americans need to believe that if they work hard, get an education, and invest in their own futures, they will reap rewards.

Persistent unemployment and wage decline for young people. In November 1997 the jobless rate for all Americans fell to 4.6 percent—the lowest in 25 years. Meanwhile, the unemployment rate for workers ages 16 to 19 remained essentially unchanged at 15.0 percent—three times the general rate. Among Hispanic teenagers unemployment reached 15.9 percent; among Black teens, 28.6 percent. The job market was tight for young adults as well, with one of every 12 Americans between the ages of 20 and 24 (8.4 percent) out of work.

Dropping out of school is a sure path to unemployment or low wages. According to data from the U.S. Bureau of Labor Statistics, of the nearly half-million high school dropouts in 1995–96, 286,000 had no job in October 1996. Not all these young people were in the labor force (that is, working or actively seeking work), but among those who were, the unemployment rate was 27.9 percent. This average masks disparities by gender and race: unemployment among high school dropouts stood at 31.1 percent for males, 21.8 percent for females, 25.3 percent for Whites, 42.5 percent for Blacks, and 19.7 percent for Hispanics.

High school graduates also had a difficult time finding work. Of the 931,000 graduates in 1995–96 who did not go on to college, 382,000 were without jobs in October 1996. About 25 percent of those in the labor force were unemployed, although jobless rates for minorities were considerably higher: 44.8 percent for Black high school graduates and 36.1 percent for Hispanics, compared with 19.3 percent for Whites.

Even for those who find work, income has fallen. Using the U.S. Census Bureau's *Historical Income Tables*, CDF calculated that for 18- to 24-year-old high school dropouts with full-time, year-round employment, earnings (measured in 1996 dollars) plunged 25.1 percent between 1974 and 1996 (27.4 percent for males and 11.3 percent for females). Workers who have completed high school typically fare better than dropouts, but a high school diploma is no longer a ticket to economic security. Earnings (again measured in 1996 dollars) for 18- to 24-year-old graduates who hold full-year, full-time jobs and have no postsecondary education fell 15.9 percent between 1974 and 1996 (20.0 percent for males and 12.1 percent for females).

This feature was prepared in cooperation with Alan Zuckerman, executive director of the National Youth Employment Coalition.

Another trend is the widening gap between young and older workers. During the late 1960s the median weekly pay of men under 25 with full-time jobs was nearly three-fourths that of older men. By 1994 it had fallen to half.

The link between youth unemployment and crime. While economic and employment prospects spiraled downward, crime by teens and young adults shot up. The number of men under age 25 in prisons and jails more than doubled between 1986 and 1995, from 178,000 to 359,000. A recent study, *Market Wages and Youth Crime* by Jeffrey Grogger, concluded that this phenomenon was not coincidental and that there is, in fact, a strong relationship between wage levels and criminal behavior.

Grogger examined data from the 1980 National Longitudinal Survey of Youth and found that the more money young men earn by legitimate means, the less likely they are to commit crimes. Grogger estimated that a 20 percent drop in wages leads to a 12 to 18 percent increase in youth participation in crime. He also observed that "wages largely explain the tendency of crime to decrease with age," because as people get older, their earning power increases.

Addressing the employment needs of at-risk youth ought to be a central part of anti-crime efforts. Unfortunately, recent congressional initiatives in the area of juvenile crime (see pp. 82–84) have focused on punishment rather than on prevention efforts that help equip young people to become productive members of society.

The National Youth Employment Coalition, in its 1994 report, *Toward a National Youth Development System: How We Can Better Service Youth at Risk*, highlighted the challenges ahead. The report noted:

> A quick-fix summer job or brief training program isn't enough to change the life of the most at-risk youth in today's world. If we hope to bring the most at-risk youth into the mainstream of American economic life, we need to craft and implement a national youth training, education, employment and development strategy that is coherent and long-term.

Federal commitment: What's missing. While a number of important local initiatives are helping young people move into the work force and become economically self-sufficient, a tremendous vacuum exists at the national level. For more than 35 years the federal government was the primary source of funds for youth employment efforts and the sponsor of numerous programs. However, in the past several years this commitment has faltered.

In 1995 Congress slashed funding for youth programs under the Job Training Partnership Act (JTPA) by 80 percent, from $600 million to less than $130 million. Funding for the JTPA Summer Youth Employment Program and for YouthBuild, another important public program, has also been under attack. Although Congress reversed earlier decisions to eliminate funding for summer jobs for youths, it provided only $871 million for 1998—the same amount as in 1997. This will pay for approximately 530,000 summer jobs—70,000 fewer than in 1995. YouthBuild, a highly successful youth training model funded through the U.S. Department of Housing and Urban Development, had its appropriations cut from $50 million in 1995 to

$20 million in 1996, then increased to $30 million for 1997 and $35 million for 1998. Advocates are making strong efforts to seek more funds for YouthBuild in the FY 1999 budget.

Job Corps remains the nation's largest training program for seriously at-risk youth, serving some 60,000 young people each year. Eighty percent of Job Corps participants are high school dropouts, 64 percent have never held a full-time job, and more than 40 percent come from welfare families. The program survived the 1995 funding assaults and efforts to fold Job Corps centers into state work force development centers, but it has not been expanded to serve larger numbers of at-risk youth. Job Corps funding for 1998 is set at $1.246 billion—about $93 million above the 1997 level.

AmeriCorps and the 1994 School-to-Work program also address youth training and employment needs but are limited in scope. AmeriCorps places more than 25,000 young people in year-long service assignments ranging from housing renovation to childhood immunization drives. In exchange, participants earn help paying for their postsecondary education. Although the program has been repeatedly targeted for elimination, AmeriCorps' backers preserved its budget allocation of $425 million for 1998. The School-to-Work initiative, funded at $400 million for 1998 ($200 million each from the Department of Labor and the Department of Education), mainly supports collaborative efforts by states, localities, and private employers to help prepare students for the labor force through work-based learning experiences.

New developments. One heartening piece of news is that the 1998 Labor-HHS-Education appropriation bill includes $250 million in advance funds for 1999 for a new Youth Opportunities grant program. The grants will pay for comprehensive education and job training for young people who live in empowerment zones and enterprise communities (small geographic areas targeted for intensive economic development activity). Release of the new funds, however, is contingent on the passage of federal legislation establishing the new program in 1998.

Another positive development, which arose from the Balanced Budget Act of 1997, is a new welfare-to-work grant program providing $3 billion in 1998–99 for employment-related services for welfare recipients. Because 30 percent of welfare recipients (close to 1 million) are between the ages of 18 and 24, a significant percentage of these new funds can be targeted to young people making the transition from welfare to the work force.

Local initiatives: What works. A number of local programs have strong track records of providing employment training and other services to young people. In 1995 the National Youth Employment Coalition, funded by the Department of Labor and private foundations, established the Promising and Effective Practices Network (PEPNet). PEPNet's mission is to identify effective youth employment programs through a self-nomination and peer review process and to help programs learn from each other about what works. Each year PEPNet recognizes outstanding programs that (1) show sound organization and management, with skilled leaders and qualified, committed staff; (2) rely on principles of adolescent development to shape program activities and goals; (3) prepare young people for the work force by building basic and work-related competencies, emphasizing the connection between education and work, providing job and community service opportunities, and forging ties with employers; and (4) demonstrate success, collecting credible data or other evidence to measure operational effectiveness and the achievement of desired outcomes.

The 32 programs identified by PEPNet as exemplary demonstrate that varied approaches are effective in preparing young people, even those most at risk, for work that leads to self-sufficiency. One recent PEPNet awardee is the Milwaukee Community Service Corps, which promotes the virtues of work and social responsibility through community service. Participants engage in projects ranging from home renovations and graffiti removal to anti-hunger campaigns and urban gardening. Some of the assignments are designed to give enrollees experience that can improve their chances of winning formal union apprenticeships and permanent, full-time jobs. The program also provides academic instruction to help participants obtain a high school general equivalency degree (GED) or pursue higher education.

Another award winner is the Academy for Career Excellence, a program of Jobs for Youth in New York City. The academy provides comprehensive educational and job training services to prepare out-of-school youths for career-track employment. Several corporations and government agencies participate by offering internships that may lead to full-time paid positions. In 1996, 65 percent of the young people in the program were placed in career-track jobs.

PEPNet has also recognized the Gulf Coast Trade Center in New Waverly, Texas. This residential training facility provides basic and vocational education, GED preparation, community service and work experience, and counseling and social services to more than 400 young people referred by the courts each year. A majority have been placed in jobs at an average wage of $7.50 per hour, 60 percent have attained a GED, and the recidivism rate has been less than 10 percent. (Additional information about the PEPNet program can be found on the Web at www.nyec.org.)

What needs to be done. The Census Bureau projects that in the next 15 years the number of young adults ages 18 to 24 will increase by almost 22 percent, from slightly under 25 million to more than 30 million. At the same time, fewer and fewer job opportunities will be available to those without the skills needed in the 21st century. A high school diploma is the minimum requirement, but it is only the first step. The Bureau of Labor Statistics predicts that job growth in the coming decade will take place generally in fields that require at least an associate's degree. Unless we improve employment prospects for young people through job training, vocational classes, and postsecondary education, a sizable number will be trapped in low-wage jobs and poverty.

We must invest in youth training, youth development, and youth employment programs, both summer and year-round, to help young people become productive members of the work force and society. We need national leadership to support and expand the innovative and creative efforts in many local communities. The federal government should design a comprehensive and coherent strategy to equip young people for careers in an increasingly competitive work environment. Without solid avenues to jobs that offer adequate economic rewards, at-risk youths are left with little hope for a better future. Moreover, the nation will keep paying a high price in terms of violence, drug abuse, teen pregnancy, and the impoverishment of vast numbers of young Americans.

ADOLESCENT PREGNANCY

After rising for years, the teen birth rate in the United States has begun to decline. According to figures released last year by the National Center for Health Statistics (NCHS), the teen birth rate has fallen four years in a row. Nonetheless, teens are still becoming pregnant and having babies at unacceptably high rates. Adolescents who become pregnant pay a heavy price, but so do their children and society in general. Teen pregnancy is a major contributor to, as well as a consequence of, the poverty that victimizes more than 14 million American children.

Many observers attribute the drop in teen pregnancy to the growing effectiveness of education and prevention campaigns. To continue the downward trend, we need to intensify and accelerate these efforts. We must promote comprehensive approaches that address both girls and boys and provide them with the motivation and opportunities to make better choices.

Adolescent Pregnancy: 1973 to 1998

Data from NCHS indicate steady decline in the teen birth rate—the number of births per 1,000 females ages 15-19—throughout the 1970s and early 1980s. In 1970 the birth rate stood at 68.3 per 1,000; by 1986 it had reached a low of 50.2 per 1,000. After 1986, however, the teen birth rate began increasing, rising to 62.1 per 1,000 in 1991. Since 1991, teen births have been edging steadily downward again. In 1995 the teen birth rate fell for the fourth year in a row, sinking to 56.8 per 1,000. This is the lowest rate since 1988, and the preliminary data for 1996 indicate a further drop, to 54.7 births per 1,000 girls.

Teen births are down in absolute numbers too. In 1995 teenagers had 512,115 babies—fewer than in any year since 1988 and fewer than in 1980, 1970, 1960, or 1950. Preliminary NCHS figures for 1996 indicate a further drop, to about 505,000 births. According to the Centers for Disease Con-

This chapter was prepared in cooperation with Melissa Ludtke, author of *On Our Own: Unmarried Motherhood in America* (Random House, 1997).

trol and Prevention (CDC), abortions among teenagers have also slowed, continuing the steady decline that began in the early 1980s.

Meanwhile, the proportion of teen births that occur outside of marriage has climbed year after year, growing from about 30 percent in 1970 to 75 percent in the mid-1990s (see figure 7.1). The birth rate for unmarried teens also went up steadily from the early 1960s until 1991, when it peaked at 44.8 births per 1,000 unmarried girls ages 15–19. Recently the rate has leveled off, but it is still almost three times its level in the early 1960s.

Experts believe that teen pregnancies are declining in part because more teens are choosing to delay sexual activity and because those who are sexually active are using contraceptives more frequently. According to NCHS's 1995 National Survey of Family Growth, the proportion of teens who have had intercourse has started to fall, after increasing steadily for more than two decades. The survey also found that teens who are sexually active are more likely to be using contraceptives. The Alan Guttmacher Institute estimates that the pregnancy rate among sexually experienced teens has dropped by almost one-fifth since the mid-1970s.

Although the recent trends are encouraging, they are less heartening when placed in a global perspective. Compared with other industrialized countries, the United States has an abysmal record. The teen birth rate here exceeds that in many European nations and is 15 times higher than Japan's rate (see figure 7.2). Various factors contribute to this disparity. For example, U.S. teens are less likely to use contraceptives or to use them effectively. They generally have a more difficult time securing contraceptive supplies and are taught about sex in less comprehensive ways and at a later age.

A Profile of Teen Pregnancy

The Alan Guttmacher Institute estimates that approximately 1 million teenagers become pregnant each year. About 85 percent of these pregnancies are unplanned, accounting for one–seventh of all unplanned pregnancies. More than half result in births, accounting for 13.1 percent of all births. About one-third end in abortion, and one-seventh in miscarriage.

Demographic characteristics of teen mothers. NCHS data show that the vast majority of the

Figure 7.1 **Rise in Births to Unmarried Teens**

Births to unmarried girls account for a growing share of all births to teens. Only one of four teens having babies in 1995 was married, compared with nearly six of seven in 1960.

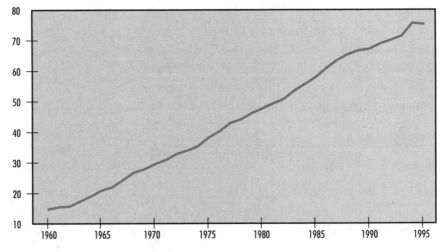

Percentage of births to females ages 15–19 that were to unmarried teens

Source: U.S. Department of Health and Human Services, National Center for Health Statistics.

512,115 babies born to teenage girls in 1995—499,873—were born to mothers between 15 and 19 years of age. Older adolescents, ages 18 and 19, were responsible for 60 percent of all teen births. However, 12,242 babies (slightly more than 2 percent of the total) were born to mothers younger than 15.

The majority of teen mothers are White. In 1995, 355,489 babies were born to White teens; 139,621 to Blacks; 9,038 to teens of Asian or Pacific Island descent; and 7,967 to Native Americans. Included in these figures are 121,636 babies born to Hispanic teens, who are not classified as a separate racial group in NCHS data.

Although White mothers outnumber all others, the rate of births is higher among minority youths (see figure 7.3). In 1995 the birth rate among Black teens ages 15–19 was 96.1 births per 1,000 girls—almost twice the 50.1 rate among Whites. However, birth rates for Black teens have fallen markedly and steadily in the past few years. The 1995 rate for this group represents an 8 percent drop from 1994 (when the birth rate was 104.5 per 1,000) and a decline of almost 17 percent since 1991 (when the rate peaked at 115.5). The 1995 rate among Hispanic teens, however—106.7

births per 1,000 girls—was about the same as in 1991.

NCHS also reports that three-fourths of the babies born to teen mothers in 1995 were born to unmarried teens—only a slight decline from 1994. This included 68.0 percent of those born to White teens, 95.3 percent of those born to Black teens, and 67.8 percent of those born to Hispanic teens.

Finally, about four in five births to teenagers are first births, and the rate at which teens have second births (as well as subsequent ones) has slowed. In 1996, 22 percent of all births to 15- to 19-year-olds were repeat births, down from 25 percent during 1990–92.

Social risk factors associated with teen pregnancy. In reviewing data from the U.S. Department of Education's National Education Longitudinal Study, Child Trends (a research organization that evaluates indicators of child and adolescent well-being) identified four key risk factors associated with having a baby before the age of 20. These factors were early school failure, early behavioral problems, family dysfunction, and poverty. The more of these factors that were present when a girl

Figure 7.2 Teen Birth Rates: International Comparisons

American teens have far more babies than their counterparts in Japan, Australia, Canada, or Europe.

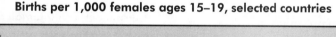

Births per 1,000 females ages 15–19, selected countries

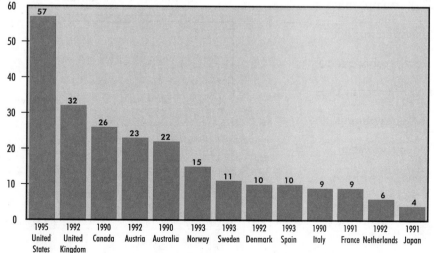

Source: Susan Williams McElroy and Kristin Anderson Moore, "Trends over Time in Teenage Pregnancy and Childbearing: The Critical Changes," in Rebecca A. Maynard, ed., *Kids Having Kids: Economic Costs and Social Consequences of Teen Pregnancy* (Urban Institute Press, 1997).

was in the eighth grade, the greater her likelihood of bearing a child during adolescence. For girls who experienced none of the risk factors, the probability of having a baby as a teenager was 11 percent. Of girls with three or more risk factors, half gave birth before age 20. Early school failure alone dramatically increased the risk; 25 percent of high school–age mothers had dropped out of school prior to the pregnancy.

Conversely, educational success can play a positive role in averting teen pregnancies. New research by Child Trends indicates that involvement in school activities or completion of high school or a general equivalency degree (GED) after a teenager has her first baby are strongly associated with postponing a second teen birth.

Sexual Activity and Contraceptive Use

Data compiled by the Alan Guttmacher Institute in 1994 indicate that by age 18 more than half of young women and three-fourths of young men have had intercourse. These rates are about 20 percentage points higher than in the early 1970s. However, as already noted, the proportion of teens who are sexually experienced has decreased slightly since 1990—the first decline in more than two decades.

Contraceptive use. The 1995 National Survey of Family Growth also found that sexually active teens are more likely to use contraception than teens in prior decades. The Alan Guttmacher Institute reported in 1997 that three-fourths of adolescents use some form of contraception the first time they have intercourse; at least seven of 10 sexually active teenage girls use contraception regularly. However, not all teens do.

In focus groups, adolescents describe their intense desire to retain personal privacy when talking about their sexual activity and say they are embarrassed to speak about sexual matters in general. They also regard health clinics, where contraceptives are most likely to be available, as places in which adults are going to judge them as morally irresponsible. These perceptions help to explain the lengthy delay—23 months on average among women ages 15–24—between the initiation of sexual relations and the first visit to a family planning clinic.

Teaching teens about sex has been found to increase their knowledge without increasing their

---

Figure 7.3 **Racial Disparity in Teen Birth Rates**

Birth rates among teenagers vary considerably by race. In 1995 the majority of teen mothers were White, but Black teens were almost twice as likely to have babies.

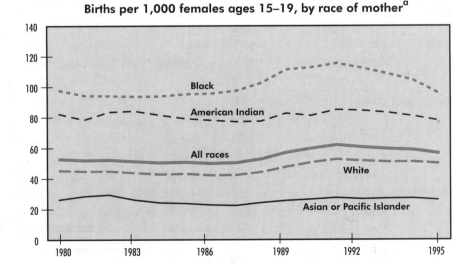

Births per 1,000 females ages 15–19, by race of mother[a]

a. Hispanic teen birth rate not shown because of incomplete data prior to 1991.
Source: U.S. Department of Health and Human Services, National Center for Health Statistics.

sexual activity, despite assumptions to the contrary. In *No Easy Answers: Research Findings on Programs to Reduce Teen Pregnancy*, the National Campaign to Prevent Teen Pregnancy reported in 1997 that making condoms and school-based health clinics available as part of pregnancy prevention efforts does not increase teens' sexual activity. However, simply providing access to contraception is not enough to prevent pregnancy. The weight of the research evidence indicates that making contraceptives available in school-based clinics—without adding other important program components that address teens' motivations—does not affect teen pregnancy or birth rates. *No Easy Answers* notes that even though abstinence-only programs may be appropriate for many young people, especially junior high and middle school youths, no published scientific research of adequate quality measures whether or not such initiatives actually delay sexual activity. The report's author, Douglas Kirby, cautions that because some young people have sexual relations and others refrain, "programs need to address both abstaining from or postponing sex and using contraceptives."

The use of condoms is recommended to teens not only to prevent pregnancy but also to protect themselves against sexually transmitted diseases (STDs). Each year 3 million teens—about one in four of those who are sexually active—acquire an STD. Increased awareness of and education about AIDS and other sexually transmitted diseases have led to increased condom use. Too often, however, teens do not practice "safe sex" when the female is taking birth control pills to protect against pregnancy; only one-quarter of the 1.7 million teens who rely on the pill also use condoms.

Coerced sex. Some sexual activity among teens is nonconsensual, as recent studies have detailed. The 1995 National Survey of Family Growth found that the younger a girl is at first intercourse, the more likely the experience was coercive. Twenty-two percent of girls who had sex before age 13 described their first experience as "nonvoluntary" (including girls who said they were raped); an additional 49 percent defined it as "unwanted." Among those who were 13 or 14 years old at the time of first intercourse, 8 percent characterized it as non-voluntary and 31 percent as unwanted. Among girls who were 15 or 16 at the time of first intercourse, 5 percent and 19 percent, respectively, labeled the experience nonvoluntary or unwanted.

The 1995 National Survey of Family Growth also helped to illuminate the vulnerability of teenage girls to the pressures of older males. When girls' first sexual partners were the same age or younger, about 25 percent of the girls described the encounter as unwanted. However, when their partners were five or more years older, 37 percent said they hadn't wanted their first sexual experience to occur. The survey also found that the greater the age gap between girls and their first partners, the less likely they were to have used contraception.

The Price That Children and Society Pay

According to 1996 Census Bureau data, one in four American children under the age of 6—6.1 million—are now growing up in poor families. Poverty is especially prevalent among children with young and poorly educated mothers. Child Trends' 1996 analysis of the National Education Longitudinal Study indicated that almost two-thirds of teen mothers had not completed high school. Because limited education is linked to poverty, the majority of babies born to adolescents will be poor. Before the passage of the 1996 welfare legislation, more than half (53 percent) of welfare spending was going to families formed by mothers in their teens. The National Campaign to Prevent Teen Pregnancy has noted that the total cost to taxpayers (including cash payments, food stamps, and health insurance) was estimated to be about $30 billion each year during the early 1990s.

Research by Child Trends and others has identified numerous problems associated with teen parenting. Babies born to teens are generally at greater risk of health problems than other babies. More than 9 percent are low birthweight (5.5 pounds or less), compared with 7 percent of all babies. Low birthweight babies are more likely to die before their first birthday or to suffer disabilities such as developmental delays, cerebral palsy, and seizure disorders.

The disadvantages do not end in infancy. Although some studies are finding that teenage mothers—when compared with peers of similar social, economic, and educational background—do as well over the long term in securing employment, furthering their education, and increasing their income, their children generally experience more difficulties throughout their youth than those born to older mothers. Recent research sponsored by the Robin Hood Foundation, comparing children whose mothers were 17 or younger with children born to 20- and 21-year-olds, highlights some of these problems. During the preschool years, signs of delays in cognitive development begin to emerge and tend to grow more evident as the children age. Preschool children of teen mothers also tend to display higher levels of aggression and less ability to control impulsive behavior. By adolescence, children of teen mothers have, on the whole, higher rates of grade failure and more delinquency (and with boys, more incarceration). They also become sexually active earlier, with one consequence being a greater likelihood of pregnancy before age 20.

What accounts for the difficulties experienced by the children of teenagers? The answer too often is early inattention or poor-quality care from their parents. Teen parents typically are emotionally immature, have high rates of family poverty, and lack the parenting skills critical to the task of nurturing infants and toddlers.

Preventing Teen Pregnancy

According to the National Campaign to Prevent Teen Pregnancy, the reasons teenagers become pregnant include lack of knowledge or skills to avoid sex or use contraceptives and lack of motivation to avoid early childbearing. Teen pregnancy is also associated with troubling relationships between teen girls and older males, sexual abuse, poor performance in school, family breakdown, and poverty. Douglas Kirby, author of the National Campaign's report *No Easy Answers*, notes that there are "no single or simple approaches that will markedly reduce adolescent pregnancy." The report found that more and better research needs to be done on what works; current studies suffer from small sample sizes, lack of comparison groups, lack of long-term follow-up, and little replication of find-

- In 1995 teen births declined to their lowest levels since 1988. Teenage girls had 512,115 babies, and the birth rate stood at 56.8 births per 1,000 females between ages 15 and 19.

- Two-thirds of teenage mothers are high school dropouts. About one-quarter drop out before they become pregnant.

- Welfare spending (including cash assistance, food stamps, and health coverage) for teenage mothers and their children was estimated at about $30 billion each year during the early 1990s.

- Children of teenagers are more likely than those born to older mothers to be poor, to suffer health problems in infancy, and to do poorly in school.

- Each year sexually transmitted diseases strike about 3 million teens—about one in four of those who are sexually active.

ings. However, *No Easy Answers* concluded that comprehensive programs that focus intensely on the many reasons teens become pregnant show the most promise for significantly reducing teen pregnancy and birth rates.

Helping teens postpone parenthood. Most experts concur that efforts to deter teens from becoming pregnant should address the major precursors of teen pregnancy—early school failure, early behavioral problems, family dysfunction, and the pressures generated by poverty. CDF's 1987 report, *Adolescent Pregnancy: An Anatomy of a Social Problem in Search of Comprehensive Solutions*, outlines six strategies for bolstering the motivation and capacity of teens to avoid too-early pregnancy. These are (1) strengthening education and basic skills training for teenagers, (2) developing teens' work-related skills through jobs and work experience, (3) generating a range of non-academic opportunities for success, to help build self-esteem and self-perception, (4) offering family life education and life planning counseling that can help teens think about their futures, (5) providing comprehensive adolescent health services in a range of settings, and (6) fostering a national and community commitment to reducing teen pregnancy, with the involvement of caring adults who can provide positive role models, values, and support for teens.

It is vital, too, to reach young people at an appropriate age, *before* they are engaged in risky behaviors. Kristin Moore, chair of the National Campaign's Task Force on Effective Programs and Research, has said, "The greater the risk of adolescent pregnancy, the earlier interventions need to be implemented."

In 1997 a national resource center was created to assist in replicating prevention programs with demonstrated effectiveness. A panel of experts convened by the Program Archive on Sexuality, Health and Adolescence has already certified the components and findings of 24 programs. Information on these programs, along with evaluative materials, is available to practitioners through Sociometrics Corporation in Los Altos, California.

Working with males. Most pregnancy prevention efforts have focused exclusively on females. More recently, male adolescents have been targeted as well. The initiatives directed at males are characterized by experimentation in method, philosophy, and target populations. Most, however, try to send a two-pronged message: It is not good to become a father as a teenager, but if you do, you have the responsibility to be a good one.

The National Center for Fathers and Families has compiled a national directory of 886 male-centered prevention programs, and *Map and Track: State Initiatives to Encourage Responsible Fatherhood*, a 1997 publication by the National Center for Children in Poverty, surveys fatherhood initiatives in the 50 states. In California, local male involvement programs are newly supported by $8 million in state funds—the largest contribution any state has made to prevention programs aimed at boys. California has also led the nation in reviving strict enforcement of statutory rape laws as a means of deterring adult men from becoming sexually involved with teenage girls.

Few of the male-focused prevention programs incorporate rigorous evaluations into their design (as do few female-oriented approaches). In addition, funding is fragile and short-term, and few programs for males have existed longer than two to three years. It is thus too early to judge their effectiveness, and questions remain about how to replicate or institutionalize any of them over the long term.

As with girls' initiatives, however, interventions for boys should be tailored to clients by age, stage of development, and cultural and religious background. Messages need to be developed to help boys redefine their understanding of "manhood" to emphasize caring, responsibility, commitment to family, self-control, and respect for women.

An Effective Local Initiative: TOP

To reduce rates of teen pregnancy, school failure, and school suspension, 107 sites in 16 states have implemented the Teen Outreach Program (TOP) for high school students. TOP serves both girls and boys, engaging them in supervised volunteer work in the community, classroom-based discussions, and activities related to key social-developmental tasks of adolescence. Students are both self-selected and recommended by their teachers.

Ingredients for success. The philosophy behind TOP is based on research findings that problem behaviors among teens occur in clusters, not as single events. The expectation, therefore, is that well-designed interventions can bring results on several fronts at the same time. The TOP approach focuses on four interrelated strategies:

- **Youth development.** To help young people achieve their full potential, TOP sets high expectations and clear standards, engages teens in meaningful activities, provides opportunities for them to contribute, and fosters lasting relationships with caring, supportive adults.
- **Community involvement.** TOP participants undertake service-related activities that reconnect them to their communities. All sectors of the community support such efforts.
- **Learner-centered education.** The classroom component of TOP is guided by a curriculum, "Changing Scenes." Young people do most of the talking, and adults act as guides in discussions about observations and emotions. Both the classroom activities and the community service projects emphasize hands-on learning.
- **Academic extensions.** Teens have an opportunity to apply what they learn in school to the positive development of their communities. Using interdisciplinary learning techniques, TOP facilitators help students connect skills learned in core school subjects to workplace requirements in their service assignments.

What sets TOP apart from many other prevention programs is that it does not explicitly focus on the problem behaviors it seeks to prevent. Instead it works on enhancing teens' competence in decision making, interacting with peers and adults, and identifying and handling their own emotions. According to Dr. Joseph Allen, professor of psychology at the University of Virginia and one of TOP's primary evaluators, this approach means that the program "may be politically acceptable in communities where programs that explicitly focus upon sexual behavior may not be feasible to implement."

Payoffs for participants. Since 1978, when the program began, TOP has made a difference in the lives of more than 12,000 young people. In the most recent nationwide evaluation, conducted between 1991 and 1995 and published in August 1997, 700 high school students at 25 sites with Teen Outreach Programs were randomly assigned to either TOP or a control group. When their circumstances were compared at the end of the nine-month program, rates of pregnancy, school failure, and academic suspension were substantially lower among those who attended TOP. They demonstrated an 11 percent lower rate of course failure in school, 14 percent fewer school suspensions, a 60 percent lower dropout rate, and 33 percent fewer pregnancies. Students said that what affected their behavior most was "feeling safe," "being listened to and respected," "having input in selecting the work they do," and being encouraged to see themselves as competent individuals who could be autonomous but still connected to other young people and adults.

The extent to which TOP can be expanded to other sites or successfully replicated elsewhere depends on a community's capacity to commit resources and human energy to reproducing TOP's critical elements. Local models can be school-led, community-sponsored, or jointly developed by educators and community leaders, but the core principles and components cannot be compromised if success is to occur.

Moving Forward: A 1998 Agenda for Action

The problems that plague so many teenagers today, including pregnancy, cannot be overcome unless we find ways to give these young people a belief in themselves and their futures. If they are to develop their full potential, they must have the motivation to defer parenthood and the tools to compete and succeed in the work force. These include an adequate education, access to a good job, and the means to attain economic self-sufficiency. Providing those opportunities requires a wide range of strategies: strengthening our educational system, restoring communities that have become hazardous to the well-being of children and families, making early childhood development programs available, and working to combat the multiple problems associated with child poverty.

We should take specific steps to:

■ Increase federal and state investments in comprehensive youth development initiatives, including job training, that are targeted to improving the economic, educational, social, and psychological condition of disadvantaged teens. The federal government should help lead the way by developing a comprehensive youth development agenda and promoting model programs.

■ Expand investments in after-school and summer programs for all teenagers, particularly those in low-income neighborhoods. These recreational and enrichment programs in struc-

tured, supervised settings can help reduce opportunities for the risk-taking behaviors that often occur after the school day ends and before parents return home from work, and during summer months.

■ Expand mentoring and tutoring programs in all communities. Volunteers—from civic groups, congregations, youth-serving organizations, local businesses, fraternities and sororities, and other community-based organizations—can provide guidance and positive role models.

■ Support and strengthen age-appropriate family life education and comprehensive school-based or school-linked services that promote adolescent health and pregnancy prevention. These programs need the extensive involvement of parents and close collaboration with education, health, and other officials. Only with a shared understanding of teens' needs and a strong local consensus about how to address them can such programs succeed.

■ Invest in research and evaluation to help develop the most effective approaches to preventing teenage pregnancy, and disseminate that information to state and local entities.

Appendix A
National Trends Among Children

TABLE A1 **Poverty Among Children***

	Children under age 18		Children under age 6	
Year	Number who are poor	Poverty rate[a]	Number who are poor	Poverty rate[a]
1959	17,552,000	27.3%	—	—
1960	17,634,000	26.9	—	—
1961	16,909,000	25.6	—	—
1962	16,963,000	25.0	—	—
1963	16,005,000	23.1	—	—
1964	16,051,000	23.0	—	—
1965	14,676,000	21.0	—	—
1966	12,389,000	17.6	—	—
1967	11,656,000	16.6	—	—
1968	10,954,000	15.6	—	—
1969	9,691,000	14.0	3,298,000	15.3%
1970	10,440,000	15.1	3,561,000	16.6
1971	10,551,000	15.3	3,499,000	16.9
1972	10,284,000	15.1	3,276,000	16.1
1973	9,642,000	14.4	3,097,000	15.7
1974	10,156,000	15.4	3,294,000	16.9
1975	11,104,000	17.1	3,460,000	18.2
1976	10,273,000	16.0	3,270,000	17.7
1977	10,288,000	16.2	3,326,000	18.1
1978	9,931,000	15.9	3,184,000	17.2
1979	10,377,000	16.4	3,415,000	17.8
1980	11,543,000	18.3	4,030,000	20.5
1981	12,505,000	20.0	4,422,000	22.0
1982	13,647,000	21.9	4,821,000	23.3
1983	13,911,000	22.3	5,122,000	24.6
1984	13,420,000	21.5	4,938,000	23.4
1985	13,010,000	20.7	4,832,000	22.6
1986	12,876,000	20.5	4,619,000	21.6
1987	12,843,000	20.3	4,852,000	22.4
1988	12,455,000	19.5	5,032,000	22.6
1989	12,590,000	19.6	5,071,000	22.5
1990	13,431,000	20.6	5,198,000	23.0
1991	14,341,000	21.8	5,483,000	24.0
1992	14,617,000	21.9	5,781,000	25.0
1993	14,961,000	22.0	6,097,000	25.6
1994	14,610,000	21.2	5,878,000	24.5
1995	13,999,000	20.2	5,670,000	23.7
1996	13,764,000	19.8	5,333,000	22.7

*Related children in families.

— Data not available.

a. Percentage of all children who are poor.

Source: U.S. Department of Commerce, Bureau of the Census.

TABLE A2 **Maternal and Infant Health**

Year	Infant mortality rate				Babies born at low birthweight[b] (percent)	Babies born to mothers who received late or no prenatal care (percent)		
	Total[a]	White[a]	Black[a]	Black-White ratio		Total	White	Black
1940	47.0	43.2	72.9	1.69	—	—	—	—
1950	29.2	26.8	43.9	1.64	—	—	—	—
1959	26.4	23.2	44.8	1.93	—	—	—	—
1960	26.0	22.9	44.3	1.93	7.7%	—	—	—
1961	25.3	22.4	41.8	1.87	7.8	—	—	—
1962	25.3	22.3	42.6	1.91	8.0	—	—	—
1963	25.2	22.2	42.8	1.93	8.2	—	—	—
1964	24.8	21.6	42.3	1.96	8.2	—	—	—
1965	24.7	21.5	41.7	1.94	8.3	—	—	—
1966	23.7	20.6	40.2	1.95	8.3	—	—	—
1967	22.4	19.7	37.5	1.90	8.2	—	—	—
1968	21.8	19.2	36.2	1.89	8.2	—	—	—
1969	20.9	18.4	34.8	1.89	8.1	8.1%	6.3%	18.2%
1970	20.0	17.8	32.6	1.83	7.9	7.9	6.2	16.6
1971	19.1	17.1	30.3	1.77	7.7	7.2	5.8	14.6
1972	18.5	16.4	29.6	1.80	7.7	7.0	5.5	13.2
1973	17.7	15.8	28.1	1.78	7.6	6.7	5.4	12.4
1974	16.7	14.8	26.8	1.81	7.4	6.2	5.0	11.4
1975	16.1	14.2	26.2	1.85	7.4	6.0	5.0	10.5
1976	15.2	13.3	25.5	1.92	7.3	5.7	4.8	9.9
1977	14.1	12.3	23.6	1.92	7.1	5.6	4.7	9.6
1978	13.8	12.0	23.1	1.93	7.1	5.4	4.5	9.3
1979	13.1	11.4	21.8	1.91	6.9	5.1	4.3	8.9
1980	12.6	10.9	22.2	2.04	6.8	5.1	4.3	8.8
1981	11.9	10.3	20.8	2.02	6.8	5.2	4.3	9.1
1982	11.5	9.9	20.5	2.07	6.8	5.5	4.5	9.6
1983	11.2	9.6	20.0	2.08	6.8	5.6	4.6	9.7
1984	10.8	9.3	19.2	2.06	6.7	5.6	4.7	9.6
1985	10.6	9.2	19.0	2.07	6.8	5.7	4.7	10.0
1986	10.4	8.8	18.9	2.15	6.8	6.0	5.0	10.6
1987	10.1	8.5	18.8	2.21	6.9	6.1	5.0	11.1
1988	10.0	8.4	18.5	2.20	6.9	6.1	5.0	10.9
1989	9.8	8.1	18.6	2.30	7.0	6.4	5.2	11.9
1990	9.2	7.6	18.0	2.37	7.0	6.1	4.9	11.3
1991	8.9	7.3	17.6	2.41	7.1	5.8	4.7	10.7
1992	8.5	6.9	16.8	2.43	7.1	5.2	4.2	9.9
1993	8.4	6.8	16.5	2.43	7.2	4.8	3.9	9.0
1994	8.0	6.6	15.8	2.39	7.3	4.4	3.6	8.2
1995	7.6	6.3	15.1	2.40	7.3	4.2	3.5	7.6

— Data not available.

a. Infant deaths before age 1 per 1,000 live births.

b. Birthweight less than 2,500 grams (5 lbs., 8 oz.).

c. Prenatal care begun in the last three months of pregnancy.

Source: U.S. Department of Health and Human Services, National Center for Health Statistics. Calculations by Children's Defense Fund.

TABLE A3 **Adolescent Childbearing**

Year	Birth rate among teens and adults[a]		Birth rate among teens[b]	
	All	Unmarried	All	Unmarried
1959	118.8	21.9	89.1	15.5
1960	118.0	21.6	89.1	15.3
1961	117.1	22.7	88.6	16.0
1962	112.0	21.9	81.4	14.8
1963	108.3	22.5	76.7	15.3
1964	104.7	23.0	73.1	15.9
1965	96.3	23.5	70.5	16.7
1966	90.8	23.4	70.3	17.5
1967	87.2	23.9	67.5	18.5
1968	85.2	24.4	65.6	19.7
1969	86.1	25.0	65.5	20.4
1970	87.9	26.4	68.3	22.4
1971	81.6	25.5	64.5	22.3
1972	73.1	24.8	61.7	22.8
1973	68.8	24.3	59.3	22.7
1974	67.8	23.9	57.5	23.0
1975	66.0	24.5	55.6	23.9
1976	65.0	24.3	52.8	23.7
1977	66.8	25.6	52.8	25.1
1978	65.5	25.7	51.5	24.9
1979	67.2	27.2	52.3	26.4
1980	68.4	29.4	53.0	27.6
1981	67.4	29.5	52.2	27.9
1982	67.3	30.0	52.4	28.7
1983	65.8	30.3	51.4	29.5
1984	65.4	31.0	50.6	30.0
1985	66.2	32.8	51.0	31.4
1986	65.4	34.2	50.2	32.3
1987	65.7	36.0	50.6	33.8
1988	67.2	38.5	53.0	36.4
1989	69.2	41.6	57.3	40.1
1990	70.9	43.8	59.9	42.5
1991	69.6	45.2	62.1	44.8
1992	68.9	45.2	60.7	44.6
1993	67.6	45.3	59.6	44.5
1994	66.7	46.9	58.9	46.4
1995	65.6	45.1	56.8	44.4

a. Births per 1,000 females ages 15–44.

b. Births per 1,000 females ages 15–19.

Source: U.S. Department of Health and Human Services, National Center for Health Statistics.

TABLE A4 **Youth Unemployment**

Year	Unemployment by age			Unemployment among 16- to 24-year-olds not enrolled in school, by level of education		
	All ages	Ages 16–19	Ages 20–24	Less than four years of high school	High school graduate only	Four years or more of college
1959	5.5%	14.6%	8.5%	—	—	—
1960	5.5	14.7	8.7	—	—	—
1961	6.7	16.8	10.4	—	—	—
1962	5.5	14.7	9.0	—	—	—
1963	5.7	17.2	8.8	—	—	—
1964	5.2	16.2	8.3	—	—	—
1965	4.5	14.8	6.7	—	—	—
1966	3.8	12.8	5.3	—	—	—
1967	3.8	12.9	5.7	—	—	—
1968	3.6	12.7	5.8	—	—	—
1969	3.5	12.2	5.7	—	—	—
1970	4.9	15.3	8.2	17.2%	9.9%	6.5%
1971	5.9	16.9	10.0	18.0	9.6	6.6
1972	5.6	16.2	9.3	16.8	9.5	7.2
1973	4.9	14.5	7.8	14.9	7.2	4.9
1974	5.6	16.0	9.1	19.2	9.8	5.0
1975	8.5	19.9	13.6	25.3	13.6	8.2
1976	7.7	19.0	12.0	24.7	12.1	7.1
1977	7.1	17.8	11.0	20.6	10.5	8.0
1978	6.1	16.4	9.6	18.8	8.8	6.3
1979	5.8	16.1	9.1	19.2	9.9	5.0
1980	7.1	17.8	11.5	25.3	12.5	5.9
1981	7.6	19.6	12.3	26.9	13.8	5.3
1982	9.7	23.2	14.9	31.8	17.3	9.2
1983	9.6	22.4	14.5	27.3	15.2	7.0
1984	7.5	18.9	11.5	25.8	11.8	5.9
1985	7.2	18.6	11.1	25.9	12.7	5.4
1986	7.0	18.3	10.7	24.3	11.5	4.8
1987	6.2	16.9	9.7	21.8	10.7	5.5
1988	5.5	15.3	8.7	20.0	10.1	4.8
1989	5.3	15.0	8.6	19.9	10.1	5.0
1990	5.5	15.5	8.8	20.0	10.4	5.2
1991	6.7	18.6	10.8	23.1	12.7	6.9
1992	7.4	20.0	11.3	24.9	13.9	6.5
1993	6.8	19.0	10.5	22.8	13.1	6.1
1994	6.1	17.6	9.7	23.1	11.9	5.5
1995	5.6	17.3	9.1	21.5	12.2	5.6
1996	5.4	16.7	9.3	22.1	12.1	5.4

— Data not available.

Source: U.S. Department of Labor, Bureau of Labor Statistics.

Appendix B
Children in the States

Child Population and Children in Poverty

State	All children, 1996		Poor children, 1993				
	Number	Percentage of state population	Number	Percentage of children in the state	State rank[a]	County with highest child poverty rate	Rate in county
Alabama	1,076,436	25.2%	288,512	26.2%	41	Perry County	51.5%
Alaska	184,387	30.4	30,628	15.9	11	Wade Hampton Census Area	48.2
Arizona	1,150,186	26.0	321,595	28.0	44	Apache County	47.5
Arkansas	659,448	26.3	170,943	26.0	39	Lee County	58.3
California	8,866,413	27.8	2,331,091	26.4	42	Fresno County	41.1
Colorado	997,938	26.1	162,858	16.5	14	Costilla County	43.6
Connecticut	797,950	24.4	131,786	16.5	14	Hartford County	20.7
Delaware	176,015	24.3	29,897	16.7	16	Sussex County	20.9
District of Columbia	109,559	20.2	38,697	33.3	49	District of Columbia	33.3
Florida	3,423,067	23.8	827,435	24.7	36	Dade County	38.4
Georgia	1,952,456	26.6	480,129	25.2	37	Clay County	49.2
Hawaii	306,523	25.9	45,984	14.9	5	Hawaii County	22.9
Idaho	348,509	29.3	54,066	15.5	9	Shoshone County	27.8
Illinois	3,155,905	26.6	643,528	20.4	30	Alexander County	42.9
Indiana	1,498,524	25.7	260,217	17.3	20	Lake County	25.5
Iowa	719,339	25.2	112,170	15.1	7	Appanoose County	26.9
Kansas	687,314	26.7	117,134	16.7	16	Wyandotte County	32.1
Kentucky	968,660	24.9	277,678	28.1	45	Owsley County	65.0
Louisiana	1,233,455	28.4	419,234	33.3	49	East Carroll Parish	62.3
Maine	299,519	24.1	60,358	19.4	26	Washington County	30.7
Maryland	1,286,190	25.4	194,218	15.1	7	Baltimore city	40.9
Massachusetts	1,421,929	23.3	269,681	18.7	24	Suffolk County	35.7
Michigan	2,537,014	26.4	607,192	23.6	34	Wayne County	41.5
Minnesota	1,247,008	26.8	185,224	14.7	4	Beltrami County	29.3
Mississippi	756,134	27.8	261,597	33.9	51	Holmes County	62.2
Missouri	1,394,199	26.0	303,044	21.6	33	St. Louis city	51.8
Montana	232,751	26.5	47,745	19.8	29	Glacier County	37.6
Nebraska	442,186	26.8	62,619	13.9	3	Thurston County	29.9
Nevada	416,750	26.0	64,454	16.7	16	Clark County	18.6
New Hampshire	295,866	25.5	34,116	11.5	1	Carroll County	17.1
New Jersey	1,986,972	24.9	311,444	15.7	10	Essex County	31.5
New Mexico	501,233	29.3	154,078	30.6	47	McKinley County	45.9
New York	4,540,534	25.0	1,226,505	26.7	43	Bronx County	53.4
North Carolina	1,833,617	25.0	354,012	19.7	27	Hyde County	38.7
North Dakota	168,643	26.2	28,056	16.2	13	Sioux County	43.5
Ohio	2,847,841	25.5	626,433	21.5	32	Scioto County	37.2
Oklahoma	880,796	26.7	226,841	25.4	38	Harmon County	45.9
Oregon	808,406	25.2	146,719	18.3	23	Josephine County	28.9
Pennsylvania	2,894,676	24.0	582,194	19.7	27	Philadelphia County	43.3
Rhode Island	235,283	23.8	49,456	20.6	31	Providence County	27.5
South Carolina	937,765	25.4	227,943	23.7	35	Allendale County	43.1
South Dakota	204,156	27.9	40,072	19.2	25	Shannon County	58.7
Tennessee	1,322,161	24.9	342,542	26.0	39	Hancock County	47.4
Texas	5,452,277	28.5	1,539,249	28.6	46	Starr County	59.3
Utah	678,803	33.9	93,257	13.6	2	San Juan County	34.6
Vermont	146,648	24.9	25,470	17.0	19	Orleans County	26.8
Virginia	1,631,836	24.4	289,223	17.8	22	Richmond city	44.1
Washington	1,436,804	26.0	248,624	17.3	20	Yakima County	33.3
West Virginia	421,933	23.1	142,138	32.6	48	McDowell County	60.4
Wisconsin	1,343,034	26.0	218,733	15.9	11	Menominee County	40.3
Wyoming	133,275	27.7	20,673	14.9	5	Goshen County	24.8
United States	69,048,323	26.0	15,727,492	22.7		Owsley County, KY	65.0

a. States are ranked by percentage of children in poverty, from lowest to highest.
Source: U.S. Department of Commerce, Bureau of the Census. Calculations by Children's Defense Fund.

TABLE B2 **Children in Poverty, by Race, 1989**

State	All races		White		Black		Hispanic[a]	
	Number	Percent	Number	Percent	Number	Percent	Number	Percent
Alabama	253,636	24.2%	89,959	12.9%	160,510	47.5%	1,829	23.4%
Alaska	19,284	11.4	8,864	7.4	1,086	14.5	809	12.2
Arizona	212,001	22.0	104,283	14.9	12,813	35.7	89,883	34.9
Arkansas	155,399	25.3	82,932	17.7	70,023	52.0	2,290	31.9
California	1,380,275	18.2	591,097	12.7	195,563	30.7	713,980	27.2
Colorado	129,565	15.3	88,222	12.2	13,677	33.8	48,497	32.7
Connecticut	79,020	10.7	36,963	6.1	23,591	28.9	30,002	41.2
Delaware	19,256	12.0	7,543	6.3	10,600	30.8	1,297	25.0
District of Columbia	28,610	25.5	799	4.9	26,339	29.1	1,677	26.3
Florida	525,446	18.7	252,793	12.0	243,435	41.0	93,288	24.6
Georgia	343,068	20.1	108,825	9.9	227,207	40.0	7,163	24.0
Hawaii	31,944	11.6	8,306	9.9	969	11.7	5,296	17.8
Idaho	49,159	16.2	41,528	14.7	281	22.5	7,705	35.4
Illinois	495,505	17.0	204,276	9.7	233,506	43.3	80,047	25.0
Indiana	203,791	14.2	141,319	11.2	55,984	40.1	7,627	21.8
Iowa	101,661	14.3	89,059	13.1	8,241	50.6	3,253	26.7
Kansas	93,066	14.3	65,528	11.5	18,665	40.3	8,233	23.5
Kentucky	234,012	24.8	193,614	22.7	38,193	47.0	1,803	26.2
Louisiana	380,942	31.4	112,404	15.4	259,228	56.5	5,908	23.3
Maine	41,897	13.8	40,429	13.6	440	25.9	435	16.2
Maryland	128,523	11.3	46,164	6.1	77,002	23.2	4,165	12.3
Massachusetts	176,221	13.2	105,129	9.2	29,547	33.3	49,645	49.1
Michigan	450,426	18.6	239,263	12.4	188,405	46.2	22,103	30.2
Minnesota	146,386	12.7	102,624	9.7	17,394	49.5	6,486	30.7
Mississippi	248,705	33.6	59,138	14.9	186,212	55.6	1,471	30.9
Missouri	230,058	17.7	152,757	13.9	71,928	41.5	4,246	20.3
Montana	44,706	20.5	33,458	17.1	221	31.1	1,874	36.0
Nebraska	58,474	13.8	44,420	11.4	8,761	43.2	3,861	27.9
Nevada	38,232	13.3	22,893	9.9	8,358	33.5	8,491	21.5
New Hampshire	20,440	7.4	19,295	7.2	351	15.3	705	16.4
New Jersey	200,726	11.3	84,110	6.4	81,788	27.8	59,531	27.8
New Mexico	122,260	27.8	67,615	22.1	3,542	35.0	70,158	35.0
New York	799,531	19.1	342,541	11.9	274,947	34.1	269,703	41.9
North Carolina	272,923	17.2	102,034	9.3	158,007	35.9	5,047	24.2
North Dakota	29,732	17.1	23,031	14.4	204	15.1	623	27.5
Ohio	493,206	17.8	315,714	13.4	163,131	45.4	15,910	32.0
Oklahoma	179,283	21.7	105,173	16.6	34,475	44.5	11,950	35.8
Oregon	111,629	15.8	91,249	14.2	5,489	36.3	14,285	33.8
Pennsylvania	432,227	15.7	270,941	11.5	124,859	40.6	38,374	46.7
Rhode Island	30,842	13.8	20,274	10.4	4,425	35.9	6,356	41.3
South Carolina	190,873	21.0	52,430	9.5	136,563	39.6	1,635	19.0
South Dakota	39,896	20.4	25,008	14.7	327	26.7	663	27.8
Tennessee	251,529	21.0	142,418	15.2	106,024	43.0	2,400	24.1
Texas	1,159,710	24.3	612,724	18.3	254,287	39.3	638,905	40.2
Utah	78,041	12.5	64,755	11.1	1,290	34.7	9,213	26.8
Vermont	17,020	12.0	16,435	11.9	211	24.9	143	11.8
Virginia	197,382	13.3	88,370	8.1	102,862	30.9	5,147	11.9
Washington	179,272	14.5	124,632	11.9	14,548	30.5	27,381	34.0
West Virginia	115,073	26.2	106,458	25.4	7,887	50.2	814	34.3
Wisconsin	188,863	14.9	110,939	9.9	53,392	55.8	12,435	33.7
Wyoming	19,190	14.4	15,532	12.6	340	31.5	2,724	28.1
United States	11,428,916	18.3	5,876,267	12.5	3,717,128	39.8	2,407,466	32.2

a. Persons of Hispanic origin may be of any race.

State	Native American		Asian or Pacific Islander		Other	
	Number	Percent	Number	Percent	Number	Percent
Alabama	1,519	24.6%	1,166	19.0%	482	28.0%
Alaska	8,621	25.7	500	8.3	213	12.6
Arizona	44,607	53.1	2,204	14.9	48,094	38.2
Arkansas	1,053	26.1	648	17.5	743	34.7
California	17,982	26.5	155,493	19.6	420,140	30.2
Colorado	3,008	35.4	3,130	17.6	21,528	36.8
Connecticut	313	21.4	917	6.6	17,236	47.1
Delaware	80	21.5	149	6.6	884	30.0
District of Columbia	55	35.7	232	16.0	1,185	31.6
Florida	2,541	26.1	5,194	12.9	21,483	31.5
Georgia	938	25.0	2,465	11.5	3,633	29.7
Hawaii	408	25.2	21,327	12.1	934	16.5
Idaho	2,056	40.5	567	20.6	4,727	40.9
Illinois	1,422	23.9	7,640	9.4	48,661	27.8
Indiana	1,132	30.2	1,124	11.6	4,232	27.8
Iowa	1,160	43.4	1,898	23.5	1,303	28.4
Kansas	1,932	26.8	2,203	22.2	4,738	26.6
Kentucky	681	41.8	867	16.5	657	26.2
Louisiana	3,166	46.9	4,414	34.0	1,730	30.3
Maine	583	28.3	326	13.6	119	19.0
Maryland	661	18.5	2,820	7.6	1,876	14.3
Massachusetts	1,309	35.3	9,330	24.1	30,906	51.9
Michigan	6,147	32.5	4,891	14.6	11,720	35.9
Minnesota	10,459	54.8	12,638	37.1	3,271	37.5
Mississippi	1,429	45.6	1,657	39.7	269	32.5
Missouri	1,483	26.2	1,984	17.7	1,906	25.0
Montana	10,238	53.4	224	17.6	565	43.3
Nebraska	2,795	57.0	724	17.9	1,774	31.8
Nevada	1,745	29.8	1,040	10.9	4,196	25.0
New Hampshire	119	25.6	370	13.4	305	22.6
New Jersey	886	26.2	4,622	5.9	29,320	33.0
New Mexico	26,643	50.1	797	18.4	23,663	36.0
New York	4,800	29.6	25,021	14.9	152,222	47.6
North Carolina	7,820	29.9	2,344	16.4	2,718	31.2
North Dakota	6,179	58.3	148	16.8	170	22.6
Ohio	1,588	30.4	3,557	14.1	9,216	39.3
Oklahoma	31,977	34.8	1,427	15.8	6,231	40.4
Oregon	4,288	32.3	3,752	19.2	6,851	37.2
Pennsylvania	1,128	31.1	8,354	20.7	26,945	54.7
Rhode Island	440	39.5	2,043	34.0	3,660	42.5
South Carolina	599	27.4	715	12.1	566	21.6
South Dakota	14,160	63.3	195	17.0	206	26.2
Tennessee	906	30.8	1,438	15.7	743	25.8
Texas	4,501	25.6	14,518	15.6	273,680	40.6
Utah	4,893	47.3	2,281	19.8	4,822	33.5
Vermont	251	36.3	70	7.3	53	20.2
Virginia	666	19.0	3,377	7.8	2,107	13.5
Washington	10,228	37.7	12,594	20.0	17,270	39.8
West Virginia	337	44.6	193	8.5	198	32.1
Wisconsin	6,505	46.1	10,819	48.8	7,208	42.5
Wyoming	1,966	49.0	84	10.0	1,268	35.2
United States	260,403	38.8	346,491	17.1	1,228,627	35.5

Source: U.S. Department of Commerce, Bureau of the Census, 1990 Census of Population and Housing, Summary Tape File 3.
Calculations by Children's Defense Fund.

TABLE B3 **AFDC/TANF Benefit Levels and Participation***

| | Maximum monthly benefit for a three-person family | | | | | | Number of welfare (AFDC/TANF) recipients | | |
| | 1970 maximum | | 1997 maximum | | | | | | |
State	Actual dollars	Inflation-adjusted value in 1997	Actual dollars	As a percentage of poverty line	1997 state rank[a]	Percentage change 1970–97	January 1993	August 1997	Percentage change
Alabama	$ 65	$ 265	$164	14.8%	50	−38.2%	141,746	70,851	−50.0%
Alaska	328	1,338	923	66.5	1	−31.0	34,951	33,082	−5.3
Arizona	138	563	347	31.2	33	−38.4	194,119	136,706	−29.6
Arkansas	89	363	204	18.4	45	−43.8	73,982	47,480	−35.8
California	186	759	565	50.9	6	−25.5	2,415,121	2,269,558	−6.0
Colorado	193	787	356	32.0	30	−54.8	123,308	59,634	−51.6
Connecticut	283	1,154	636	57.2	4	−44.9	160,102	151,542	−5.3
Delaware	160	653	338	30.4	35	−48.2	27,652	20,560	−25.6
District of Columbia	195	796	398	35.8	24	−50.0	65,860	63,627	−3.4
Florida	114	465	303	27.3	38	−34.8	701,842	394,343	−43.8
Georgia	107	437	280	25.2	41	−35.9	402,228	241,478	−40.0
Hawaii	226	922	712	55.7	2	−22.8	54,511	74,480	36.6
Idaho	211	861	317	28.5	36	−63.2	21,116	6,846	−67.6
Illinois	232	946	377	33.9	26	−60.2	685,508	555,668	−18.9
Indiana	120	490	288	25.9	40	−41.2	209,882	107,436	−48.8
Iowa	201	820	426	38.3	19	−48.0	100,943	75,106	−25.6
Kansas	222	906	429	38.6	18	−52.6	87,525	47,860	−45.3
Kentucky	147	600	262	23.6	43	−56.3	227,879	148,609	−34.8
Louisiana	88	359	190	17.1	47	−47.1	263,338	129,273	−50.9
Maine	135	551	418	37.6	23	−24.1	67,836	45,138	−33.5
Maryland	162	661	377	33.9	26	−43.0	221,338	149,028	−32.7
Massachusetts	268	1,093	565	50.9	6	−48.3	332,044	195,473	−41.1
Michigan	219	893	459	41.3	14	−48.6	686,356	419,777	−38.8
Minnesota	256	1,044	532	47.9	11	−49.1	191,526	152,765	−20.2
Mississippi	56	228	120	10.8	51	−47.5	174,093	86,910	−50.1
Missouri	104	424	292	26.3	39	−31.2	259,039	179,955	−30.5
Montana	202	824	438	39.4	15	−46.8	34,848	24,573	−29.5
Nebraska	171	698	364	32.8	28	−47.8	48,055	37,985	−21.0
Nevada	121	494	348	31.3	32	−29.5	34,943	28,854	−17.4
New Hampshire	262	1,069	550	49.5	9	−48.5	28,972	16,952	−41.5
New Jersey	302	1,232	424	38.2	21	−65.6	349,902	252,200	−27.9
New Mexico	149	608	389	35.0	25	−36.0	94,836	61,435	−35.2
New York	279	1,138	577	51.9	5	−49.3	1,179,522	989,200	−16.1
North Carolina	145	592	272	24.5	42	−54.0	331,633	222,883	−32.8
North Dakota	213	869	431	38.8	16	−50.4	18,774	10,404	−44.6
Ohio	161	657	341	30.7	34	−48.1	720,476	433,792	−39.8
Oklahoma	152	620	307	27.6	37	−50.5	146,454	73,837	−49.6
Oregon	184	751	460	41.4	13	−38.7	117,656	54,083	−54.0
Pennsylvania	265	1,081	421	37.9	22	−61.1	604,701	417,881	−30.9
Rhode Island	229	934	554	49.9	8	−40.7	61,116	54,628	−10.6
South Carolina	85	347	200	18.0	46	−42.3	151,026	78,316	−48.1
South Dakota	264	1,077	430	38.7	17	−60.1	20,254	12,233	−39.6
Tennessee	112	457	185	16.7	49	−59.5	320,709	157,924	−50.8
Texas	148	604	188	16.9	48	−68.9	785,271	468,611	−40.3
Utah	175	714	426	38.3	19	−40.3	53,172	30,990	−41.7
Vermont	267	1,089	639	57.5	3	−41.3	28,961	22,048	−23.9
Virginia	225	918	354	31.9	31	−61.4	194,212	117,360	−39.6
Washington	258	1,053	546	49.1	10	−48.1	286,258	237,198	−17.1
West Virginia	114	465	253	22.8	44	−45.6	119,916	75,313	−37.2
Wisconsin	184	751	517	46.5	12	−31.1	241,098	97,383	−59.6
Wyoming	213	869	360	32.4	29	−58.6	18,271	4,279	−76.6
United States[b]	184	751	377	33.9		−49.8	14,115,000	9,995,000	−29.2

*AFDC—Aid to Families with Dependent Children. TANF—Temporary Assistance for Needy Families.

a. States are ranked by ratio of maximum monthly benefit to poverty line, from highest to lowest.

b. Median for benefits: total for enrollment.

Source: U.S. Department of Health and Human Services, Office of Family Assistance, and U.S. Congress, Congressional Research Service. Calculations by Children's Defense Fund.

TABLE B4 **Number of Children Participating in Food Stamps and Child Nutrition Programs, FY 1997***

State	Food stamps[a]	Supplemental Food Program for Women, Infants, and Children (WIC)				School lunch program[b]	School break-fast program	Child and Adult Care Food Program (CACFP)	Summer food program
		Women	Infants	Children	Total				
Alabama	273,000	26,989	35,549	56,361	118,899	548,170	147,312	36,080	57,017
Alaska	27,000	5,393	5,109	13,035	23,537	47,912	7,961	6,814	0
Arizona	233,000	34,222	38,507	73,920	146,649	420,221	129,561	41,031	23,410
Arkansas	136,000	22,682	23,007	41,622	87,311	310,676	115,492	22,006	11,483
California	2,042,000	287,832	278,318	658,074	1,224,224	2,487,706	819,476	280,312	189,236
Colorado	125,000	18,882	19,059	37,127	75,068	308,628	48,183	38,394	14,347
Connecticut	107,000	11,111	15,383	32,874	59,368	241,378	48,833	20,515	23,092
Delaware	30,000	3,242	4,383	7,958	15,583	67,048	16,013	11,974	8,862
District of Columbia	48,000	3,713	5,003	8,075	16,791	50,994	32,734	4,630	16,614
Florida	715,000	79,278	95,124	180,526	354,928	1,267,613	379,753	80,678	234,033
Georgia	422,000	56,162	59,292	114,700	230,154	1,024,717	345,287	85,750	92,370
Hawaii	53,000	6,876	7,746	16,185	30,807	144,518	37,584	8,753	3,628
Idaho	40,000	6,982	7,895	16,597	31,474	139,532	23,318	6,362	2,843
Illinois	545,000	47,505	71,615	116,835	235,955	995,916	187,614	81,176	122,587
Indiana	188,000	33,770	37,508	61,430	132,708	598,357	100,022	43,623	14,851
Iowa	84,000	14,625	14,294	37,374	66,293	387,053	53,776	27,794	5,785
Kansas	88,000	12,688	13,449	28,817	54,954	307,851	64,534	53,319	6,943
Kentucky	212,000	28,469	29,479	64,753	122,701	521,347	172,461	26,983	28,400
Louisiana	362,000	33,782	41,111	64,363	139,256	666,607	235,975	56,621	55,838
Maine	51,000	5,942	5,864	14,886	26,692	104,290	23,514	14,744	5,759
Maryland	200,000	22,381	26,182	42,957	91,520	375,663	79,562	51,659	32,926
Massachusetts	190,000	26,937	27,392	64,490	118,819	484,069	96,612	50,856	39,707
Michigan	460,000	48,391	52,548	117,013	217,952	762,515	158,503	75,773	38,700
Minnesota	152,000	19,815	21,300	53,155	94,270	544,936	75,501	94,339	23,213
Mississippi	220,000	22,051	29,914	48,159	100,124	402,540	169,024	27,094	34,291
Missouri	276,000	32,823	33,425	65,390	131,638	578,146	142,312	42,833	32,359
Montana	37,000	4,831	4,265	12,583	21,679	84,130	14,516	12,660	3,845
Nebraska	52,000	7,555	9,190	16,795	33,540	211,318	24,496	39,273	6,815
Nevada	52,000	9,193	9,545	18,576	37,314	101,692	28,843	5,147	5,148
New Hampshire	27,000	4,038	4,834	10,307	19,179	94,454	14,523	6,776	2,008
New Jersey	282,000	33,686	34,826	72,979	141,491	542,470	75,811	38,418	58,966
New Mexico	125,000	11,407	11,971	30,305	53,683	189,730	69,621	45,158	53,273
New York	964,000	101,776	118,805	258,682	479,263	1,706,622	444,614	173,792	424,203
North Carolina	304,000	49,193	51,992	93,307	194,492	790,030	235,418	92,890	39,327
North Dakota	17,000	3,632	3,601	9,659	16,892	83,940	10,984	17,853	2,014
Ohio	488,000	58,666	75,630	120,034	254,330	971,432	168,182	74,590	38,549
Oklahoma	164,000	26,118	27,475	54,815	108,408	366,567	124,007	44,443	14,892
Oregon	131,000	22,075	17,067	50,242	89,384	255,736	72,504	36,132	13,678
Pennsylvania	513,000	53,816	56,800	147,521	258,137	1,006,874	170,170	63,369	120,155
Rhode Island	48,000	4,706	5,318	12,551	22,575	57,291	7,861	6,602	12,419
South Carolina	191,000	30,193	30,349	58,425	118,967	458,361	161,442	26,304	68,635
South Dakota	24,000	4,852	5,059	12,023	21,934	104,657	14,114	11,909	5,390
Tennessee	284,000	36,575	37,814	76,507	150,896	605,239	180,131	38,595	37,310
Texas	1,320,000	166,057	174,519	343,030	683,606	2,279,760	784,624	155,199	120,764
Utah	58,000	14,866	14,712	27,747	57,325	258,104	26,866	40,720	20,766
Vermont	27,000	3,762	2,959	9,412	16,133	51,118	11,897	8,593	2,811
Virginia	261,000	29,623	33,563	66,905	130,091	632,961	162,611	39,993	28,332
Washington	247,000	34,117	35,330	75,967	145,414	439,792	104,229	53,954	27,887
West Virginia	124,000	12,657	12,457	29,599	54,713	209,778	87,714	11,808	18,027
Wisconsin	159,000	23,403	24,566	60,929	108,898	518,083	42,050	51,765	20,930
Wyoming	17,000	3,112	2,843	6,482	12,437	55,976	7,494	7,392	656
United States	13,195,000	1,662,452	1,803,946	3,712,058	7,178,456	25,864,518	6,755,639	2,393,448	2,265,094

*Data reflect average participation each month that the program operates.

a. State enrollments are rounded to the nearest 1,000; the U.S. total may not equal the sum of the state numbers because of this rounding.

b. All children receiving a federal subsidy for lunch, including children receiving free and reduced-price lunches.

Source: U.S. Department of Agriculture, Food and Consumer Service.

TABLE B5 **Child Support Enforcement, FY 1995**

State	Total caseload	Cases with court orders		Cases with collection		State rank[a]
		Number	Percent	Number	Percent	
Alabama	371,071	212,554	57.3%	78,718	21.2%	25
Alaska	53,350	39,428	73.9	9,147	17.1	34
Arizona	285,123	83,324	29.2	33,255	11.7	47
Arkansas	130,332	87,460	67.1	33,784	25.9	16
California	2,367,404	1,029,305	43.5	328,691	13.9	42
Colorado	195,336	122,869	62.9	29,305	15.0	40
Connecticut	227,221	136,899	60.2	36,884	16.2	36
Delaware	55,541	38,107	68.6	15,513	27.9	13
District of Columbia	93,304	38,670	41.4	9,801	10.5	50
Florida	1,020,738	1,020,738	100.0	160,766	15.7	38
Georgia	515,830	250,352	48.5	97,351	18.9	31
Hawaii	52,748	28,023	53.1	13,157	24.9	18
Idaho	62,194	47,890	77.0	18,196	29.3	11
Illinois	721,151	212,502	29.5	77,926	10.8	49
Indiana	777,706	533,236	68.6	76,308	9.8	51
Iowa	182,669	139,580	76.4	39,173	21.4	24
Kansas	129,458	76,173	58.8	44,210	34.2	7
Kentucky	305,178	165,182	54.1	50,157	16.4	35
Louisiana	366,600	138,886	37.9	49,420	13.5	43
Maine	75,898	59,075	77.8	27,034	35.6	4
Maryland	362,345	262,768	72.5	83,258	23.0	21
Massachusetts	218,126	162,060	74.3	58,375	26.8	14
Michigan	1,508,480	716,196	47.5	232,564	15.4	39
Minnesota	225,696	172,232	76.3	91,247	40.4	1
Mississippi	285,662	124,438	43.6	36,391	12.7	44
Missouri	375,299	263,347	70.2	69,092	18.4	32
Montana	43,781	23,945	54.7	9,034	20.6	26
Nebraska	138,878	78,528	56.5	26,515	19.1	30
Nevada	74,311	45,455	61.2	16,098	21.7	23
New Hampshire	44,494	31,699	71.2	15,673	35.2	5
New Jersey	536,610	360,694	67.2	129,161	24.1	20
New Mexico	92,570	20,709	22.4	14,713	15.9	37
New York	1,282,835	728,255	56.8	192,935	15.0	40
North Carolina	442,765	209,346	47.3	97,664	22.1	22
North Dakota	37,357	25,083	67.1	9,355	25.0	17
Ohio	906,266	602,324	66.5	253,432	28.0	12
Oklahoma	118,132	64,565	54.7	21,715	18.4	32
Oregon	253,447	136,660	53.9	48,806	19.3	29
Pennsylvania	882,374	566,415	64.2	271,496	30.8	10
Rhode Island	77,801	38,257	49.2	9,810	12.6	45
South Carolina	218,243	91,674	42.0	56,820	26.0	15
South Dakota	30,479	27,568	90.4	9,993	32.8	9
Tennessee	622,292	301,001	48.4	69,794	11.2	48
Texas	736,413	343,823	46.7	143,174	19.4	28
Utah	110,092	77,660	70.5	21,479	19.5	27
Vermont	19,336	15,448	79.9	6,731	34.8	6
Virginia	363,058	216,649	59.7	136,411	37.6	3
Washington	360,317	292,304	81.1	120,051	33.3	8
West Virginia	117,204	46,058	39.3	28,453	24.3	19
Wisconsin	411,085	324,889	79.0	157,555	38.3	2
Wyoming	46,294	17,791	38.4	5,642	12.2	46
United States	18,930,894	10,848,094	57.3	3,672,233	19.4	

a. States are ranked from highest to lowest collection rate.

Source: U.S. Department of Health and Human Services, Office of Child Support Enforcement. Calculations by Children's Defense Fund.

TABLE B6 **Fair Market Rent and the Minimum Wage, 1998**

State	Lowest monthly rent[a]	Hourly minimum wage[b]	Lowest rent as a percentage of minimum wage	State rank[c]
Alabama	$357	$5.15	41.6%	1
Alaska	763	5.65	81.0	50
Arizona	553	5.15	64.4	41
Arkansas	397	5.15	46.3	7
California	479	5.15	55.8	28
Colorado	501	5.15	58.4	34
Connecticut	610	5.18	70.7	43
Delaware	602	5.15	70.1	42
District of Columbia	812	6.15	79.2	48
Florida	470	5.15	54.8	25
Georgia	423	5.15	49.3	12
Hawaii	986	5.25	112.7	51
Idaho	532	5.15	62.0	38
Illinois	439	5.15	51.1	20
Indiana	404	5.15	47.1	8
Iowa	423	5.15	49.3	12
Kansas	486	5.15	56.6	29
Kentucky	391	5.15	45.6	4
Louisiana	393	5.15	45.8	6
Maine	490	5.15	57.1	32
Maryland	488	5.15	56.9	30
Massachusetts	554	5.25	63.3	40
Michigan	488	5.15	56.9	30
Minnesota	451	5.15	52.5	21
Mississippi	386	5.15	45.0	3
Missouri	382	5.15	44.5	2
Montana	478	5.15	55.7	27
Nebraska	517	5.15	60.2	37
Nevada	681	5.15	79.3	49
New Hampshire	653	5.15	76.1	44
New Jersey	675	5.15	78.6	47
New Mexico	429	5.15	50.0	17
New York	475	5.15	55.3	26
North Carolina	421	5.15	49.0	11
North Dakota	490	5.15	57.1	32
Ohio	410	5.15	47.8	9
Oklahoma	391	5.15	45.6	4
Oregon	548	5.50	59.8	36
Pennsylvania	423	5.15	49.3	12
Rhode Island	655	5.15	76.3	45
South Carolina	425	5.15	49.5	16
South Dakota	538	5.15	62.7	39
Tennessee	438	5.15	51.0	19
Texas	417	5.15	48.6	10
Utah	458	5.15	53.4	23
Vermont	684	5.25	78.2	46
Virginia	423	5.15	49.3	12
Washington	512	5.15	59.7	35
West Virginia	434	5.15	50.6	18
Wisconsin	467	5.15	54.4	24
Wyoming	456	5.15	53.1	22

a. For a two-bedroom apartment in the metropolitan county with the lowest fair market rent (as determined by HUD) in the state.

b. Minimum wage as of September 1, 1997.

c. States are ranked by the ratio of rent to minimum wage, from lowest to highest.

Source: U.S. Department of Housing and Urban Development (HUD) and U.S. Department of Labor. Calculations by Children's Defense Fund.

TABLE B7 **Early Prenatal Care and Low Birthweight, 1995**

| State | Incidence of early prenatal care, by race of mother[a] | | | | | | Incidence of low-birthweight births, by race of mother[b] | | | | | |
| | All races | | White | | Black | | All races | | White | | Black | |
	Rate	State rank[c]	Rate	State rank[c]	Rate	State rank[c]	Rate	State rank[d]	Rate	State rank[d]	Rate	State rank[d]
Alabama	81.7%	33	87.8%	12	69.5%	32	9.0%	47	7.1%	45	13.0%	21
Alaska	83.4	23	85.7	27	85.3	2	5.3	1	5.1	1	12.4	14
Arizona	72.1	49	73.2	50	68.9	35	6.8	19	6.6	36	13.1	24
Arkansas	76.6	47	80.8	43	62.1	49	8.2	40	6.8	39	13.1	24
California	78.5	41	78.5	46	76.3	11	6.1	13	5.5	8	12.0	8
Colorado	80.4	38	81.1	41	72.9	18	8.4	41	8.0	51	15.9	40
Connecticut	87.8	6	89.5	5	76.3	11	7.1	23	6.3	26	12.7	17
Delaware	85.3	10	88.5	9	74.4	16	8.4	41	7.0	43	12.9	19
District of Columbia	59.8	51	76.9	48	54.5	51	13.4	51	5.6	12	15.9	40
Florida	82.6	30	85.9	26	71.3	25	7.7	35	6.4	29	12.1	10
Georgia	84.2	15	88.8	7	75.5	14	8.8	46	6.5	33	13.1	24
Hawaii	83.7	19	88.8	7	91.9	1	7.0	21	5.3	5	11.1	4
Idaho	79.9	39	80.1	44	78.3	6	5.9	9	5.8	13	• •	• •
Illinois	80.8	36	84.4	34	67.1	37	7.9	38	6.1	20	14.5	39
Indiana	80.9	35	82.5	39	66.9	38	7.5	28	6.9	42	13.0	21
Iowa	87.1	8	87.7	14	72.2	22	6.0	11	5.8	13	11.1	4
Kansas	85.7	9	86.8	19	75.0	15	6.4	18	5.9	15	12.2	12
Kentucky	84.3	13	85.7	27	71.2	27	7.6	30	7.1	45	12.8	18
Louisiana	80.7	37	88.3	10	70.0	31	9.7	49	6.7	37	14.0	34
Maine	89.1	4	89.4	6	78.2	7	6.1	13	6.0	18	• •	• •
Maryland	87.9	5	92.4	1	77.7	8	8.5	43	6.2	22	13.5	28
Massachusetts	89.3	3	90.8	3	78.7	5	6.3	15	5.9	15	10.4	2
Michigan	83.6	20	86.8	19	69.5	32	7.7	35	6.3	26	14.0	34
Minnesota	83.6	20	86.3	24	62.9	48	5.9	9	5.5	8	12.1	10
Mississippi	77.2	46	87.0	18	66.1	43	9.8	50	7.0	43	13.0	21
Missouri	85.2	11	87.7	14	71.7	23	7.6	30	6.5	33	14.1	37
Montana	81.5	34	83.5	37	85.0	3	5.8	8	5.9	15	• •	• •
Nebraska	84.1	16	85.2	32	70.5	29	6.3	15	6.0	18	12.0	8
Nevada	75.7	48	76.6	49	65.9	45	7.4	25	6.7	37	13.6	29
New Hampshire	90.0	1	90.1	4	82.9	4	5.5	4	5.5	8	• •	• •
New Jersey	82.8	27	86.4	23	67.3	36	7.6	30	6.2	22	13.1	24
New Mexico	69.5	50	71.6	51	60.6	50	7.5	28	7.7	50	10.5	3
New York	78.0	44	81.5	40	66.5	40	7.6	30	6.4	29	12.4	14
North Carolina	83.5	22	88.3	10	71.3	25	8.7	44	6.8	39	13.8	32
North Dakota	83.9	17	85.2	32	76.8	10	5.3	1	5.1	1	• •	• •
Ohio	84.7	12	87.3	17	69.5	32	7.6	30	6.5	33	13.9	33
Oklahoma	78.2	43	80.9	42	66.1	43	7.0	21	6.4	29	12.5	16
Oregon	78.8	40	79.2	45	72.8	19	5.5	4	5.4	6	10.3	1
Pennsylvania	83.4	23	86.5	22	65.3	47	7.4	25	6.2	22	14.2	38
Rhode Island	89.7	2	91.1	2	77.4	9	6.8	19	6.3	26	11.3	7
South Carolina	78.5	41	85.5	30	66.2	42	9.3	48	6.8	39	13.7	30
South Dakota	81.9	32	85.6	29	72.7	20	5.6	7	5.5	8	• •	• •
Tennessee	82.8	27	86.2	25	71.1	28	8.7	44	7.2	47	14.0	34
Texas	77.3	45	77.6	47	73.7	17	7.1	23	6.4	29	12.2	12
Utah	84.3	13	85.3	31	66.4	41	6.3	15	6.2	22	• •	• •
Vermont	87.3	7	87.5	16	70.3	30	5.4	3	5.4	6	• •	• •
Virginia	83.8	18	87.8	12	71.7	23	7.7	35	6.1	20	12.9	19
Washington	82.7	29	83.6	36	75.8	13	5.5	4	5.2	4	11.1	4
West Virginia	82.0	31	82.6	38	66.8	39	7.9	38	7.6	49	16.5	42
Wisconsin	83.4	23	86.6	21	65.5	46	6.0	11	5.1	1	13.7	30
Wyoming	83.1	26	83.9	35	72.7	20	7.4	25	7.3	48	• •	• •
United States	81.3		83.6		70.4		7.3		6.2		13.1	

• • Number too small to calculate a reliable rate.
a. Births to mothers who received care beginning in the first three months of pregnancy, as a percentage of all births among base group.
b. Newborns weighing less than 2,500 grams (5 lbs., 8 oz.), as a percentage of all births among base group.
c. States are ranked from highest to lowest incidence of early prenatal care.
d. States are ranked from lowest to highest incidence of low-birthweight births.
Source: U.S. Department of Health and Human Services, National Center for Health Statistics. Calculations by Children's Defense Fund.

TABLE B8 **Teen Birth Rates***

State	1990	1991	1992	1993	1994	1995
Alabama	71.0	73.9	72.5	70.5	72.2	70.3
Alaska	65.3	65.4	63.9	56.8	55.5	50.2
Arizona	75.5	80.7	81.7	79.8	78.7	75.7
Arkansas	80.1	79.8	75.5	73.9	76.3	73.5
California	70.6	74.7	74.0	72.7	71.3	68.2
Colorado	54.5	58.2	58.4	55.2	54.3	51.3
Connecticut	38.8	40.4	39.4	39.2	40.3	39.3
Delaware	54.5	61.1	59.6	59.7	60.2	57.0
District of Columbia	93.1	114.4	116.1	128.8	114.7	106.8
Florida	69.1	68.8	66.3	64.8	64.4	61.7
Georgia	75.5	76.3	74.5	73.0	71.7	71.1
Hawaii	61.2	58.7	53.5	53.0	53.5	47.9
Idaho	50.6	53.9	51.7	50.7	46.6	49.0
Illinois	62.9	64.8	63.6	63.0	62.8	59.9
Indiana	58.6	60.5	58.7	58.6	57.9	57.5
Iowa	40.5	42.6	40.8	41.1	39.7	38.6
Kansas	56.1	55.4	55.7	55.7	53.5	52.2
Kentucky	67.6	68.9	64.7	64.0	64.5	62.5
Louisiana	74.2	76.1	76.5	76.1	74.7	69.9
Maine	43.0	43.5	39.8	37.1	35.5	33.6
Maryland	53.2	54.3	50.7	50.1	49.7	47.7
Massachusetts	35.1	37.8	38.0	37.9	37.2	34.3
Michigan	59.0	59.0	56.5	53.2	52.1	49.2
Minnesota	36.3	37.3	36.0	35.0	34.4	32.4
Mississippi	81.0	85.6	84.2	83.3	83.0	80.6
Missouri	62.8	64.5	63.2	59.8	59.0	55.5
Montana	48.4	46.7	46.2	45.7	41.2	41.8
Nebraska	42.3	42.4	41.1	40.5	42.8	37.6
Nevada	73.3	75.3	71.4	73.4	73.6	73.3
New Hampshire	33.0	33.3	31.3	30.7	30.1	30.5
New Jersey	40.5	41.6	39.2	38.1	39.3	38.0
New Mexico	78.2	79.8	80.3	81.1	77.4	74.5
New York	43.6	46.0	45.3	45.7	45.8	44.0
North Carolina	67.6	70.5	69.5	66.8	66.3	64.1
North Dakota	35.4	35.6	37.3	36.8	34.6	33.5
Ohio	57.9	60.5	58.0	56.8	55.0	53.4
Oklahoma	66.8	72.1	69.9	68.6	65.9	64.0
Oregon	54.6	54.9	53.2	51.2	50.7	50.7
Pennsylvania	44.9	46.9	45.2	44.3	43.8	41.7
Rhode Island	43.9	45.4	47.5	49.8	47.7	43.1
South Carolina	71.3	72.9	70.3	66.0	66.5	65.1
South Dakota	46.8	47.5	48.3	44.3	42.8	40.5
Tennessee	72.3	75.2	71.4	70.2	71.0	67.9
Texas	75.3	78.9	78.9	78.1	77.6	76.1
Utah	48.5	48.2	46.3	44.5	42.7	42.4
Vermont	34.0	39.2	35.6	35.2	33.0	28.6
Virginia	52.9	53.5	51.8	49.8	50.7	48.7
Washington	53.1	53.7	50.9	50.2	48.2	47.6
West Virginia	57.3	57.8	56.0	55.6	54.3	52.7
Wisconsin	42.6	43.7	42.1	41.1	38.8	37.8
Wyoming	56.3	54.2	49.6	49.6	48.2	47.2
United States	59.9	62.1	60.7	59.6	58.9	56.8

*Number of births per 1,000 females ages 15–19.
Source: U.S. Department of Health and Human Services, National Center for Health Statistics.

TABLE B9 **Infant Mortality, by Race of Mother, 1995***

State	All races		White		Black	
	Rate	State rank[a]	Rate	State rank[a]	Rate	State rank[a]
Alabama	9.8%	48	7.1%	38	15.2%	16
Alaska	7.7	29	6.1	17	• •	• •
Arizona	7.5	25	7.2	39	17.0	23
Arkansas	8.8	40	7.2	39	14.3	10
California	6.3	11	5.8	8	14.4	11
Colorado	6.5	12	6.0	12	16.8	22
Connecticut	7.2	19	6.5	28	12.6	4
Delaware	7.5	25	6.0	12	13.1	6
District of Columbia	16.2	51	• •	• •	19.6	33
Florida	7.5	25	6.0	12	13.0	5
Georgia	9.4	44	6.5	28	15.1	14
Hawaii	5.8	5	• •	• •	• •	• •
Idaho	6.1	8	5.8	8	• •	• •
Illinois	9.4	44	7.2	39	18.7	32
Indiana	8.4	38	7.3	42	17.5	25
Iowa	8.2	35	7.8	47	• •	• •
Kansas	7.0	17	6.2	19	17.6	27
Kentucky	7.6	28	7.4	45	10.7	2
Louisiana	9.8	48	6.2	19	15.3	17
Maine	6.5	12	6.3	25	• •	• •
Maryland	8.9	41	6.0	12	15.3	17
Massachusetts	5.2	1	4.7	1	9.0	1
Michigan	8.3	36	6.2	19	17.3	24
Minnesota	6.7	16	6.0	12	17.6	27
Mississippi	10.5	50	7.0	35	14.7	13
Missouri	7.4	23	6.4	27	13.8	8
Montana	7.0	17	7.0	35	• •	• •
Nebraska	7.4	23	7.3	42	• •	• •
Nevada	5.7	4	5.5	4	• •	• •
New Hampshire	5.5	3	5.5	4	• •	• •
New Jersey	6.6	15	5.3	2	13.3	7
New Mexico	6.2	10	6.1	17	• •	• •
New York	7.7	29	6.2	19	13.9	9
North Carolina	9.2	42	6.7	30	15.9	20
North Dakota	7.2	19	6.7	30	• •	• •
Ohio	8.7	39	7.3	42	17.5	25
Oklahoma	8.3	36	8.0	49	15.1	14
Oregon	6.1	8	5.9	10	• •	• •
Pennsylvania	7.8	32	6.2	19	17.6	27
Rhode Island	7.2	19	7.0	35	• •	• •
South Carolina	9.6	47	6.7	30	14.6	12
South Dakota	9.5	46	7.9	48	• •	• •
Tennessee	9.3	43	6.8	33	17.9	30
Texas	6.5	12	5.9	10	11.7	3
Utah	5.4	2	5.3	2	• •	• •
Vermont	6.0	7	6.2	19	• •	• •
Virginia	7.8	32	5.7	7	15.3	17
Washington	5.9	6	5.6	6	16.2	21
West Virginia	7.9	34	7.6	46	• •	• •
Wisconsin	7.3	22	6.3	25	18.6	31
Wyoming	7.7	29	6.8	33	• •	• •
United States	7.6		6.3		15.1	

*Infant deaths (before age 1) per 1,000 live births.

 • • Number too small to calculate a reliable rate.

a. States are ranked from lowest to highest rate.

Source: U.S. Department of Health and Human Services, National Center for Health Statistics. Calculations by Children's Defense Fund.

TABLE B10 **Health Insurance Coverage and Immunization Status of Children**

State	Children lacking insurance throughout the year, 1994–96[a]			Children covered by Medicaid, FY 1996[b]		19- to 35-month-old children fully immunized, 1996[c]	
	Number	Percent	State rank[d]	Number	Percent	Percent	State rank[e]
Alabama	179,000	15.1%	37	357,152	27.1%	75%	36
Alaska	22,000	10.8	20	52,497	23.8	69	49
Arizona	281,000	22.4	49	454,952	32.8	70	45
Arkansas	139,000	19.3	46	199,713	25.0	72	42
California	1,804,000	18.7	44	3,682,510	34.8	76	32
Colorado	161,000	14.9	35	208,303	17.4	76	32
Connecticut	90,000	10.6	18	212,762	23.0	87	1
Delaware	24,000	12.7	27	56,946	26.9	80	10
District of Columbia	19,000	15.7	40	80,335	58.9	78	20
Florida	652,000	17.5	42	1,245,241	30.5	77	23
Georgia	329,000	15.4	39	771,308	32.8	80	10
Hawaii	22,000	6.7	2	21,943	5.9	77	23
Idaho	51,000	13.4	28	82,762	19.5	66	50
Illinois	332,000	9.8	12	1,109,535	29.9	75	36
Indiana	180,000	11.2	23	360,442	20.3	70	45
Iowa	88,000	11.4	25	171,964	20.1	80	10
Kansas	76,000	10.3	17	161,121	19.8	73	40
Kentucky	160,000	15.0	36	348,045	29.3	76	32
Louisiana	277,000	20.3	47	466,503	31.0	79	15
Maine	45,000	14.0	32	96,652	27.3	85	3
Maryland	158,000	11.3	24	320,632	21.0	78	20
Massachusetts	141,000	9.3	8	419,973	25.3	86	2
Michigan	220,000	8.1	6	805,828	26.9	74	38
Minnesota	94,000	7.1	4	369,339	25.4	83	7
Mississippi	156,000	18.6	43	318,420	34.3	79	15
Missouri	184,000	12.3	26	468,126	28.5	74	38
Montana	27,000	10.7	19	58,925	20.7	77	23
Nebraska	45,000	9.4	10	111,327	21.2	80	10
Nevada	86,000	19.1	45	91,112	18.7	70	45
New Hampshire	32,000	10.2	14	60,418	17.7	83	7
New Jersey	295,000	13.9	30	465,523	20.1	77	23
New Mexico	126,000	22.9	50	224,007	37.1	79	15
New York	680,000	13.9	30	1,753,424	32.6	79	15
North Carolina	284,000	14.2	34	644,270	29.2	77	23
North Dakota	14,000	7.9	5	34,868	17.2	81	9
Ohio	309,000	10.1	13	877,582	26.0	77	23
Oklahoma	201,000	20.8	48	253,374	23.7	73	40
Oregon	123,000	14.0	32	170,906	17.6	70	45
Pennsylvania	288,000	9.3	8	936,185	27.5	79	15
Rhode Island	24,000	9.7	11	76,001	27.7	85	3
South Carolina	174,000	16.8	41	313,790	27.3	84	6
South Dakota	19,000	8.5	7	54,018	22.1	80	10
Tennessee	219,000	15.1	37	633,961	39.6	77	23
Texas	1,440,000	24.1	51	1,847,355	28.1	72	42
Utah	75,000	10.2	14	128,353	15.6	63	51
Vermont	11,000	7.0	3	61,559	35.6	85	3
Virginia	197,000	11.0	21	439,778	22.2	77	23
Washington	171,000	11.0	21	543,411	31.6	78	20
West Virginia	47,000	10.2	14	261,343	50.0	71	44
Wisconsin	92,000	6.4	1	334,921	21.1	76	32
Wyoming	20,000	13.4	28	35,153	21.5	77	23
United States	11,300,000	15.1		23,254,568	28.0	77	

a. Averages of the number and percentage of uninsured children under age 18 from 1994 through 1996 for states, and for 1996 for the United States.

b. Includes any persons under age 21 enrolled in Medicaid for any length of time in FY 1996.

c. Four or more doses of DPT or DT, three or more doses of poliovirus vaccine, one or more doses of any measles-containing vaccine, and three or more doses of Hib vaccine,

d. States are ranked from lowest to highest percentage of children lacking insurance.

e. States are ranked from highest to lowest percentage of immunized children.

Source: U.S. Department of Commerce, Bureau of the Census, U.S. Department of Health and Human Services, Health Care Financing Administration, and U.S. Department of Health and Human Services, Centers for Disease Control and Prevention. Calculations by Children's Defense Fund.

TABLE B11   **Head Start Enrollment and Race of Enrollees, 1996**

State	Total enrollment	Race of enrollees (percentage distribution)				
		White	Black	Hispanic	Asian or Pacific Islander	Native American
Alabama	15,897	22%	76%	2%	0%	0%
Alaska	3,179	21	5	4	2	68
Arizona	17,063	18	6	40	1	36
Arkansas	10,978	50	45	4	0	0
California	95,172	17	16	59	7	1
Colorado	9,786	34	10	51	2	3
Connecticut	6,375	22	45	31	1	0
Delaware	2,030	20	65	14	0	0
District of Columbia	3,266	0	85	13	1	0
Florida	29,885	18	62	19	1	0
Georgia	20,942	21	73	5	1	0
Hawaii	2,615	17	6	7	70	0
Idaho	3,405	50	1	40	1	8
Illinois	35,641	26	55	17	1	0
Indiana	13,492	64	31	5	0	0
Iowa	6,942	78	13	6	2	1
Kansas	6,582	52	28	15	2	3
Kentucky	15,988	78	20	1	1	0
Louisiana	20,750	17	82	1	1	0
Maine	4,121	92	2	3	1	3
Maryland	10,733	20	70	8	2	0
Massachusetts	12,593	42	22	29	6	1
Michigan	36,849	49	40	8	1	2
Minnesota	14,928	50	14	19	8	9
Mississippi	22,212	12	86	0	1	1
Missouri	16,887	58	39	2	1	0
Montana	4,338	50	1	3	1	45
Nebraska	4,464	56	17	17	1	8
Nevada	2,619	27	32	28	1	11
New Hampshire	1,264	91	4	4	1	1
New Jersey	14,157	14	56	29	1	0
New Mexico	7,964	17	3	60	1	20
New York	46,609	30	36	31	3	1
North Carolina	17,792	25	65	7	1	3
North Dakota	2,957	55	2	2	1	40
Ohio	50,919	52	44	3	1	0
Oklahoma	16,019	47	22	6	1	24
Oregon	8,836	50	6	36	2	6
Pennsylvania	29,965	49	40	10	1	0
Rhode Island	2,779	52	22	19	4	2
South Carolina	11,199	8	87	3	0	3
South Dakota	4,057	42	2	2	1	53
Tennessee	15,337	55	42	2	1	0
Texas	58,199	14	31	54	1	0
Utah	5,330	61	2	26	3	7
Vermont	1,440	94	1	1	2	1
Virginia	14,516	35	47	15	3	0
Washington	14,578	36	9	39	7	8
West Virginia	7,507	89	11	0	0	0
Wisconsin	15,628	46	31	9	7	7
Wyoming	1,729	61	3	20	1	14
United States	798,513	32	36	25	3	4

Source: U.S. Department of Health and Human Services, Head Start Bureau.

TABLE B12 **Public Schools Offering Extended Day Programs, 1993–94**

State	Number	Percent
Alabama	1,274	23.9%
Alaska	478	16.9
Arizona	1,057	43.2
Arkansas	1,084	11.8
California	7,319	30.6
Colorado	1,329	26.4
Connecticut	964	29.5
Delaware	169	20.0
District of Columbia	160	47.0
Florida	2,348	46.9
Georgia	1,723	36.2
Hawaii	234	74.6
Idaho	573	11.9
Illinois	3,884	18.3
Indiana	1,869	37.0
Iowa	1,518	11.2
Kansas	1,450	18.1
Kentucky	1,327	49.0
Louisiana	1,446	18.5
Maine	721	12.7
Maryland	1,185	43.5
Massachusetts	1,689	26.1
Michigan	3,159	19.1
Minnesota	1,492	28.6
Mississippi	957	11.1
Missouri	2,082	27.9
Montana	890	7.7
Nebraska	1,296	4.8
Nevada	365	43.7
New Hampshire	445	13.6
New Jersey	2,195	29.5
New Mexico	663	21.6
New York	3,904	22.7
North Carolina	1,927	42.8
North Dakota	582	9.6
Ohio	3,636	19.1
Oklahoma	1,763	16.7
Oregon	1,184	23.8
Pennsylvania	3,128	13.4
Rhode Island	295	7.4
South Carolina	1,081	27.7
South Dakota	661	5.3
Tennessee	1,522	20.5
Texas	5,890	20.6
Utah	674	9.6
Vermont	318	12.3
Virginia	1,698	23.2
Washington	1,806	19.5
West Virginia	898	8.4
Wisconsin	2,014	18.8
Wyoming	411	11.2

Source: U.S. Department of Education, National Center for Education Statistics.

TABLE B13 **Participants in Federal Education and Disability Programs**

| State | Title I 1994–95 | Individuals with Disabilities Education Act (IDEA) 1995–96 school year | | | | Supplemental Security Income (SSI) | |
		Total	Ages 3–5	Ages 6–17	Ages 18–21	Child recipients, Nov. 1997	Child cases terminated Aug. 1996–Dec. 1997[a]
Alabama	120,629	98,266	8,594	84,440	5,232	26,988	4,939
Alaska	8,615	17,604	2,015	14,958	631	1,008	89
Arizona	131,342	76,121	7,893	65,263	2,965	12,955	1,254
Arkansas	90,324	53,880	7,520	44,024	2,336	16,140	4,279
California	1,490,633	565,670	54,795	489,168	21,707	80,986	5,350
Colorado	46,772	69,850	7,153	59,786	2,911	9,252	986
Connecticut	47,003	76,226	7,359	65,412	3,455	5,677	681
Delaware	9,884	15,624	1,905	13,025	694	2,587	243
District of Columbia	11,744	7,058	387	6,081	590	2,979	211
Florida	256,916	310,184	27,080	271,078	12,026	60,441	8,242
Georgia	148,013	135,042	13,314	117,164	4,564	28,918	3,222
Hawaii	14,294	16,029	1,306	14,177	546	1,088	30
Idaho	24,092	23,826	3,091	19,989	746	3,292	598
Illinois	201,760	255,905	24,967	220,648	10,290	44,446	8,741
Indiana	88,116	133,962	12,261	115,629	6,072	18,698	3,011
Iowa	27,540	66,247	5,837	57,148	3,262	6,450	1,269
Kansas	37,521	53,602	6,135	45,404	2,063	7,242	1,817
Kentucky	126,143	82,889	14,683	64,997	3,209	22,816	3,158
Louisiana	120,317	91,059	9,588	76,743	4,728	34,038	8,687
Maine	23,350	31,872	3,553	26,956	1,363	2,789	295
Maryland	59,452	100,863	9,486	87,489	3,888	13,824	1,610
Massachusetts	83,322	157,196	14,241	135,126	7,829	16,580	2,240
Michigan	154,971	188,768	18,241	161,511	9,016	39,866	6,241
Minnesota	90,579	98,311	10,781	83,697	3,833	10,959	1,292
Mississippi	150,451	66,804	6,607	57,399	2,798	22,037	4,598
Missouri	108,512	121,407	8,395	107,763	5,249	18,815	4,318
Montana	20,361	18,364	1,766	15,834	764	2,226	367
Nebraska	32,589	39,308	3,312	34,460	1,536	4,104	610
Nevada	15,469	28,202	3,166	24,146	890	3,599	223
New Hampshire	13,330	25,150	2,165	21,827	1,158	1,940	170
New Jersey	149,766	197,062	16,639	171,551	8,872	22,099	2,362
New Mexico	66,263	47,578	4,563	41,256	1,759	6,352	831
New York	453,585	394,841	48,536	323,144	23,161	78,293	15,517
North Carolina	101,967	147,078	16,671	125,794	4,613	30,279	4,931
North Dakota	13,511	12,355	1,169	10,567	619	1,238	123
Ohio	201,796	227,529	18,204	197,241	12,084	51,357	8,416
Oklahoma	70,433	71,728	5,312	63,161	3,255	11,696	1,212
Oregon	48,523	65,022	6,097	56,338	2,587	6,887	456
Pennsylvania	273,033	210,929	20,586	179,234	11,109	43,342	5,188
Rhode Island	16,269	25,072	2,333	21,461	1,278	2,909	557
South Carolina	61,579	86,522	10,319	73,090	3,113	17,420	2,718
South Dakota	14,476	15,512	2,176	12,703	633	2,687	241
Tennessee	123,595	126,461	10,151	109,981	6,329	22,674	4,028
Texas	715,284	441,543	32,262	386,842	22,439	54,479	9,065
Utah	40,951	52,463	4,861	45,686	1,916	4,299	526
Vermont	10,952	11,246	1,215	9,518	513	1,329	194
Virginia	68,163	141,759	13,284	122,388	6,087	22,305	4,162
Washington	74,807	106,890	12,565	89,825	4,500	12,498	1,191
West Virginia	38,612	46,487	4,842	39,277	2,368	8,293	1,359
Wisconsin	69,366	106,413	13,545	87,990	4,878	19,803	3,877
Wyoming	7,992	12,549	1,556	10,490	503	1,106	177
United States	6,374,967	5,572,328	544,482	4,778,879	248,967	944,130	145,904

a. Child SSI cases terminated as a result of the 1996 welfare law (see chapter 1 for details).
Source: U.S. Department of Education and Social Security Administration.

TABLE B14 **Child Abuse and Neglect***

State	Child victims of abuse and neglect			Type of abuse or neglect, 1995 (percentage distribution)					
	1990	1995	Percentage change	Physical abuse	Neglect	Medical neglect	Sexual abuse	Psychological abuse	Other abuse
Alabama	16,508	18,120	9.8%	31.0%	44.1%	0.0%	18.4%	6.5%	0.0%
Alaska	–	8,142	–	29.7	54.6	0.0	13.2	2.2	0.3
Arizona	24,244	25,154	3.8	31.4	49.9	2.6	6.2	2.2	7.6
Arkansas	7,922	8,169	3.1	35.0	36.0	0.0	22.8	0.0	6.2
California	78,512	166,418	112.0	31.1	47.9	0.0	15.7	5.0	0.3
Colorado	7,906	7,602	–3.8	23.2	48.9	5.4	11.9	10.6	0.0
Connecticut	12,481	23,762	90.4	16.7	48.3	0.0	0.0	0.0	34.9
Delaware	2,065	2,300	11.4	16.8	33.3	3.6	8.7	14.1	22.9
District of Columbia	3,210	5,916	84.3	8.0	79.5	6.7	1.1	0.1	4.7
Florida	79,086	77,976	–1.4	17.1	42.5	2.9	7.8	3.8	25.9
Georgia	34,120	57,250	67.8	17.6	59.5	5.4	9.3	5.0	3.1
Hawaii	1,974	2,635	33.5	18.6	20.0	1.7	6.3	3.4	50.0
Idaho	2,667	10,743	302.8	34.0	41.6	0.0	18.8	0.0	5.3
Illinois	37,539	49,217	31.1	9.4	32.7	12.5	8.1	1.0	36.2
Indiana	26,818	22,493	–16.1	20.4	55.6	5.5	18.5	0.0	0.0
Iowa	8,215	9,967	21.3	29.8	51.3	2.3	11.7	1.4	3.6
Kansas	–	3,264	–	25.7	24.8	2.1	29.3	3.4	14.7
Kentucky	22,239	28,630	28.7	25.4	61.7	0.0	8.1	0.0	4.9
Louisiana	15,383	14,194	–7.7	21.7	66.9	0.0	7.1	3.6	0.7
Maine	4,133	4,628	12.0	15.6	35.3	0.0	9.2	39.9	0.0
Maryland	–	–	–	–	–	–	–	–	–
Massachusetts	28,621	25,375	–11.3	21.3	70.0	0.0	5.2	3.1	0.3
Michigan	25,774	21,165	–17.9	21.3	62.0	0.3	8.1	0.8	7.6
Minnesota	9,256	10,142	9.6	28.5	55.4	5.2	8.6	2.3	0.0
Mississippi	–	5,588	–	29.0	53.6	0.0	11.9	1.9	0.3
Missouri	21,732	17,764	–18.3	17.8	50.7	3.0	15.1	1.9	11.4
Montana	–	4,194	–	32.0	57.8	0.0	10.2	0.0	0.0
Nebraska	5,595	3,510	–37.3	27.1	61.8	0.0	11.2	0.0	0.0
Nevada	7,703	7,791	1.1	13.5	45.8	2.6	3.0	5.1	30.0
New Hampshire	1,056	1,059	0.3	24.8	46.5	0.0	26.4	2.3	0.0
New Jersey	19,546	9,279	–52.5	30.2	38.9	15.9	9.0	1.8	4.2
New Mexico	4,379	8,842	101.9	24.2	68.6	0.0	7.2	0.0	0.0
New York	57,931	57,699	–0.4	13.5	23.0	2.9	4.2	1.4	55.1
North Carolina	24,880	30,935	24.3	4.6	87.1	2.4	5.3	0.4	0.2
North Dakota	2,893	3,340	15.5	27.4	54.8	4.5	0.0	0.0	13.3
Ohio	49,434	58,416	18.2	23.0	51.5	0.0	16.3	9.2	0.0
Oklahoma	–	11,700	–	18.2	49.5	3.4	9.0	8.9	11.1
Oregon	8,126	8,991	10.6	15.7	28.9	0.0	14.5	7.4	33.4
Pennsylvania	7,951	6,891	–13.3	41.5	1.6	0.0	39.8	13.6	3.5
Rhode Island	5,393	4,437	–17.7	27.0	62.1	2.3	8.2	0.4	0.0
South Carolina	–	11,439	–	15.0	41.5	3.9	6.8	1.7	31.1
South Dakota	4,132	2,526	–38.9	19.0	62.5	0.0	9.9	8.6	0.0
Tennessee	11,473	12,166	6.0	20.7	39.9	3.6	21.8	5.1	8.8
Texas	53,939	46,768	–13.3	26.8	46.9	3.8	13.3	5.6	3.6
Utah	8,524	8,848	3.8	22.0	18.4	1.2	23.6	13.7	21.1
Vermont	1,500	1,122	–25.2	24.6	26.5	1.5	45.9	1.5	0.0
Virginia	14,174	10,416	–26.5	22.5	56.4	2.1	13.0	4.3	1.7
Washington	–	20,264	–	29.3	46.2	3.7	13.2	7.1	0.6
West Virginia	–	–	–	–	–	–	–	–	–
Wisconsin	14,165	17,118	20.8	27.4	34.5	2.2	33.4	2.6	0.0
Wyoming	2,478	1,508	–39.1	22.8	46.1	1.2	10.1	3.0	16.8

* Data comparisons should not be made between years or among states. Duplicated counts and differences and changes in practice and policy prevent meaningful comparisons.

– Data not available.

Source: U.S. Department of Health and Human Services, National Center on Child Abuse and Neglect.

TABLE B15 **Children Under 18 in Foster Care**

State	Last day FY 1990	Last day FY 1991	Last day FY 1992	Last day FY 1993	Last day FY 1994	Last day FY 1995	Percentage change FY90-FY95
Alabama	4,420	4,383	4,133	3,938	3,788	3,590	-18.8%
Alaska	3,852	1,942	1,496	2,029	1,876	1,783	-53.7
Arizona	3,379	3,618	3,909	4,107	4,271	5,640	66.9
Arkansas	1,351	1,326	1,981	2,296	2,196	2,374	75.7
California	79,482	80,880	83,849	88,262	93,321	96,617	21.6
Colorado	3,892	5,519	4,390	5,700	5,957	7,258	86.5
Connecticut	4,121	4,202	4,252	4,557	4,648	7,045	71.0
Delaware	663	655	638	707	746	843	27.1
District of Columbia	2,313		2,152	2,145	1,981	2,088	-9.7
Florida	10,664	10,235	9,928	9,568	9,284	9,002	-15.6
Georgia	15,179	15,500	16,999	17,277	17,239	17,876	17.8
Hawaii	1,659	1,600	1,214	1,574	1,818	2,454	47.9
Idaho	548	877	1,235	1,342	906	1,068	94.9
Illinois	20,753	23,776	29,542	33,815	41,161	47,862	130.6
Indiana	7,492	8,126	8,455	8,669	9,883	10,145	35.4
Iowa	3,425	4,609	3,606	3,411	3,526	3,952	15.4
Kansas	3,976	7,112	7,838	4,593	4,501	4,744	19.3
Kentucky	3,810	6,422	6,966	3,363	3,567	3,760	-1.3
Louisiana	5,379	5,799	5,722	5,607	5,831	5,962	10.8
Maine	1,745	1,814	1,944	2,150	2,236	2,473	41.7
Maryland	6,473	4,859	5,816	6,107	6,936	7,399	14.3
Massachusetts	11,856	13,232	13,147	13,382	13,574	13,591	14.6
Michigan	9,000	11,282	11,121	10,382	10,606	10,889	21.0
Minnesota	7,310	7,898	7,895	9,700	10,379	8,452	15.6
Mississippi	2,832	2,830	3,169	3,293	3,425	2,940	3.8
Missouri	8,241	7,143	8,171	8,625	8,873	9,331	13.2
Montana	1,224	1,494	1,691	1,447	1,414	1,695	38.5
Nebraska	2,543	2,660	2,985	3,222	3,274	3,213	26.3
Nevada	2,566	1,563	1,664	2,831	2,440	1,823	-29.0
New Hampshire	1,505	2,095	2,630	2,509	1,975	1,477	-1.9
New Jersey	8,879	8,451	8,024	7,673	7,771	8,014	-9.7
New Mexico	2,042	2,304	2,118	2,097	2,174	2,050	0.4
New York	63,371	65,171	62,705	59,658	58,658	52,395	-17.3
North Carolina	7,170	9,619	10,275	11,024	11,859	12,760	78.0
North Dakota	393	695	759	805	875	867	120.6
Ohio	18,062	17,298	17,099	15,922	15,922	17,800	-1.5
Oklahoma	3,435	3,803	2,892	2,953	6,707	3,017	-12.2
Oregon	4,261	3,996	4,031	4,119	4,599	5,138	20.6
Pennsylvania	16,665	17,508	18,491	18,976	19,735	20,559	23.4
Rhode Island	2,680	3,311	2,755	2,830	3,139	3,309	23.5
South Carolina	3,286	3,698	5,066	4,656	4,761	5,234	59.3
South Dakota	567	613	674	710	631	665	17.3
Tennessee	4,971	5,217	5,312	5,835	6,186	6,520	31.2
Texas	6,698	7,200	9,965	10,880	11,315	11,700	74.7
Utah	1,174	1,405	895	1,465	1,622	1,936	64.9
Vermont	1,063	1,088	1,162	1,236	1,336	1,430	34.5
Virginia	6,217	6,590	6,305	6,229	6,429	6,844	10.1
Washington	13,302	13,956	11,327	8,394	9,189	9,715	-27.0
West Virginia	1,997	1,997	2,315	2,483	2,483	2,877	44.1
Wisconsin	6,037	6,403	6,812	7,045	8,058	7,832	29.7
Wyoming	484	605	907	620	957	2,241	363.0
United States	404,407	424,379	438,427	442,218	466,038	480,249	18.8

Source: American Public Welfare Association. Calculations by Children's Defense Fund.

TABLE B16 **Firearm Deaths Among Children Ages 0-19, by Cause**

State	Total[a]		Homicide[a]		Suicide		Accidental		Unknown	
	1994	1995	1994	1995	1994	1995	1994	1995	1994	1995
Alabama	148	119	78	61	34	38	30	15	6	5
Alaska	28	19	7	7	14	8	7	4	0	0
Arizona	125	140	60	92	45	36	10	10	10	2
Arkansas	62	85	33	48	23	28	2	3	4	6
California	887	843	698	650	119	129	58	53	12	11
Colorado	67	63	26	28	35	26	3	8	3	1
Connecticut	53	29	35	23	14	5	4	1	0	0
Delaware	8	10	3	7	3	3	2	0	0	0
District of Columbia	77	75	75	73	1	2	1	0	0	0
Florida	229	204	150	132	67	56	10	12	2	4
Georgia	188	154	111	94	55	46	16	14	6	0
Hawaii	9	3	0	2	8	1	1	0	0	0
Idaho	25	29	5	7	14	14	6	7	0	1
Illinois	398	320	327	250	52	50	15	16	4	4
Indiana	118	117	59	59	44	40	13	15	2	3
Iowa	39	28	7	7	27	18	4	3	1	0
Kansas	63	49	33	28	22	16	6	5	2	0
Kentucky	73	59	22	20	33	27	18	12	0	0
Louisiana	211	174	137	115	49	37	15	19	10	3
Maine	14	6	6	0	8	5	0	1	0	0
Maryland	95	143	81	118	11	20	2	1	1	4
Massachusetts	46	40	36	32	9	8	1	0	0	0
Michigan	238	202	153	129	63	52	13	14	9	7
Minnesota	42	54	17	22	19	24	5	8	1	0
Mississippi	106	101	61	48	20	26	22	21	3	6
Missouri	164	139	99	84	30	40	29	11	6	4
Montana	23	20	4	4	11	13	7	2	1	1
Nebraska	22	24	6	14	10	7	4	3	2	0
Nevada	42	44	20	17	15	21	4	5	3	1
New Hampshire	6	10	1	2	5	7	0	1	0	0
New Jersey	63	55	44	43	13	11	3	0	3	1
New Mexico	49	37	21	17	24	20	3	0	1	0
New York	331	234	251	170	57	43	19	16	4	5
North Carolina	157	150	79	77	60	53	15	19	3	1
North Dakota	12	12	1	2	10	9	1	1	0	0
Ohio	154	132	71	64	62	46	20	19	1	3
Oklahoma	78	74	43	30	25	34	6	8	4	2
Oregon	55	57	19	18	26	28	9	10	1	1
Pennsylvania	156	159	96	100	50	50	7	7	3	2
Rhode Island	6	6	4	6	1	0	1	0	0	0
South Carolina	80	66	49	26	15	24	16	14	0	2
South Dakota	14	13	0	2	10	7	4	4	0	0
Tennessee	127	137	65	75	38	40	23	16	1	6
Texas	523	462	319	289	151	126	38	32	15	15
Utah	45	54	14	14	30	37	0	2	1	1
Vermont	7	6	0	0	6	5	1	1	0	0
Virginia	116	106	67	65	37	29	9	10	3	2
Washington	93	75	43	37	37	29	8	7	5	2
West Virginia	25	28	4	10	14	15	4	3	3	0
Wisconsin	78	74	34	30	28	31	15	4	1	9
Wyoming	18	14	5	1	11	10	2	3	0	0
United States	5,793	5,254	3,579	3,249	1,565	1,450	512	440	137	115

a. Excluding firearm deaths by legal intervention (such as by law enforcement officials).
Source: U.S. Department of Health and Human Services, National Center for Health Statistics, Division of Vital Statistics. Calculations by Children's Defense Fund.

Selected Web Sites

Listed below are selected Web sites that may be useful to child advocates. Many of the sites have links to other sites. Keep in mind that the Web changes rapidly; although all of these addresses were accurate at press time, some of them may have changed since. CDF does not endorse any of the sites, nor vouch for the accuracy of any of the information found there.

Government Agencies

U.S. Department of Agriculture	http://www.usda.gov/
U.S. Department of Education	http://www.ed.gov/
U.S. Department of Health and Human Services	http://www.os.dhhs.gov/
U.S. Department of Justice	http://www.usdoj.gov/
U.S. Department of Labor	http://www.dol.gov/
White House	http://www.whitehouse.gov/
Links to state governments	http://www.nasire.org/ss/STstates.html
Links to county governments	http://www.naco.org/members/counties/stlist.htm

Statistical Agencies

Bureau of Labor Statistics	http://stats.bls.gov/
Census Bureau	http://www.census.gov/
Centers for Disease Control and Prevention	http://www.cdc.gov/
Health Care Financing Administration	http://www.hcfa.gov/
National Center for Education Statistics	http://nces.ed.gov/
National Center for Health Statistics	http://www.cdc.gov/nchswww/index.htm
Social Security Administration	http://www.ssa.gov/

Advocacy Groups

Bread for the World	http://www.bread.org/
Center on Budget and Policy Priorities	http://www.cbpp.org/
Child Trends	http://www.childtrends.org/
Child Welfare League of America	http://www.cwla.org/
Children Now	http://www.childrennow.org/
Children's Defense Fund	http://www.childrensdefense.org/
Families USA	http://www.familiesusa.org/
Food Research and Action Center (FRAC)	http://www.frac.org/
Kids Count	http://www.aecf.org/aeckids.htm
Stand For Children	http://www.stand.org/

Other Useful Sites

GPO Access (Federal Register)	http://www.access.gpo.gov/
IFAS (e-mail members of Congress)	http://www.ifas.org/activist/index.html
Thomas (federal legislation)	http://thomas.loc.gov/

Index